NOT IN FRONT OF THE AUDIENCE

Homosexuality on stage

Nicholas de Jongh

London and New York

First published 1992
by Routledge
11 New Fetter Lane, London EC4P 4EE
Simultaneously published in the USA and Canada
by Routledge
a division of Routledge, Chapman and Hall, Inc.
29 West 35th Street, New York, NY 10001

© 1992 Nicholas de Jongh

Typeset in 10 on 12 point Palatino by
Falcon Typographic Art Ltd, Edinburgh
Printed in Great Britain by
TJ Press (Padstow) Ltd, Padstow, Cornwall

British Library Cataloguing in Publication Data
De Jongh, Nicholas Raymond
Not in front of the audience: homosexuality on stage
1. New York. London (England).
Homosexuality, related to theatre, history
I. Title
792.09421

Library of Congress Cataloging in Publication Data
De Jongh, Nicholas
Not in front of the audience: homosexuality on stage
Nicholas de Jongh.
p. cm.
Includes index.
1. Drama–20th century–History and criticism.
2. Gay men in literature. 3. Homosexuality in literature.
4. Homosexuality and literature.
5. Theater–Great Britain–History–20th century.
6. Theater–United States–History–20th century.
7. Theater and society–Great Britain.
8. Theater and society–United States.
I. Title.
PN1861.D43   1992
822'.9109353–dc20   91–16819

ISBN 0–415–03362–4
ISBN 0–415–03363–2 pbk

To My Mother

CONTENTS

CONTENTS

PLATES

(Between pages 82 and 83)

PREFACE

This study attempts to explore a neglected terrain. It considers how the theatres of London and New York treated the subject of homosexuality and depicted homosexuals in the course of over half a century. I have not included lesbians and lesbianism within the ambit of this study since I felt that such a pioneering study deserved and required the attention of a woman rather than a man.

I wanted to investigate the ways in which playwrights, actors and directors were influenced by prevailing mythic constructions of homosexuality as the epitome of evil, danger and corruption, and how such constructions were destroyed and replaced in the aftermath of Gay Liberation. But the theatre's treatment of homosexuality was a microcosm of its governing attitudes. It promoted plays of rigid orthodoxy, driving home messages of political, social and sexual conformity to the status quo. Between 1925 and 1956 the playhouses of both theatre capitals preserved the notion that the stage was frivolity's medium – evening escapism for the leisured and richer classes. The play was a version of Christian morality in which vice was always put down and the theatre of happy endings tended to reign supreme.

Since the playhouses were controlled by business syndicates and commercially motivated impresarios, a theatre of dissent barely existed. The businessmen all promoted the ideology of the ascendant classes. And since the playhouses in both London and New York were, until the 1960s, subject to a close form of censorship which forbade the depiction of homosexuals on stage or even the discussion of homosexuality, those rare dramatists who wished to challenge the ban or to urge heterodox ideas upon suspicious audiences were either ignored or had to rely upon a series of cryptic signifiers to suggest what they were forbidden to place in front of the audience. Even in the 1960s, by which time there was a kind of revolution against the fashionable and frivolous theatre of orthodoxy, when a new generation expected the theatre to fulfil new functions, to urge dissent, when the profit motive was no longer the greatest goad and state subsidy for the performing arts was being promoted, the theatres of London and New York were still reluctant to discard the old iconography of the homosexual and its mythic constructions of homosexuality. But America, fired by a whole new culture of protest and liberation strategies, began to register the shocks of change, some of them even manifest in plays about homosexuality. And in London, the termination of the Lord Chamberlain's control of theatre in 1968, released playwrights into a virgin territory of freedom to speak, show and suggest. As this book went to press, the Lord Chamberlain's correspondence in relation to the censorship of the theatre from 1901 to 1968 was at last placed in the public domain. I was fortunate to be the first person to explore these files and to see the way in which the Lord Chamberlain had covertly imposed political, social and sexual censorship; he upheld the values and beliefs of a governing aristocratic class while professing impartiality.

In dealing with twentieth-century interpretations of male homosexuality, I have to some extent relied upon Jung's notion of the masculine and the feminine as profound archetypal principles, although in so doing I do not altogether reject the complementary assertion that some apparent gender traits are in fact the results of cultural conditioning rather than of biological imposition.

An example may make this point clearer. In the Cold War 1950s homosexuality was vehemently characterised as an acquired, addictive practice, as disease or sin; homosexual acts, according to a senior Home Office official, were said to induce a state of ecstasy sufficient to divert men from heterosexuality. But there was still reckoned to be a way to curb the incidence of what had come to be described as an epidemic of homosexuality. The psychologist Gordon Westwood, expressing a popular belief of the period, explained that the emergence of homosexual desire in the young male could be discouraged through what he described as 'ideal family life'. This 'ideal' depended upon the influence of a 'tolerant, virile and decisive father' and a mother who was 'gentle, patient and passive'. This notion of passivity as either a characterising or ideal aspect of the female is now regarded as part of an outmoded cultural ideology.

This study delves into old theatrical worlds, standards and values. Writing from the perspective of a gay man, I was struck by a quaint incongruity. Since the late sixteenth century the theatre has been described as rampantly homosexual. Ian McKellen, writing an introduction to the thirty-eighth edition of the *Bedside Guardian*, confessed, not quite jokingly I think, that his dreams of belonging drove him to become an actor. 'I'd heard', he wrote, 'everyone in the theatre was queer.' Yet that 'queer' theatre of which he had heard such shouts and whispers was for much of this century enthusiastic in its incitements to hate homosexuals.

Nicholas de Jongh, February 1991

ACKNOWLEDGEMENTS

Many people have helped me write this book by providing information, advice, support and opinion. Needless to say, the text's inadequacies, opinions and defects are my own.

I would like to thank the following: John Ashbery; Frith Banbury; Keith Baxter; Kenneth Butler; Sir Peter Hall; Robert Harris; John Haynes; Derek Jarman; Jeremy Kingston; Karen and Fiona Mellor; Helen Montagu; Anthony Page; Robert Peden; James Roose-Evans; Martin Sherman; Max Stafford-Clark; Simon Watney; Hugh Whitemore; at Routledge: Julia Hall, Helena Reckitt and Moira Taylor. Dr Anthony Stevens cajoled, persecuted and encouraged me in a campaign to persuade me to finish the book. My greatest gratitude is owed to him.

1

FROM THE PLAYHOUSE
TO THE OLD BAILEY

INTRODUCTION

A young man, ostensibly in search of a cure for his addiction to drugs, breaks down in a doctor's consulting room. High on guilt and shame, he confesses that he is really a victim of homosexual desires which he cannot control. 'I'm one of those damned creatures who are called degenerates and moral lepers for a thing they cannot help,' he helpfully explains.[1] An affected, middle-aged bachelor dons a pair of gardening gloves to arrange a bouquet of irises and tulips in a vase.[2] A long-haired, sensitive 18-year-old schoolboy, who acts female roles in the school plays and is nicknamed 'Grace', attempts suicide with a kitchen knife, after failing to rise to the challenge posed by the local prostitute.[3] A colonel in the Austro-Hungarian army, who has been blackmailed to spy for the enemy, drags his boy-friend out of bed and warns the young man that he has nothing to look forward to except a future of 'dyed, whispy hair . . . disease . . . rolling thighs and a big bottom'.[4] A 'shamefully beautiful', young man lies happily in bed in the arms of his older lover.[5] An enraged, middle-aged man demands that the homosexuals of New York fight for recognition of and pride in a 'gay culture that isn't just sexual. Being defined by our cocks is literally killing us,' he shouts.[6]

We are considering revelatory scenes and images. An enormous gulf separates the first, taken from a 1927 play written by that early camp sex-symbol, Mae West, and banned before it reached Broadway, and the last, from Larry Kramer's theatrical polemic about AIDS, *The Normal Heart* (Plate 8), which succeeded on both sides of the Atlantic. Within this period

1

a process of social change takes place which helps transform the nineteenth-century form of theatre bequeathed to the twentieth. This change is most dramatic and negotiated at speed; the theatrical images to which I refer are symptoms, although small ones, of this process. In these sixty years, negative myths – those traditional notions of what homosexuality entailed and the ways in which it was represented on stage – were challenged, discredited and lost much of their authority. Medical, religious and social injunctions, anathematising and repressing homosexuals, were losing their potency. The stage reflected these changes.

In 1925, where this book begins, homosexuality was, in Britain and America, sin, crime and illness. Homosexuals were pariahs and outcasts, scarcely fit to be depicted upon the stage. The slang, the jargon, by which they were described – 'queens' and 'queers', 'fairies' and 'faggots', 'poofs', 'pansies' and 'puffs', 'sissies' to a man – echoed from the real world on to the stage. But there was no consistent interpretation of what supposed threat the homosexual was thought to pose to the heterosexual male. He might be depicted on stage as the epitome of effeminacy, an object of scorn and contempt. He was also reckoned a sinister and potent agent of the devil, a proselytiser, who encouraged young men to that dangerous addiction, homosexuality. The homosexual as he emerged in theatrical form was therefore pathetic, introjecting society's view of him and succumbing to guilt and self-pity. He was also threatening. By 1985, when *The Normal Heart* was seen, homosexuals were still depicted as unorthodox, subjected to the stress that may be induced when your sexuality causes problems of self-acceptance. But homosexuality was no longer regarded as illness or disease, and not inevitably as crime.

This book is a survey of the change as refracted, principally, through the commercial theatre of London and New York. It is a partial and limited account, since it deals with male homosexuality and not with lesbianism, which deserves and merits independent scrutiny. It seeks to trace the way in which a monolithic, commercial theatre, redolent of orthodoxy and conservatism, came to mirror the new attitudes to homosexuality. Not until the 1960s did this theatre begin to be affected by the theatrical revolution of the 1950s, which broke out at the Royal Court in the London of 1956, and whose social, political and aesthetic values were affected by Bertolt Brecht and a new generation of European writers: John Osborne's *Look Back In Anger*, a tirade and battle-cry on behalf of a new generation, set the new wave pounding against the old theatrical order. New York's off-off-Broadway theatre, created in the later 1950s, in lofts and studios, was partially influenced by the Royal Court's example.

The principal plays, with which I deal, have an identifying theme in common. They describe situations and pose moral dilemmas where homosexual desire, whether latent or manifest, precipitates a crisis. Until the 1960s they tend to be plays of orthodoxy and conformity. They reflect the myths and assumptions by which homosexuality was defined and derogated. There is usually a tension between the unorthodox desire and the orthodoxy which the dramatist endorses. The homosexual character is seen as a man in revolt from family, from marriage, from the approved fixtures and fittings of life.

In the period 1925–58, since homosexuality is reckoned the archetype of evil, the triumphalism of the Christian ethic, so beloved of the commercial theatre, is ensured. Suicide, alcoholism, murder, mental breakdown, death, imprisonment, ostracism, blackmail or mere misery are the ends to which homosexuals are brought at a play's lysis. Most of the protagonists are victims of negative emotions engendered by shame, fear, guilt, bewilderment, depression or hysteria. Since in this thirty-three-year period depiction of homosexuals on stage was prohibited, dramatists, directors and actors collaborated to fashion a homosexual iconography, a series of signifiers and codes that corroborate what the play texts could only imply. Since the stereotype of homosexuality was generally reckoned to be synonymous with effeminacy, a series of signs and words alerted audiences to a character's true sexuality. The homosexual character might be signified by appearance, manner, diction and behaviour. These signifiers would all be aspects of effeminacy or femininity, the polar opposite of the archetypal masculine. So the homosexual character on stage would usually be slim, slender or willowy, not broad, athletic or powerful. He would have paid exaggerated attention to his clothes. In the 1920s, in particular, the over-dressed man was synonymous with the homosexual, and his concern with how he looked would be taken as a sign of narcissism, which was supposed to be a signifier of homosexuality.

In manner the character would manifest significant signs which in a woman would be admired. He would be gentle or poetic, nervous and artistic, emotional and loquacious. His diction, rather than his deportment, would be camp, which in Susan Sontag's appealing definition was founded upon 'love of the unnatural, of artifice and exaggeration, something of a private code, a badge of identity'.[7]

Oscar Wilde's verbal camping enabled him to subject the world to the discipline of his transforming skills, to hold authentic emotion at an arm's length, to exalt style (though not at content's expense), to outlaw spontaneity. And in plays of the period camp speech, camp design, camp costume became in their mannered, consciously wrought extravagances a mode of dissociation from the conventional and mundane.

In this period the homosexual characters, smuggled on stage with the light camouflage of innuendo, circumlocution, and allusion, would be tellingly ranged against various celebrations of an idealised male archetype: the authoritative and unemotional male, who was liable to be athletic, muscular, clean-cut. The male theatrical stars of the popular and classical theatre were variants on this type: Gerald du Maurier and Ronald Squire, on the West End stage of the 1920s, epitomised the suave and sophisticated, without ever decking themselves in camp. John Gielgud broke the supremacy of these actors within the decade. But his personality and his style – the temperament bowed by overwhelming emotion, the body stiffly slim, elegant – were reckoned suitably in the service of Shakespearean heroes who could be written down as neurotics. And Laurence Olivier, Ralph Richardson and Michael Redgrave, in the 1930s, reaffirmed the salience of the male archetype, both on stage and on screen. In America a similar pattern was apparent.

The commercial theatre responded to the incitements of the Cold War and to McCarthyism. Senator McCarthy was notoriously influential in urging that the Communist and homosexual alike were potential spies and traitors.[8] They were invisible betrayers. The homosexual was no longer defined in terms of the pre-war stereotype. He might pass as heterosexual. And in the mid-1950s the highly popular *Tea and Sympathy* on

Broadway and *Serious Charge* in London are typifying plays. They respond to the new alarums by dealing with the growing pains of the heterosexual, who is accused of homosexuality on the basis of circumstantial evidence and suffers mightily, before being reaffirmed in the ranks of the sexual majority. These plays seemed to provide a critique of McCarthyism but they did little to contradict the idea that it was wrong to subject homosexuals to the persecution meted out to falsely accused heterosexuals.

In the later Cold War phase, between 1958 and 1967, before the veto upon portraying homosexuals on stage was lifted, the theatre began to be affected by the shock of the new. It was subject to structural change, to the transforming vitality of new-wave playwrights who both appealed to a new generation and wished to give the theatre a social and political function it lacked. Plays about homosexuality no longer accepted the notion of the homosexual as archetypically evil or dangerous. As the first tentative steps towards gay identity and community were taken, the stage began to depict the homosexual as the model of the pathetic-unfortunate.

In the final period, between 1968 and 1985, plays about homosexuality changed utterly. The negative myths, by which homosexuals were judged, began to be eroded. Gay dramatists and gay or gay-sympathising actors were reluctant to represent homosexuals in terms of the old stereotypes. The major plays began to recover or reconstruct history from a new perspective – to consider the damage done, the destruction caused by the persecutions meted out to homosexuals. The gay hero was born, just as a gay theatre, created by gay writers, companies and audiences, was being sought both in America and in Britain. And in the long emergency of the AIDS epidemic, when homosexuality had once more begun to be seen as the archetype of evil and danger, a few rare plays like Larry Kramer's *The Normal Heart* attempted to impart a radical potential function to the drama.

THE ORIGINS OF HATRED

The theatre, in its depiction of homosexuals, reflected the values and beliefs of the world beyond it. The Judaeo-Christian tradition of characterising sodomy as inherently evil and the cause of social downfall finds its earliest known expression in the biblical curses upon Sodom and Gomorrah. In the England of Henry VIII sodomy, whether practised between two males, or male and female, or with animals, was regarded as a crime against nature, and also a form of debauchery to which anyone might succumb, a potential for wickedness in mankind.[9] In such theorising may be detected the germs of the Freudian postulate that a bisexual component or potential exists in us all.

The idea of the homosexual as a category of person did not exist. The very word 'homosexual' was not created until the late nineteenth century. Acts of buggery were not only regarded as wicked, but thought to inspire divine retribution. As man was a microcosm of the universe, so one man's sodomitical fall from grace threatened the whole community.[10] The sodomite, diagnosed as a man outside nature's frame, with no fixed abode in heaven or hell, became one of the plausible scapegoats for catastrophes befalling communities. 'Famine, plague, flood, and fire' were 'acts of God directly provoked by the moral condition of those upon whom they fell'.[11] Settlers in the North America of the seventeenth and eighteenth century imported the same theories.

The contemporary gay historian, Arthur Gilbert, has provided an amplifying reason for this fear of buggery. The anal, he suggests, was evil. Hell had been pictured from Dante to Van Eyck as a privy teeming with excrement. Defecation was a symbolic and literal reminder to man of his similarity to animals, of the decaying process to which all living matter was subject after death. Buggery was thus emblematic of an unholy trinity–evil itself, death and bestiality.[12]

While there were religious and cultural reasons for stigmatising sodomy, the process by which the sodomite, and later the homosexual, was demonised or categorised as monstrous still survives. The Jungian theory of Shadow Projection offers an explanation of the psychic system by which we scapegoat. Jung diagnosed humanity's aggressive and cruel drives as the 'dark side or shadow of the psyche'. The superego, that complex of coercive agents in the self, ensured that we would observe the controls of our culture and that these drives would usually be repressed in the unconscious. The shadow itself could be regarded as an aspect of our collective nature, though not a clearly articulated archetype. Shadow Projection, the device by which we unconsciously attribute to others those negative characteristics denied or repressed in ourselves, offloads those instincts. The archetype of evil, rather than the individual's own shadow, is projected upon those we are schooled to fear or regard as our enemies. Contemporary Jungians have argued that Shadow Projection is a motor force for 'all racist and international prejudice and for our facility for turning opponents into devils. It explains the readiness with which we can convince ourselves that our enemies are not men or women like us, but monsters unworthy of all humane consideration.' And it is just such Shadow Projection that had helped to depict homosexuals as characters on stage as emblems of the wicked and dangerous.[13]

There are interrelated traditions by which the homosexual came to be characterised as effeminate and the actor ranked as homosexual. The process is subtle. The translators of the 1611 Authorised Version of the Bible rendered the Greek word 'which could be associated with homosexuality' as 'effeminate'. Effeminacy had no specific association with sodomy. The figure of the perfumed Elizabethan city gallant, elegantly attired in expensive clothes, who appeared in late-sixteenth-century satires, could be transported to the stage of London in 1929, where he would be naturally accepted as a contemporary stereotype of the homosexual. But for the Elizabethans effeminacy was redolent of a generalised debauchery and of 'luxurious living'.[14]

The London playhouse of the Elizabethan and Jacobean period was branded as 'a prelude to the brothel'. The theatre and the bawdy house were liable to be in close proximity; the impresario of the stage also functioned as the keeper of the brothel. The Curtain theatre, opened in 1576, was within three years being described as a pulling parlour for 'every knave and his quean'.[15] In Puritan eyes and minds the drama was an incitement to fornication and adultery, and often led to the horrors of sexually transmitted disease.

But there was a more specific accusation made against the playhouses and the actors performing in them. And the charges were not only levelled by Puritans. Theatres were condemned as the haunts of the sodomite – the sodomite defined quite literally as a passionate theatre-goer 'who is at every play and every

7

night sups with his ingles [catamites]'.[16] Phillip Stubbes, the fierce Puritan, even characterised the playhouse as an almost exclusive resort for males seeking out males for sexual purposes: 'Everyone brings another homeward of their way, very friendly, and in their secret conclaves covertly they play the Sodomites or worse'.[17] The actor, engaged in an occupation which had scant respectability, was reckoned likely to be engaged in a relationship with his patron which today would be understood in terms of homosexual prostitution. The tradition characterising the theatre as immoral, and its players liable to be sexual outlaws, endured. Clement Scott, the late-Victorian critic, suggested it was 'nearly impossible for a woman to remain pure' once she put a foot upon the stage.[18] And when, in 1990, Britain's mass-circulation newspapers stirred a malicious controversy about the sexuality of the monarch's youngest son, they suggested that the theatrical circles in which he worked were predominantly homosexual.[19]

By the end of the seventeenth century the molly houses of London were attracting a clientele who were males sexually attracted to males.[20] They were clearly effeminate in a sense which would, in the twentieth century, be regarded as stereotypically homosexual. 'They rather fancy themselves women, imitating all the little vanities that custom has reconciled to the female sex.' At the drag ball at the molly house the men 'were a mixture of wanton males and females, assuming effeminate voices and airs . . . their faces patched and painted . . .'.[21]

It looks as if, at a time before the word 'homosexual' even existed, there was beginning to exist what we would term a nascent homosexual subculture and identity. These people were defined according to their 'ways of dressing, of talking, distinctive gestures and distinctive acts'.[22] They were categorised (or could be) by that way of identifying and assigning to a category on the basis of a series of behaviourial signs – the stereotype.

This stereotype was elaborated and refined. In the eighteenth century effeminacy, a lack of physical strength and, sometimes though not invariably, a dandy-like attention to costume and appearance, were taken as symptoms of the male attracted erotically to males. The late-Victorians, when the medical profession was beginning its categorising business, used the new word 'homosexual' and rated it as illness and disease, a threat to that fount of respectability and uniformity, the family unit, which in its working-class and petit-bourgeois form was reckoned the suitable vehicle for maintaining the labour force, harnessed to burgeoning capitalistic enterprise.[23]

The three trials of Oscar Wilde in 1895 gave great and lurid public manifestation to what fresh statutory legislation and medical stipulation regarded as the increasingly prevalent vice of homosexuality. When he arrived at the Old Bailey for a date that hubris had arranged, Wilde was artistry and fame writ both large and flamboyant. He had flouted convention, and high society had put up with the flouting. Supercilious, disingenuous and lethal in the witness box, he exuded confidence from a great height, only to fall mightily in the end upon a prison sentence. Wilde, aesthete, dandy and hedonist, gave the homosexual a recognisable face. He had been accused of effeminacy in the past; now he was proved to be so. He was the first of the flaunters. Plump, unmuscular, languid, affected and upper-middle-class, though from the alien territory of Ireland, he was the antithesis of the manly virtues, the utter repudiation of the masculine archetype as it was defined. In his public life he had made a bonfire of the masculinities, as freshly celebrated and cultivated by the country's sporting, adventuring man of action (and sometimes of not too much intelligence). He had betrayed his gender.

Wilde's trials reinforced prevailing myths associating homosexuality with danger to the family, to marriage and to heterosexual males. The vices of seduction and proselytisation were supposedly the homosexual's constant companions. Wilde himself was both husband and father. True to his own words, he had resisted everything except temptation. He had deserted the marriage bed, risking blackmail and ostracism, to feast lavishly from the mouths and forbidden parts of the heterosexual panthers of the sexual underworld, to pleasure himself with those working-class youths who had been inducted into the oldest profession. So the homosexual stepped furtive and afraid into the twentieth century. He was engulfed in those negative myths and traditions that bore the authority of centuries. He was freshly discovered as a pathological case too. He was weak, sly, and he could not control his emotions. In him, no male virtues blazed a trail to heroism. He was the enemy within and he would have to be controlled. We will recognise his face and deportment again when he steps out scandalously into the nice and wholesome terrain of the twentieth-century theatre.

THE THEATRICAL CONTEXT: TRADITION, ECONOMICS AND THE IBSEN REVOLT

The plays about homosexuality and homosexual desire that feature on the London and Broadway stages between 1925 and 1965 were conventional in their form and in their sexual ideology. Yet, as we will see, they are spiritually related to the new genre of 'The Woman with a Past' society dramas of the 1880s and, more important, to the modern theatre movement of social analysis, dissent and nonconformity that Ibsen inaugurated and Shaw and Granville-Barker maintained. We will, therefore, be considering a situation in which plays that convey traditional myths and messages about homosexuality, and support moral and social orthodoxy, are nevertheless imbued with radical elements.

The fashionable and late-nineteenth-century theatre, from which Ibsen was to make such violent points of departure, was consciously prescriptive and restrictive. Its plays were like flattering mirrors, reflecting their audiences in the prettifying lights in which they wished to see themselves. Since this theatre's aesthetic was to amuse and divert, it regarded as taboo any image or discussion that cast any aspersion upon the ruling class whose life was celebrated on stage.

Broadway and the West End may at first glance seem clean different things, since the two countries are so different in their political and cultural arrangements. But from the mid-nineteenth century, when steam engines and transatlantic steamers shrank America's great spaces and the ocean, a two-way traffic of plays and players busily developed. Although Broadway had become the acknowledged theatre capital of the country by 1900 and discovered a native drama of its own, it looked to London and to Europe as a source of theatre. In 1880 the city's population was scarcely half a million, while London was eight times the size.[24]

The prime London playhouses were controlled by actor-managers, those on Broadway by businessmen. By the turn of the century the British theatre's new-found respectability was confirmed by a wave of Queen Victoria's wand, when the stage-struck sovereign knighted Henry Irving – the first actor to be so elevated. The actor, whose status had been scarcely higher than that of a tradesman, was upwardly mobile. In the first years of the twentieth century what had been a trade became a profession, and increasingly, one for gentlemen. But not until the knighthood bestowed upon Ian McKellen in 1991 was it considered either respectable or possible for an actor to admit his homosexuality and flourish.

The architecture and arrangements of London and Broadway theatres reflected the social and hierarchical nuances implicit in playgoing. Playhouses were segregated zones, with separate entrances for the well-heeled patrons of the stalls, the dress and family circles. The dominant motive of the men who owned, leased or controlled these theatres in London and New York, from 1880–1960, was profit. Their values and those of their audiences ensured that the plays of the period tended to reflect the social and political orthodoxies of a ruling class.

William Archer, the radical Victorian critic, described this theatre as no more than a capitalist adventure, with speculators allured by the chance of profits. And he railed against 'the imperative of success' which was 'the one object of managerial effort'. But he also rained down contempt upon the theatre-going public. 'Modern Englishmen cannot be got to take the drama seriously,' he wrote.[25] Walt Whitman, some three decades earlier, had similarly hankered for a new American theatre purged of 'English managers, English actors and English plays' which would 'attack and hold up to scorn, bigotry, fashionable affectation and all unmanly follies'.[26] He hankered in vain. By 1900 a 'species of commercial tyranny' had become the constant factor of American theatre with 'a ruthless theatrical syndicate' controlling it.[27]

Although the Shubert brothers, a collection of producers, ranged themselves in opposition against this syndicate, it would be fifty years before its hold upon the New York theatre was reduced by the invoking of the anti-trust laws.[28] The commercial theatre in twentieth-century London followed a similar ideological pattern, with the playhouses controlled by major theatrical corporations. The fact that the commercial theatres of London and New York have been run by small, powerful coteries of interlinked businessmen and reactionary

11

impresarios meant that the dominant theatre of Broadway and the West End before the 1960s was dependent upon the box-office power of stars.

In Britain the theatre's ability to challenge political, social or sexual orthodoxy was checked by the device of censorship in advance of production. Since 1737 an Act of Parliament, engineered by a Prime Minister piqued by the sneers and satires of Henry Fielding, had entrusted the licensing and censoring of plays to the Lord Chamberlain, a senior official in the monarch's household. As a result the stage was purged of the nutrient of true controversy. The political, the social, the religious, the sexual were barred from the stage. The stage's permitted diction was a thin, grey gruel from which all the robust, natural stuff of ordinary speech and expletives had been taken. In England it was not until 1968 that the Lord Chamberlain was relieved of his play-censoring duties and returned to his natural business of cherishing royal swans and arranging royal furniture. While he reigned over the theatre homosexuality was scarcely allowed to be depicted or discussed upon the stage: not until 1958 did the Lord Chamberlain permit plays discussing the matter of homosexuality, and even then he ruled out 'embraces' and those plays which were, as he mysteriously put it, 'violently homosexual' or contained 'practical demonstrations of love between homosexuals'. In America, after 1927, New York's stage legislature outlawed any plays which dealt with 'the subject of sex degeneracy or sex perversion'. This act was not repealed until 1967. The bounds of conventional sexual decorum were rarely penetrated.[29]

Ibsen's *Ghosts* was the great late-nineteenth-century play that challenged the idea that the upper-middle-class family was a repository and example of morality. It dissented from the idea that the reigning sexual and social orthodoxies were inherently good. The family unit emerged in the play as the fount of unhappiness and suffering. In London the Lord Chamberlain ruled that it could not be presented before a public audience, and on Friday, 13 March 1891 it was premièred for one night only, before club-members of the newly formed Independent Theatre. It was a device to avoid the Chamberlain's censoring powers and one which would often be used in the twentieth century.

Mrs Alving in *Ghosts* is the nineteenth-century model of the sexually submissive and self-sacrificial upper-middle-class married woman. She has exalted respectability, or the outward signs of it, at the expense of personal happiness and fulfilment. But the play and Mrs Alving herself are beset not so much by ghosts, as by the long-gestated consequences of her early married life. For the dead past, as incarnated by her indolent, promiscuous husband, rises up in the stricken form of her adult son who returns home suffering in the terminal stage of syphilis, for which she has been the unwitting vector.

Oswald's case history is not convincing in strict clinical terms. It is manipulated to deliver Ibsen's accusation that the bulwarks of family life were liable to be built upon foundations no more secure than sand; the very system by which two sexes were required to behave in life and marriage – with the socially and sexually submissive female allowed no independent life – was being put in question. Mrs Alving in maintaining the fiction of a respectable marriage has defied such sexual stereotyping. She has managed the family estate while her lecherous, lazy husband has whiled his life away.

We are beginning to move closer to that theatre and those predicaments with which this book is concerned. The lines of connection are being arranged. 'Ghosts!', exclaims Mrs Alving, in that most famous and chilling declaration of the play, which is also naturalism's credo:

> I almost believe we are all Ghosts, Pastor Manders. It is not only what we have inherited from our fathers and mothers that walks in us. It is every kind of dead idea and lifeless old beliefs. They are not alive but they cling to us for all that and we can never rid ourselves of them . . . There must be ghosts the whole country over, as thick as the sands of the sea. And then we are, all of us, so wretchedly afraid of the light.
>
> (2.107)

In Ibsen, inheritance, the living ghost in the works of each woman and each man, dominates our lives while the environmental fabric of our existence helps shape a process of struggle. It is this struggle that becomes the motor of the modern drama. It is in the struggle of Ibsen's *Brand* that

Raymond Williams discerns a new 'structure of feeling' in the drama.[30]

> It is for a general human liberation that this exceptional man struggles. And this is, then, decisively a modern consciousness ... It is by acting against the common condition and against even the process of detailed relationship which ties men to this, that this singular man ... expresses the ideal of humanity. It is man against men; the individual against society.

It is in this turmoil, in this engagement, that the Ibsen anti-hero and the heroine, who often struggle against the stereotypes, are actively engaged or passively caught. In these liberation ardours and impasses the first phases of a theatre of revolt are detected. It is a feminist revolt, before all else, since the Ibsen heroine bears the chief burdens of conformity and struggles against it. The plays that in the twentieth century contend with the inflammatory subject of homosexual desire clearly belong in this Ibsenite tradition of turmoil and engagement, however reactionary in structure and sexual and social ideology they are, however disapproving of that revolt against the 'common condition'.

These plays about homosexuality interpret such desires, and the action that may follow hard upon them, as drives that separate and outlaw the desirer from all the usual supports and securities of life. Family and friends are set against the homosexual. The family threatens to withdraw approval and support. Family life, with its permanent offer of secure fixtures and fittings in society, is ranged against homosexual existence, which is envisaged as a friendless limbo, where there is no community, no rules or any chance of relationship or lasting happiness.

The homosexual anti-hero – there are of course no heroes – is also interestingly a close relation of the 'woman with a past', as enticingly decked out in the fashionable society dramas of Pinero, Wilde and Jones. These are writers who had been inspired by the genre of fast French courtesan plays, by a *demi-monde* of adultery without too much guilt and with airs of flagrant naughtiness. The homosexual anti-hero is cast as the man with no future, sure to be punished by play's end, with sexual orthodoxy and the secure straight and narrow thoroughly approved. The plays which depend upon the woman with a past also trade in a sexuality which is both forbidden and dangerous – though not, of course, as depraved as the homosexual's. And the plays are composed to satisfy through titillation, albeit in the most seemly fashion. With true hypocrisy, the sexual allure and potency of the sexually adventurous woman is sumptuously revealed and then excoriated. In these plays, also, adultery and freelance acts of fornication are permitted to men but not to women.

Contrary to the governing code of the plays, the woman with a past, even though she belongs or belonged to the right class, tries to challenge the idea that women may not be sexually promiscuous and respectable at one and the same time. *The Second Mrs Tanqueray* (Pinero, 1893) offers a male fantasy of reparation and atonement by which Paula does the decent thing and commits suicide, thereby signifying that she can never be integrated into respectable society and the proper joys of family life. The man to whom her stepdaughter is committed does not have to take this drastic course. A succession of these plays admit the allure of the woman with a past – even to the point of taking her in marriage or thinking of such a desirable action – and then doom or thwart such an eventuality. Heterosexual male supremacy is reinforced. It is such a reinforcing of sexual orthodoxy that we are about to witness in the principal plays about homosexuality, from the mid-1920s to the late 1950s.

2

THE DEVIANT, THE DAMNED AND THE DANDIFIED: 1925–1939

SOURCES OF INSPIRATION

The theatre is public, open and corporate, where the novel is private, closed and personal. The dramatists of the inter-war years, who managed to secure productions for plays contending with homosexual desire, adapted some of the strategies of subterfuge already employed by novelists brooding upon similar themes. The dramatists tended, though not exclusively, to rely upon the same view of homosexual desire that affected Marcel Proust's *A la recherche du temps perdu*, Joseph Conrad's *Victory*, Thomas Mann's *Death in Venice* and André Gide's *The Immoralist* (which, indeed, emerged in dramatised form upon the stages of New York and London in the mid-1950s). They had interpreted such desire as a self-destructive passion, inducing an unwelcome host of negative emotions. And the diction of such works, 'a language of reticence and evasion, obliqueness and indirection', came to figure as techniques of canny defiance for playwrights.[1] For the 1927 New York state legislation which prevented the depiction of plays dealing with homosexuality, and a similar veto in Britain, imposed a need for analogous forms of theatrical reticence.

For those dramatists seeking to establish a clandestine stage iconography for the homosexual, Oscar Wilde's *The Picture of Dorian Gray* was an obvious inspiration: here was a negative theory of homosexuality and a stereotype to bear it. Wilde (after Huysmans) had set the 'real' life of 'bourgeois respectability and conventional morality' against a homosexuality which was seen as an evasion of such things – an escape to art and to artiness.[2]

16

From *Dorian Gray* emanated a sense of homosexual desire as dangerous, evil and life-destroying. Dorian's beautiful face was no more than a deceiving mask; it so seduced and dazzled the smitten that they missed the ugliness of the man within. The novel, in Richard Ellman's sharp phrase, was 'a negative version' of Wilde's own homosexual existence.[3] Dorian, the aesthete or rather dilettante, the fully-fledged dandy and practising narcissist, was pitched a world away from the Victorian male icons of admiration. He was sensitive, delicate, artistic, passionate for perfumes, jewellery and embroidery. Dorian's characteristics would only be celebrated and cherished in a woman.

Wilde's diction of artifice and exaggeration, the exaltation of style at the expense of content, the sense of life as role-play, would emerge as the sign of camp sensibility in some of the key homosexual characters of the modern stage. But by the later 1920s conceptions of homosexuality were beginning to be affected by that great destabiliser of sexual myths, Sigmund Freud. *The Interpretation of Dreams* had been published in English during the First World War, and within a decade the subconscious, the libido, repression and the Oedipus complex were becoming known as dynamic aspects and influencers of the human psyche.

For the writer, Freud was recognised as a visionary explorer leading the journey towards the unknown regions, that murky world beneath the surface of life. On Freud's eightieth birthday, Thomas Mann delivered a tribute signed by 197 major artists of the day, which praised him, in most significant words, for penetrating 'to truths which seemed dangerous because they revealed what had anxiously been hidden'.[4]

One of these dangerous truths related to Freud's theory of homosexuality, a concept articulated in his *Three Essays on a Theory of Sexuality* (1905). The revolutionary nature of Freud's insight lay in his rejection of the idea of the innate heterosexuality of humans: the sexual aim (the form of activity) and the object (that to which we are drawn sexually) were not ordained in advance. Homosexuality was simply 'a variation of the sexual function, produced by a certain arrest of the sexual development'.[5] Heterosexual object choice remained, in his estimate, the desired cultural norm, and homosexuality was to be interpreted as a failure to achieve that destination; but

17

he was seeking to dispose of the idea of homosexuality as an illness of either body or mind.

The extent to which Freudian theory attracted disciples and adherents may be gauged by the fact that even in a bastion of conservatism and frivolity, like the theatre, Freud was exerting some influence. In 1936 Laurence Olivier, the new leading young man at the Old Vic, was contracted to play Hamlet. Eagerly he accepted the suggestion of the director, Tyrone Guthrie, that he should create a Prince based upon the interpretation of Freud's biographer, Ernest Jones, who argued that Hamlet's delaying tactics could be attributed to the Prince's Oedipus complex.[6] A year later, when Guthrie was directing Olivier's Iago to the Othello of Ralph Richardson, Dr Jones was consulted once again. As a result, the production depended upon the idea that Iago nurtured an unconscious sexual passion for the Moor, a passion transposed to hatred and malevolence. Richardson was, however, never told of the scheme and reacted with horror to the kiss that Olivier threatened to give him in rehearsal.[7]

But Freud's attempt to integrate homosexuality within an accepted and acceptable realm of human behaviour had negative or malign repercussions as well. If heterosexuality had, in a sense, to be learned or at least developed, then it could be argued that the unlucky, the susceptible and the plain youthfully curious might be coaxed away from the path that led to the Freudian notion of full-blown maturity, marriage and the producing and nurturing of children. Both in America and in Britain, there developed a belief that you did not have to be born homosexual; you could become so through enticement.[8] The nineteenth-century theory of homosexual activity as a form of willed deviancy was born again. Even though Freud himself had dethroned the notion of heterosexuality's inevitability and naturalness, Freudian analysts were tending to interpret homosexuality as a psychiatric problem.

THE THEATRICAL CONTEXT

It seems another world now, and not just a single lifetime away from us. Flappers and chorus girls, gangsters and silly asses in monocles, *femmes fatales* and heart-throbs fill its stages. The audience, well-heeled and high-heeled, sumptuous in their starched and careful formalities, regarded the playhouses as after-dinner relaxations. The stars were remote icons to be reverenced.

The 1920s were darkened by deep problems of adjustment and recuperation from the devastations of the First World War. The grim economic facts of depression and fascist ambition that marked the 1930s could already be detected in the preceding decade; but the richer and privileged sections of post-war youth were gladly absorbed by the new cult of pleasure. The new Jazz age, with its sexy liberating dances, was characterised by its hectic exuberance, by a determined flight into high spirits. Gay was the defining stance, a gaiety which ran in opposition to a parental generation's sexual and social rigidity. The old forms, the old taboos were to be broken, in art as in life. The cultural revolt against the prevailing orthodoxies, in which the children of the early years of the century had been reared, was also a revolt against patriarchy and those values patriarchy enshrined.

Noël Coward's *The Vortex*, with its loose, amoral and privileged cocktail set, is the authentic voice and style of a new generation. George V who was shown the script by an anxious Lord Chamberlain pronounced the play 'disgusting' but unfortunately, he judged, it was impossible to ban. The original veto upon the play was placed because of objections to the sight of what was falsely described as a 'nymphomaniac mother' enjoying affairs with men of her son's age. Coward persuaded the Chamberlain that it was 'a moral tract'.[9] There may be more to it than met the eye (see chapter 4), but the play's popularity stemmed mainly from its power to shock and enthral.

The governing spirit of the middle-class audiences of London and New York was sensational, prurient, eager for glimpses of the New Immorality, but wishing to be told that this was immorality presented in a moral cause. Somerset Maugham's *Our Betters*, first seen in New York in 1917, caused an outbreak of indignation, engendered by the fact that a married American woman was discovered on stage caught in the arms of a gigolo – not in bed, but worse, in a summer-house. When, in 1923, the play was sent to the Lord Chamberlain, his advisory committee recommended it for production, on the grounds that it seemed to condemn rather than incite fornication and adultery among the aristocracy into which the American woman had married.

The popular plays of the period, whether the cynical, satirical view of upper-middle-class sexual mores, organised by Maugham and Frederick Lonsdale, or the reassuring sentimentalities of George Kaufman and Moss Hart, only went so far. They flirted with sexual naughtiness; adultery and fornication might threaten either marriage or family, but the happy ending waited in the wings for its reconciling entrance. Social orthodoxy was affirmed. The seekers after happiness, in the theatres' escapist pleasure-palaces, were satisfied. 'The drums tap out sensational bulletins', W.H. Auden wrote in an epigraph for *On The Frontier*, his three-act political melodrama, on which he collaborated with Christopher Isherwood, 'frantic the efforts of the violins, to drown the song behind the guarded hill.' And it was the frantic violins of this frivolous theatre which prevailed over the warning sounds of reality, the signs of the great Depression, the symptoms of anti-semitic persecutions and privations, the inexorable menace of Hitler's expansionist Germany.

The theatre in Britain thus seemed to exist in a temperamental opposition to the prevailing artistic spirit of the 1930s literary generation that Auden led. In that decade -- in poetry pre-eminently but in literature too -- there flourished writers who attempted to create a politicised art that would reach beyond the bourgeoisie to the working classes. The new poetry, whose governing voice was Auden's, the *Left Review*, *New Writing*, the founding of the Left Book Club -- these were the influential artistic sounds of the decade, of a struggle to relate the personal world to the political. If there were so few and so unsuccessful examples of an analogous theatre, the reason had to do with political control of the theatre, and with the economics of the theatre and those who controlled it.

Clifford Odets's *Waiting for Lefty*, written for one of those workers' theatre groups that sprang to life in the depressed 1930s, Lillian Hellman's *The Children's Hour* or Elmer Rice's *Street Scene* were examples of a fringe theatre, of a political and social drama known in London only in such rare outposts as the Communist Unity Theatre, the Embassy and small club theatres. But the British theatre, and indeed literature and the cinema, were subject to sweeping forms of censorship, kept under vigilant surveillance as if they were dangerous children who at any time might make a dash for the precipice. The nature of these controls and their extent are indicative of the high-level anxiety that all sexual candour and explicitness engendered – let alone any attempt to grapple with homosexuality. In 1928 Radclyffe Hall's lesbian novel, *The Well of Loneliness*, was prosecuted in Britain, and in 1929, in America, was subject to a seizure order. The prosecution evidence in Britain hinged upon the discreet and euphemistic sentence 'And that night they were not divided.' Britain's Attorney-General, the government's senior law-officer, led the prosecution case, asking whether it could be doubted that any innocent young man could be corrupted by such a lurid sexual picture.[10] The Attorney's question was a useful reflection of governmental beliefs and standards. Sir Archibald Bodkin, the Director of Public Prosecutions between 1920 and 1930, threatened the respectable publishing house of Allen & Unwin with prosecution for publishing a work of 'filth' by Sigmund Freud, unless an undertaking was given that the book would be disseminated only to doctors, lawyers and university lecturers.[11]

In America the destruction order for *The Well of Loneliness* was not approved, but the National Office for Decent Literature of the Catholic church ordered that homosexual novels should be placed on an index of banned books; publishers and newspapers tended to practise a form of self-censorship ensuring that the very word 'homosexuality' was exiled from the public prints. A direct veto upon the depiction of homosexuals on screen was enshrined in the Motion Picture Production code of 1934 and the veto was only circumvented by what the American film-historian Vito Russo has called 'the harmless sissy' – the effeminate man could be regarded as a fantasy creation since 'homosexuality did not officially exist.' In Britain the British Board of Film Censors operated a system of political and social censorship. It would not permit anything on celluloid which the Home Secretary, Sir Herbert Samuel, termed subversive of 'decent ordered family life'.[12]

Homosexuality, in the commercially motivated reckonings of some heterosexual dramatists and theatre producers, could be treated as one of those deviancies of the freshly immoral times. Mae West who wrote *The Drag* (1927) and Frederick Lonsdale in *Spring Cleaning* (1925) were alert to the shock tactics of putting homosexuals on stage, since they could be summoned up as signs of fast and naughty living for the new audiences.

Yet any close viewer of the plays about homosexuality placed upon the stages of New York and London in the inter-war period will still be struck by a certain diversity, by a sense that there were slight but significant attempts to qualify the predominating sense of the evil, sinister homosexual.

Even *The Drag*, performed before censorship's curtain fell, enabled heterosexual audiences to glean the news that a form of homosexual community already existed in New York, that the idea of the isolated, friendless homosexual was not necessarily true. And J.R. Ackerley's *The Prisoners of War*, in London, escaped the Lord Chamberlain's ban, perhaps because its author created a convincing homosexual anti-hero, who lacked almost all the signs of homosexual stereotyping. A sequence of plays treating homosexuality as a moral, social and family problem was organised to imply, for those who wished to take the message, that some of the crucial difficulties experienced by homosexuals were not inherent but socially conditioned.

A TOUCH OF THE FORBIDDEN

In the London high summer of 1925, a young actor, who liked to wear 'light grey flannels braced much too high', silk socks, broad-brimmed, black, soft hats, and his hair 'much too long, and overwashed to make it fluffy and romantic' took over Noël Coward's role of Nicky Lancaster in *The Vortex*.[13] John Gielgud had arrived. Within a month, the dandyish Gielgud was in the midst of a swarm of young bohemians, intellectuals and homosexuals who were present at something more subversive. They were attending a Sunday night performance at the Royal Court Theatre of a new play by an unknown young writer. The play lacked altogether the crowd-pulling tactics and sensational elements that animated *The Vortex*, but it was a real milestone in modern theatre. Coward's play, for all its thematic daring and novelty, was oblique in its depiction of a young man who may be homosexual.

J.R. Ackerley's *The Prisoners of War* was the first twentieth-century play produced upon the London or Broadway stage to deal with homosexual desire, a desire that animated the entire action. That the Lord Chamberlain permitted the play a licence, allowing it to move from its Sunday night performance, for members of the 300 Club, to the Playhouse Theatre in the West End, remains something of a mystery that still bemuses Sir John. He recently gave a graphic impression of the conventions of the London theatre of the 1920s, when he referred to the 'courage' of the producer in transferring the play to the West End, and of how it might have flourished at the Playhouse if a popular star of the period had 'dared to play such a controversial part' as that of the wretched anti-hero.[14]

J.R. Ackerley is one of those rare literary figures who win their greatest fame after death. It was achieved with his post-humously published autobiography, *My Father and Myself*, that most candid homosexual confession and a revelation of sexual irregularity in an Edwardian middle-class family. Ackerley, as his autobiography makes wretchedly clear, was a paradigm of that homosexual guilt and unhappiness experienced by his class and period. He was also a characteristic example of an artistic sensibility and a temperament that came of age and had some influence in the 1920s. Martin Green illuminatingly defined those who manifested this temperament as 'children of the sun', adult children in revolt against the patriarchal system and values that their fathers incarnated and against the orthodoxies of the male archetype.[15] The structure of their lives involved a rejection of marriage, of parenthood and of responsibility and power. Instead, they centred their lives on art and renounced the materialism of their fathers.

Green conjectured that these children of the sun were spurred by a narcissistic worship of the adult male. They were related by temperament to the aesthete and the dandy. The dandy was defined by a self-consciousness that was not regarded as masculine. He regarded his body and his personality as bare frames on which he should hang a series of ostentatious and affected designs. The dandy is and was inherently camp, being concerned with artifice and exaggeration. The aesthete, of whom the dandy rates as a derivative, may have affinities of style and manner but his terrain is different. The dandy is concerned with superficialities, with the creation of effect; the aesthete with the appreciating and judging of that 'something which is outside himself'. The dandy is his own work of art; the aesthete savours and judges real ones.[16] By the 1920s the dandy-aesthete was reckoned, in a swift organising caricature, as a likely homosexual.

Ackerley, no mean sportsman, masculine in manner and deportment, scarcely ranked as either dandy or aesthete. But he did belong in the category of the children of the sun: sensitive, narcissistic, neurotic, shy and artistic, he was the antithesis of his businessman father, who relished dirty jokes and whose life was bounded by a narrow materialism. *The Prisoners of War* did not, surprisingly, rely upon the figure of the aesthete or the dandy. It was a play well ahead of its time, and its stage history was an index of all those difficulties attendant upon bringing the subject of homosexuality on stage.

The play was based upon the hard facts of Ackerley's experience as a prisoner of war immured in a Swiss hotel, where he became bothered and bewildered by the sexy body of a consumptive young soldier. The text charts a downhill emotional journey from sexual longing to fury and final breakdown. As such, the play looked unlikely to find any place in the theatre of the 1920s. 'I do not think that any theatre would undertake a play of so harrowing and distressing a character,' the Master of Magdalene wrote to Ackerley. A leading London theatre agent confirmed this view. The Stage Society and the Everyman Theatre in Hampstead gave the writer dusty answers. But Mrs Phyllis Whitworth, who ran the less well-known 300 Club, offered him a Sunday night production at the Royal Court Theatre, since she was committed to plays which were judged 'difficult' and uncommercial.[17]

In January 1925, weeks before the play was to be produced, Ackerley was asked to see Mrs Whitworth. It transpired that she had read the play in dangerous innocence. Word had now come to her that *The Prisoners of War* was being talked about in London as 'the new homosexual play'. As a result, she had been inundated with ticket requests. On rereading the text she had realised it was 'open to misconstruction'. Open? Ackerley, a middle-class socialist with a lifelong predilection for shocking the bourgeoisie, at once told her the play was simply about a love affair between two men.[18]

The reference to 'talk in London' alluded to the bohemian and coterie underworld of homosexuals that discreetly flourished and developed in the inter-war years, both in London and New York. Julian Symons, heterosexual and an influential literary editor of the 1930s, has suggested that the post-war spirit of sexual emancipation enjoyed by a younger generation of bohemians meant that unmarried heterosexuals were freely living together, with sexual pleasure the prime pursuit for either partner. 'The Thirties might also be called the homosexual decade', he asserts, 'in the sense that in these years homosexuality became accepted as a personal idiosyncrasy.'[19] He was referring, however, to the sheltered and very narrow literary and artistic circles of the period. There was, therefore, a yawning gulf between the coteries of bourgeois artists and a commercial theatre that appealed to a quite different bourgeoisie.

It says something for Mrs Whitworth's courage that she was still persuaded to persevere with a play that she feared would cause trouble, even though presented in club conditions. For she was, on the surviving evidence, an unsophisticated and highly conventional woman. Robert Harris, at 90 the last surviving member of the original cast, recalls her hissing to him, when Ackerley's sister arrived to watch a rehearsal and profusely embraced her brother, 'You see! Incest as well.'

Harris's own memories, as a very spry and intellectually alert nonagenarian, suggest that the director, Ackerley's Cambridge friend, Frank Birch, avoided all mention in rehearsal of the play's real theme. 'One never thought of it as a homosexual play. I don't even remember it disturbing any of us,' Harris told me. 'I suppose you're right,' he conceded as I read some of the stage directions to him. 'I don't remember it disturbing any of us. Isn't it amazing?'[20]

The 'us' was a very interesting set of young actors, of a calibre that suggests how eager the brighter performers of the period were to escape from the conventional West End. George Hayes, no star but a leading Shakespearean at Stratford, played Ackerley's *alter ego*, Captain Conrad; the handsome, young Harris, who had recently played Oberon to Edith Evans's Titania at Drury Lane was cast as the love-object; the two other young officers, who seemed immersed in each other, were played by the fashionable young Canadian, Raymond Massey (who himself had been wounded fighting in the First World War), and Carleton Hobbs, who was to become the most famous and durable of all BBC radio actors after the Second World War.

The form of Ackerley's play, for all its thematic daring, is traditional. The designer, James Whaley, whose imagination was later given scope for greater leaps of daring when he directed the film of *The Bride of Frankenstein* in 1935, created a conventional stage-set, a room with a view, as if in Ibsen country, with 'snow-capped glaciers . . . avalanche paths and cascading streams' (1.93). A maid and a non-commissioned officer were in attendance, taking the place of the usual servants who attend in the drawing-room comedies of the 1920s.

The diction, with its quaint period jargon ('Drunk be blistered . . . Ruddy sharks . . . You silly stiff', 1.94), was redolent of the public schools from which most of the young men had recently come and of the war with which they had finished. And it may have been the quasi-public-school milieu of the internment hotel, the masculine demeanour of the officers, that confused the Lord Chamberlain into thinking that nothing truly impure was in the air.

None the less, even if the play is cast in allusive, symbolic terms, caution was sometimes thrown to the winds when signs of desire reared up shamelessly in the stage directions. Men were required to do these things to men on stage: a head of curls was caressed; hands were held too long to count as wholesome handshaking, or placed heavily on a favoured shoulder; fingers were brought into play, linked in a contact that lasted through several sentences of conversation. Worse, some of these gestures lacked innocence. 'Look out, someone might come,' warns the 19-year-old Lieutenant Grayle whose curls Captain Conrad 'affectionately strokes' (1.10.27).

The stage directions alert us to the fact that because Grayle had been 'educated at a good public school' he knows how to contain such advances (1.102). Harris's recollections suggest that actors and director alike were unaware of the significance of these stage directions. Hugh Walpole, T.E. Lawrence, John Lehmann and Siegfried Sassoon were all moved by the play in performance, for despite its governing melodrama Ackerley powerfully reflected a homosexual sense of being an anxious, repressed, permanent outsider in a heterosexual world. Captain Conrad's underlying sense that he would never achieve homosexual love was a typical, if not general, view. For twenty-five years of his adult life Ackerley went in dogged pursuit of what he described in his 1967 autobiography as 'the ideal friend' – a phrase evocative of public-school passion. He looked for sex in all the right places; but it was love he was after. He thought the casual pick-up would lead, could lead, to the love of a lifetime; but his sexual specifications might have been framed to ensure that the happy ending he sought would never be achieved. He was attracted to working-class, predominantly heterosexual young men, and dreamed of an unconditional devotion that they would generously give him. His ideal, he explained, was a man, with the body of a young boxer whom he loved, and the personality of the Alsatian bitch who, in middle age, filled an emotional void no human occupied.[21]

In his quest, and its underlying demands, we see a fairly typical process through which some middle-class homosexuals went within this period. Ackerley, permanently troubled by premature ejaculation, in dread of uncleanliness in the sexual Others he took to bed, and of bad breath in himself, never removed his clothes while having sex. 'Repelled' by effeminacy in men, he even disliked the word 'homosexuality' 'since it included prostitutes, pansies, pouffs, and queens'. London, 'puritanical and joyless', offered him merely a sexual terrain of 'tatty pubs in Soho and elsewhere, the haunts of queens, prostitutes, pimps, pickpockets, pansies, debauched service-men, and detectives; a few dull clubs frequented by elderly queers and some dark and smelly urinals, which were not to my taste'. These are Ackerley's autobiographic confessions and conclusions, written in a melancholic old age, and though there is some obvious factual truth, it is a partial account. Sadly, it seems as if Ackerley introjected society's contemptuous and appalled view of homosexuality, while convincing himself that he had risen above it. In his homosexual Mission Impossible and in his prematurely seminal penis are the symptoms of deep sexual anxiety and shame.[22]

The relationship between Ackerley's homosexual life and the implicit perceptions of homosexuality in The Prisoners of War was very strong. The play was an eerie premonition, if in exaggerated form, of what Ackerley's life would come. Captain Conrad ended up deep in a nervous breakdown, preposterously attached to a pot of azaleas; Ackerley ended up in dogged devotion to the whims of his possessive

Alsatian. His memoirs provide a fine explanatory context for the play.

Ackerley's strategy in delineating the personality and dilemma of Captain Conrad was rather subtle. The Captain may not be a 'sport', may hate women and never join in the 'hunt' for women in Interlaken, but he seems as masculine as the next officer. The sequences of exploitation and dejection that he suffers in his longing for Grayle, who makes use of his room and his cigarettes, are powered by oblique innuendo. Their scenes together are charged by Conrad's angry emotionalism, and the intensity of the emotion is most indicative. And when that emotionalism gives way to breakdown the middle-aged, maternal Mrs Prendergast gives the game away. 'He was so nervy and high strung he was like a woman in some way' (3.ii.132). Conrad's state of mind is more significant than that ruffling of hair. For it was one of the controlling myths about homosexuality, retailed for most of this century, that emotionalism and nervousness were stereotypical signs of homosexuality, while emotion repressed or denied approvingly was reckoned a sign of the ideal male. Running in counterpoint to Conrad's veiled wooing of Grayle is a more open quasi-sexual emotional contest between Lieutenant Tetford and Grayle for the good-looking Captain Rickman. Rickman exploits Grayle, just as Grayle exploits Conrad, by encouraging the friendship so that he may fleece him at cards.

Thirty years on, Ackerley angrily protested to a friend that there was but one homosexual in his play. The rest were 'entirely normal'. What was more, it was quite 'unthinkable' for any audience to imagine Tetford and Rickman going off together, since they were merely 'pals'.[23] Old men are, of course, liable to forget or betray their earlier selves and their writings. Ackerley had both forgotten and betrayed. His daringly allusive stage directions supply a sexual subtext for the two men's final-act discussion of the 'golden future' which they will share together in the Canadian outback (3.i.129). Rickman is required to 'link' a finger in Tetford's 'dangling hand' and then to grip it. 'The poetry in him sensed by Tetford but unsuspected by Conrad is released,' Ackerley specified (3.i.128).

All this released poetry, this thrusting and passing of mysterious somethings between two young men contemplating a future together, is scarcely the stuff of sexual innocence; and it is, of course, easy to mock these metaphors – they are necessary codes. But there is something more. Relations between Tetford and Rickman are, relatively speaking, open and clear. When Conrad comes in, while the two men are doing something entirely erotic – holding hands – they let go of each other 'without embarrassment' (111.ii.129). But when Conrad does something just as suspect, stroking Grayle's curls, the second Lieutenant warns him 'Look out. Someone might come in' (1.103). Tetford and Rickman are open, honest and unashamed; Conrad and Grayle are guilty and furtive.

The diction of both Grayle and Conrad is public-school – adolescent, petulant and emotional, suffused with displays of the temperamental. Tetford and Rickman are in their speech adult, direct, emotionally balanced and assertive. Ackerley mutes the sexual intimations of Conrad's desiring by its relative restraint:

> You'll stick by me, won't you? You could help me no end, you know, if you were decent to me. It's the sort of thing I'm most anxious to talk to you about . . . This is a decent room too and we shall be quite comfortable together. It's when I'm like this that I want you most. You'll stick by me, eh?
>
> (1.102)

But the Grayle-Conrad interchanges are otherwise adolescent and fraught with guile. 'I'm going to Rickman', rages Grayle, 'who knows how to behave like a man' (hence perhaps his attraction) 'and doesn't sulk like a kid. You were quite right. I like him better. I'm tired of you and your rotten temper. I don't want to speak to you again' (1.105). Tetford, by contrast, is direct and aggressive in defending his own interests. 'You'll go on missing him,' he tells the bereft Conrad. 'You're made that way but if your pal Grayle thinks he's going to relieve me of Eric, he's mistaken' (2.100).

It looks at the end of the play as if Ackerley was handing out rewards and punishments. The two men whom he disliked or despised – his *alter ego*, Conrad, endowed with Ackerley's own emotionalism, and Grayle – can be identified as being in some sense effeminate or lacking in masculinity. Neither of them was allowed a happy ending. But the archetypically masculine Tetford and Rickman are allowed to look forward to homosexual happiness together.

The London theatre critics, although some of them rightly referred to the play's 'morbidity', responded to that first-night performance with high enthusiasm. 'A piece', wrote the most influential critic of the period, the homosexual James Agate, in his *Sunday Times* review, 'of which one would not miss a moment, incident or personage.' And he, in company with a few other reviewers, alluded to the play's sexual innuendo. 'It jumps to the eyes that the problem is not one of depression but of repression.'[24] The reviewers who admired the play were surely celebrating its novelty-value and daring.

Nigel Playfair, one of the few producers of the inter-war period interested in classic theatre and new plays, took a chance upon *The Prisoners of War*, successfully submitted it for licence and presented it at a very unfashionable West End location, the Playhouse, where it ran for twenty-six performances. Harris believed that only a lack of publicity prevented success. But the play, for all its homosexual intimations, won Ackerley a coterie reputation. He was written into *Vogue* magazine's Hall of Fame, with pictures along with Viscount Haldane and Leonide Massine. It was as if the play's forbidden themes had passed notice.

In the same year that *The Prisoners of War* was produced, the latest play by one of the West End's most popular playwrights reached the St Martin's theatre. Frederick Lonsdale, a jovial *arriviste* in high society, was making a small fortune. He wrote comedies of aristocratic manners, where dukes were commonplace, and relied upon his audiences' inveterate snobbery and lubriciousness. Lonsdale's upper-class characters were invested with social glamour and Wildean epigrams. He appeared to condone adultery and fornication, but his plays were cunningly organised to allow the triumph of orthodoxy and convention, with the amoral defeated. It was surely for this reason that the Lord Chamberlain allowed him to introduce the first clearly defined homosexual character to take the stage, although just for a few trivial scenes.

Spring Cleaning, presented in 1925 with an assortment of West End stars, traded on the excitement inspired by fornicators and adultery. Its shock tactic was to introduce a common prostitute, a tart with heart of course, into an upper-middle-class drawing room where she gets the moral better of her so-called betters. This is not surprising: *Spring Cleaning*'s principal young people are very fast-living cocktail drinkers, who have swallowed what pride they had, and go for the main chance. 'I'm going to have fun with lots of men before I settle down and marry one of them,' says young Fay who lays claim to an uncle who is a Duke (1.29).[25]

The play proclaims its studied sexual sophistication in the very first moments when a butler nonchalantly ignores the fact that he has seen his married mistress sealed to the lips of Ernest, a middle-aged lecher. But the sophistication and the play's apparent sexual liberality are false: there is no missing the playwright's misogyny, the sense that philandering women are contemptible, while males like Ernest (played by one of the decade's most popular stars, Ronald Squire) may be forgiven attempts to steal wives. Ernest is, in fact, a middle-aged male's fantasy of himself as a male sex symbol, unashamed to flaunt his lack of conscience. 'Will you ever marry?' he is asked. 'Not as long, old friend,' he ripostes, 'as other men are willing to' (2.69).

Into this cocktailing company there comes the first of the flamboyant homosexuals to take the modern stage. Lonsdale makes no bones about it; there is none of Ackerley's closetting and concealments. 'Bobby Williams enters,' the stage directions read. 'He is an effeminate boy of 22.' And if that is not signal enough, Lonsdale provided the clinching evidence: 'He is very overdressed' (1.24). Bobby is a crude example of obvious period camp. 'How sweet you look. [*picks up a cushion*] Oh how divine. What a perfectly gorgeous cushion. I must get some like this at once' (1.24). Bobby's world is bounded by fashion and interior furnishings, and he speaks in the hectic extreme:

> I've had a terrible row with my hosier. I've been trying to get a certain colour undervest for ages, and the brute got them for me. But because Reggie Vale liked them, he gave them to him. You've no idea what terrible things I said to the beast.
>
> (1.25)

This rank stereotype of homosexuality is patronisingly accepted by the fast young female things, while he arouses contempt and loathing in the males: 'What a dreadful fellow this is' (1.25); 'That caricature of a human being' (2.75); for one of the girls he is 'a powder-puff' (1.31); for Mona, the prostitute, he is 'a fairy' (2.75); and Bobby predictably threatens to faint when a whole group of the cocktailers are faced with the threat of being locked in the drawing room.

Yet Lonsdale has a strange, equivocal admiration for the chap. It is manifest in Bobby's defence of himself. He may be trivial, he may incite Lonsdale's contempt for being effeminate; but he, unlike the rest of the posturers, has the courage to be unconventional, to be effeminate. He is a Julian Clary of his times: he ranges himself against the 'stuffies, fearing people, respectable ones' (1.26). He ignores the slings and arrows of outrageous abuse: 'I never mind what anybody says. I never have' (1.30). He is in revolt against the orthodoxies to which the others will ultimately return. The rules of society leave him cool: 'It's such fun to see one's friends in the witness box,' he says, encouraging one of the cocktail girls to do the indecent thing and leave her husband for life and fun (1.36).

Lonsdale's relative sexual candour was of a sort which the New York stage also condoned. *Spring Cleaning* had already been presented on Broadway eighteen months earlier, running for 292 performances. Yet when *The Prisoners of War*, with its plea for sexual liberation, was presented on Broadway for just eight performances at the Ritz in 1935, the discourse of the critics and the responses of the audience were contemptuous in tone. Although only the *New York Times* critic, Brooks Atkinson, used the word 'homosexual', other reviewers selected derogatory phrases and circumlocutions to describe Conrad's sexual hankerings, referring to the 'epicene', 'the middle sex' and 'the elfin strain'. Audiences laughed in the wrong places.[26] In London there existed a coterie, bohemian-artistic theatre-going audience who would treat a play like Ackerley's, for all its melodramatics, sympathetically; Broadway lacked such an audience. While the Lord Chamberlain disallowed plays that dealt with homosexuality, he was quite prepared to sanction an unequivocal depiction upon the stage of a homosexual, introduced principally as an object of derision.

The Drag, briefly seen in America in 1927, written by the

American actress Mae West, was a far more extreme example of the prevailing tendency to disparage or sensationalise homosexual existence. Mae West, mistress of the *double entendre* and the single come-on, had founded her acting career upon lack of sexual inhibition. But *The Drag*, rescued from half a century of oblivion in modern times by Kaier Curtin and William Hoffman, only flashed – albeit scandalously and sensationally – across the American stage. It has never been published, and West refused to allow it to appear in a recent volume of plays about homosexuality.[27]

The Drag is a melodramatic, quasi-morality play in which a deceitful, married homosexual is murdered, shot dead by his jealous and discarded lover, who has turned to drugs to assuage his sense of loss. West is traditional in her description of homosexuality as a form of degeneracy or illness. And the murdered homosexual, Rolly, is presented as a dangerous proselytiser, forever ingenious in his attempt to seduce an innocent young heterosexual. Rolly, however, is not an effete, weak young thing. He passes as heterosexual, has married as a cover and leaves his wife to suffer pangs of sexual frustration in a bed where nothing is consummated. While Rolly's former lover, the drug-addicted David, inspires a little pity and is true to homosexual stereotype, West reserves her anger for the likes of Rolly, whose innocent wife, Claire, is unaware of what her husband's lack of sexual interest may signify.

Rolly's father-in-law, a doctor specialising in addictions and perversions, delivers Miss West's judgement. 'In this civilised world, we are not civilised enough to know why or for what purposes these poor degenerates are brought into the world. Little did we know that a fine strong boy like Rolly was one of them.'[28] Homosexuality is finally diagnosed as some strange malady whose signs may be concealed successfully, and so leaves heterosexual women vulnerable to exploitation by deceiving homosexuals, who buy respectability with marriages of convenience.

The Drag was not only significant in itself, but played a crucial role in assisting the campaign to bring about New York State's ban upon plays dealing with homosexuals. It appeared at an inauspicious moment. 'Don't relax Mayor! Wipe out those evil plays now menacing Future of the Theatre,' begged the headlines in the *New York World* on 23 November

1927. The *World* was appealing against *The Captive* in which a 35-year-old husband saw his hair turn grey when his wife was enticed by a lesbian. 'Under cover of friendship a woman can enter any household whenever and however she pleases . . . she can poison and pillage everything before a man whose home she destroys is even aware what's happening to him', the husband complains.[29] You never knew when your wife would be snatched away by her diabolical best friend, for sexual purposes unknown to upstanding, married men.

The Drag had the good fortune to be tried out in New Jersey in the midst of the uproar over *The Captive*. It stirred murky clouds of scandal, some fascinated comment in the New York press and expressions of outrage from politicians and religious leaders; a Cardinal and a Rabbi, Baptists, Methodists and Protestants united in an ecumenical chorus of outrage. One February night, when *The Drag* was poised *en route* for Broadway, the actors and managers of three New York plays were arrested in several fell swoops, and charged, according to press reports, with 'being a public nuisance' and 'tending to corrupt the morals of youths and others'. Mae West was appearing appropriately that night in *Sex*, and *Sex* was one of the raided three. In such circumstances, and with *The Drag* similarly threatened if it showed itself on Broadway, there was no longer any chance of the play coming to town.[30]

West was no sexual pioneer, however much she claimed at the time to be bringing homosexuals out of the cold, and giving chorus boys the chance of a lifetime to prance in drag on stage. In her autobiography, *Goodness Had Nothing to Do with It*, published forty years later, when she had little left to trade upon except her past, West claimed she had wanted to alert all America to the danger within, a danger unseen. She had set her simple sights in *The Drag* against those homosexuals who could not be recognised or identified at a knowing glance, the sort of chap to whom the average girl might even be married. Such men were secretly in concert (she thought) to bring America to its knees, jeopardising the country's future survival. For they had it in their wicked minds to convert the male masses to homosexuality and enlist innocent youths in their sexual ranks.

If the tenor of West's play was predictable and its characterisation of homosexuals traditional, the central drag scene was not. Rolly's homosexual party-goers, crude sexual opportunists, are also depicted as temptation for heterosexual young men to whom they gladly succumb: 'I'm the type that men prefer. I can at least go through the navy yard without having the flags drop to half-mast' one of them boasts.[32] The mistress of sexual abundance never believed, as far as she was concerned, that enough was as good as a sexual feast. *The Drag* was to alert upstanding American women that men aspired to steal their meat. West's alarm call would sound, in more general terms, across the stages of Broadway and the West End.

PERVERTS IN DISGUISE

The Green Bay Tree by Mordaunt Shairp (1933, Plate I) was the most dishonest and morally disreputable play about homosexuality to reach the stages of London and Broadway between the wars. It was also the most commercially successful and critically applauded. The play's message, conveyed in easily decipherable theatre-code, appeared to describe the enfeebled struggle of a young man to leave his rich, middle-aged protector and embark upon a marriage. Although it is not explicitly suggested that the relationship between Julian, the young man, and his protector, Mr Dulcimer, is sexual, there is no missing the sense of homoerotic corruption that permeates the whole play. Since Mr Dulcimer, he explains, bought Julian for £500 at the age of 11, from impoverished working-class parents, and since Julian is shown addicted to an idle life of luxury in a sumptuous, Mayfair apartment, there is no missing the insinuation that the youth has been successfully enticed, that he will never be able to achieve a heterosexual mode. Worse, Julian's pathetic attempts to escape to heterosexuality are thwarted by the older man's devilish cunning.

The audience is incited to believe that Julian's addiction to 'luxury' and 'pleasure' has contaminated him; these words are endowed with special meaning and, it becomes clear, are synonymous with homosexuality. Photographs of an epicene Laurence Olivier in the Broadway production of 1933, with his first wife, Jill Esmond, playing the girl he never marries, make a sexual point tellingly. Mr Dulcimer, therefore, emerges as a diabolical thwarter of heterosexual desire, a secret subverter of the juvenile, working-class male. The play's crisis is precipitated by Julian's wish to marry. A battle of wills and wiles is joined, in which the possessive Dulcimer is pitted against Julian's fiancée and Julian's real father. Nothing directly states that Dulcimer is homosexual; but, all the signs suggest he is, and that his relationship with Julian is homoerotic.

Shairp invites us to interpret the play as a modern morality parable, a reworking of Dr Faustus, in which Dulcimer emerges as an updated Mephistopheles, offering Julian the infirm glories of the world, in the form of money and luxury, while never allowing him beyond midnight, and into a new day of marriage, parenthood and a heterosexual version of fulfilment. The attachment between Dulcimer and Julian is also conceived as an unnatural refuge from the heterosexual life, and approved mature patterns of work, duty, marriage and responsibility. 'Support a wife. That sounds rather dreary,' Julian exclaims to his patron (1.i.62). Julian claims to long for independence, but he knows he cannot achieve it. 'I can't move a step without you,' he confesses to Dulcimer (1.i.62). His symptoms of stress become apparent in his perfunctory attempts to study, to make himself employable. But he lacks any application. He has, thanks to Dulcimer's years of training, become good for nothing much. Homosexuality, through the older man's precious, affected example, is depicted as a sterile evasion of real life; all the pleasures that money may buy are here represented as glamorous devices to soothe an existence empty of purpose. For once in the snobbish plays of the period the upper-class mode is denounced, though chiefly because it is also homosexual.

The stage directions for *The Green Bay Tree* are lavishly spattered with instructions which indicate how far Dulcimer is to be played as the epitome of Wildean camp. He is in the tradition of Dorian Gray, dilettante and dandy. The sumptuous room is redolent of 'luxury and fastidiousness', relished by a 'complete dilettante', with a 'sensitive personality' and 'a delicate appreciation of beauty' (1.i). Dulcimer is elegance incarnate in his double-breasted dinner jacket, and matching manners. His personality will 'fascinate, repel and alarm' (1.i.55). Dulcimer and his rich life-style are insistently evocative. He seeks out pleasure as his constant companion. He exists in a small artistic whirl, wafting from one 'heart-rending private view' to a box at the opera for 'the most exquisite love story ever imagined' (1.i.57). Life poses no greater problems than the arrangement of 'amethyst cushions' around the 'amber' swimming pool in his country villa or the decoration of the cupids in his country home (1.i.57). His senses are continually gratified: champagne, liqueurs and cocktails are served in every scene; soft lights and sweet music are regularly summoned up. Even the desserts are camp: 'A coupé Evelyn Laye' turns out to be the most exquisite and refined ice-cream imaginable. And a camp butler serves up 'a large and very exquisitely designed ice-pudding shaped like a small rose tree in bloom' (2.ii.82).

Dulcimer was played in London in 1933 for six months at the St Martin's Theatre by Frank Vosper, a popular actor of the decade – bohemian, gay and charming, according to John Gielgud, and much admired as a highly sinister Claudius to one of Gielgud's Hamlets.[33] Here he was required to be suave, affected and quietly dangerous: the nickname of 'Dulcie', by which he is addressed, crudely advertised what is already apparent. He also expresses himself in terms that seem disparaging of heterosexual aspirations. 'There is always something terrifying in the remorselessness of nature, something shattering in all this reassertion of the principle of life,' he tells Julian (1.i.57). Dulcimer prefers 'To see nature controlled and at my feet.' He is thus ranged against the life force itself. It is precisely the principle of reassertion, symbolised by Julian's wish to marry, against which Dulcimer contends.

Julian's 'natural' father 'Owen' is depicted in crudely approving terms that recall early seventeenth-century Puritan pamphlets and their distinction between a corrupt, decadent metropolitan life, as exemplified by Dulcimer, and pure, honest country existence represented by Owen. Julian's father is a part-time lay preacher who has repented his earlier drunken life and now rails against the lures of the cinema. He works in a dairy 'full of fresh eggs and glasses of milk' – no corrupting homosexual liqueurs available there (2.i.75). Mr Dulcimer reads the Bible merely for its 'style' – as befits an amoral aesthete (1.i.69), while Owen lives by it. Dulcimer offers Julian Mayfair luxury, a life free of work, but full of holidays and opera; his real father a hard diet of 'prayer and moral purpose' (2.i.75).

Leonora, heterosexuality's other vigilant missionary, engaged in a quest to rescue Julian's body for herself, and his soul from sexual damnation, supplies those elements of masculinity missing in both Dulcimer and Julian. Not only is she nicknamed 'Leo,' as if she were as good as any man, she is 'clean-cut, strong-willed, decisive' – the very attributes you would expect of a Boy's Own hero (1.i.63). She is 'quite free from pose' – the camp quality with which Dulcimer is so over-endowed (1.i.63).

'I must have comfort, I must have pleasure, I must have money to spend,' Julian tells Leonora in the tones of today's impenitent yuppie (3.i.91). Mr Dulcimer exploits Julian's weakness. 'You know that luxury is the breath of your life,' he warns his protégé. In its full context Dulcimer's innuendo becomes clearer: 'You know that luxury is the breath of your life. You couldn't do without it for a second. What you are feeling is childish revulsion against yourself. Self-loathing is always painful, but fortunately one outgrows it' (2.ii.88). The references to 'self-loathing' and 'revulsion against yourself' are inappropriate criticisms of someone living in luxury, but the words are apt and to the point if they really refer to a man who cannot escape his homosexuality. 'Go and get married,' Dulcimer challenges Julian, 'Disregard your temperament, your disposition, your everything that cries out against it. Can you do it?' (2.ii.88). Something more than luxury is at stake. Julian's response – 'Why do you torment me like this?' – admits as much (2.ii.88). Leonora draws an even more pointed connection between Julian's addiction to luxury and to his sexual personality. 'Do you think it's pleasant for me', she exclaims, 'to find out that the man I love isn't a man at all, but only a bundle of sensations!' (3.i.92). To live in luxury is thus to be unmanned or unmanly. And in the most sexually pointed sentence of the play she taunts him with the prospect of a future 'in Piccadilly with a painted face' (3.i.92) if he abstains from marriage and all 'that is normal and healthy' (3.i.93). The sexual innuendo could not be made clearer.

Leonora's mission to save Julian by preaching the virtues of moral hygiene fails. At the play's climactic struggle for possession of Julian's first-rate body and his third-rate personality, the Faustian nature of the battle is indicated, with Dulcimer a homosexual anti-Christ. 'I'm not under the spell,' Leonora insists, but even she feels the force of Dulcimer's 'snake-like' fascination (2.ii.82). Worse, when news of Dulcimer's return to London is announced, Julian notices that Leonora looks as if she had 'seen the devil' (2.ii.78). Even the stage direction alludes to 'the spell' that the older man is able to cast (2.ii.86). Finally Leonora and Owen spill the truth as they speak in identical terms. 'This man has got hold of Julian body and soul,' she cries. Owen, as befits a preacher, is even more fervent: 'This man is wicked. He's evil. You don't realise how evil he is! I want you to get away before he destroys your soul altogether' (3.i.95).

But it is not Julian's soul for which audiences were invited to feel anxiety. It is his body that seems under threat, for all the evidence to the contrary. And Shairp finally proves that anxiety justified. 'If you take him away', Dulcimer tells Leonora, 'I'm lost. Like you I have feelings, but with Julian in my life I am never troubled by them. He keeps them content and satisfied' (2.ii.94). And with lights dimmed, Dulcimer, playing Chopin at the piano, reasserts his power over Julian in a form that owes more to the erotic than to the artistic. 'Have you ever played the harmonium, Dulcie?', Julian asks in 'dreamy' tones, 'It's not an instrument you can stroke, like you're stroking that piano.' The youth ends up 'weeping' and pliant. The 'spell' as Shairp once more terms it, has worked (2.ii.86).

Even when Owen intercedes, conveniently grabbing an 'exquisitely jewelled revolver' from Dulcimer's attaché case and shooting his son's benefactor dead, Dulcimer triumphs posthumously. Julian becomes Dulcimer's double, at once adopting his manners and his diction. The play's anti-hero has been likened to 'the wicked in great power . . . spreading himself like a green bay tree', and the play's last scene thus affirms the triumph of that homosexual corruption which Dulcimer personifies (2.i.75).

The Green Bay Tree's commercial success depended upon its titillating powers, its teetering on forbidden terrain; its frequent revival on Broadway in the years between 1945 and 1951 was a sign of this capacity. The reviewers of productions in both theatre capitals matched Shairp's reticence. 'A wealthy degenerate', said the *New Statesman*, describing Dulcimer as created by Frank Vosper. 'One may read anything one chooses, or very little . . . into Dulcimer's feeling for his ward,' Brooks Atkinson wrote, after the Broadway opening in the *New York*

Times. 'The author more or less lets the point go by default, devoting himself in the main to an attack on luxury.'[34] Similarly, in the London *Star*, A.E. Wilson had concluded 'If the object was to arouse powerful detestation for two abominable people a kind of success may be concluded.' But he would not specify the nature of the abomination. Only Ivor Brown, in the *Observer*, confessing himself weary of laughing at 'effeminate men with all the mincing movements of their kind', came close to any sort of sexual diagnosis and judgement: 'He [Dulcimer] is there as the objectively studied specimen of a rare and unhappy species.' Others were not so sure: 'One may wish that Mr Shairp had been more forthright in clarifying his issue and had not hesitated to call a spade a spade,' lamented the New York *Evening Post* reviewer.[35] However, in neither country did one critic authoritatively challenge or question what Shairp had asserted.

INCITEMENTS TO PITY

Both on Broadway and in the West End there were antidotes to Mordaunt Shairp's defamations of homosexuality. Laurence Olivier, before going to take the role of Julian in New York, played in Keith Winter's *The Rats of Norway*, which Gladys Cooper, the former Edwardian chorus girl who had graduated to the straight theatre, presented at the Playhouse Theatre in 1933. The play resorted to cryptic imagery of a sort more subtle than Shairp's, revealing an emotional rapport between two schoolmasters, which even their love affairs with attendant young women cannot abate.

There were more vital attempts to invite pity for homosexuals, interpreting such sexual desiring as a social dilemma rather than a symptom of inherent evil or illness. The most daring and provocative of these efforts was a play seeking to rescue Oscar Wilde from the terminal ignominity into which he had been cast just forty-one years earlier. It was also the first play in the twentieth century to bring frank discussion of homosexuality to the stage.

Leslie and Sewell Stokes, the play's authors, did so by relying upon court transcripts of Wilde's Old Bailey court cases. The Lord Chamberlain would not license the play for public production and it was, therefore, staged at the famous Gate

Theatre Club close to Charing Cross station. Here, in the 1930s, banned plays regularly saw the light of evening, watched by club members only: here Eric Portman and Flora Robson had, for the first time in Britain, startlingly rendered O'Neill's *Desire Under the Elms* in 1931, a play which like Lillian Hellman's *The Children's Hour* and Pirandello's *Six Characters in Search of an Author* had been refused a licence by the Lord Chamberlain.

Among the small-part actors who played in *Oscar Wilde* was a young man who, after the Second World War, turned to directing and managed to maintain his passion for new and radical dramatists like John Whiting and Rodney Ackland while working as the principal director for the company which specialised in conventional and traditional West End theatre. He directed a series of star vehicles ridden by the likes of Edith Evans, Peggy Ashcroft, Sybil Thorndike, Michael Redgrave, Ralph Richardson and Paul Scofield.

Frith Banbury is now 78. He is homosexual and was a conscientious objector during the Second World War. He has managed to observe the conventions and standards of West End commercial theatre for five decades, both as outsider and insider. By the time *Oscar Wilde* was produced, he estimates that the theatre's old guard, represented by stage leaders like Gerald du Maurier 'who was very anti-gay', had been all but superseded; but that did not mean that a new generation of theatre managers and directors was generally sympathetic to homosexual actors.

> It was not permissible to put homosexuality on the stage and if we wanted to get on in the West End we did not choose to parade our sexual preference except where we knew it was perfectly OK to be so – either with those who were gay or who did not mind.[36]

It was a matter of theatre economics as well and of producer power.

> I wanted jobs. If they knew you were gay they'd think 'He's gay. He's not male enough. He's not a sexual draw for the part.' Therefore you were in the closet. But it was never a great strain, because I had a perfectly adequate sex life. Not pick-ups. And I never felt guilty.

Banbury's testimony runs counter to the prevailing idea of the homosexual introjecting guilt and shame. He was lucky in his serenity and his ability to ignore the conventions by which Britain was ordered. So he happily went without a thought for his reputation to audition for *Oscar Wilde*.

At the time he was playing in repertory at Perranporth in Cornwall. Norman Marshall, who ran the Gate, had offered him the role of Eustace. A portly, shy young actor who was in the Perranporth company with him asked for a chance to read the play. He handed the script back to Banbury a day or two later looking grim. 'You must *not* read it,' Robert Morley warned, 'You'll never get another job. It's a horrible homosexual part.' Banbury was not put off. He was offered and accepted the part of Eustace. But once rehearsals had begun in London, the actor chosen to play Wilde left the cast abruptly. No one was available. Frank Pettingell, a bright and fattish heterosexual who dared to play homosexual parts, was not free. Who else could be summoned at short notice and in such circumstances? 'I do know an actor,' Banbury said, mentioning his friend Morley. 'Oh no,' said Marshall, 'Terrible actor.' But in the end, and in the emergency, Morley took the role. There was no one else. 'My only hope', he said at the time, Banbury recalls, 'is to persuade people that I'm not like Oscar Wilde but that Oscar Wilde was like me.'

He managed the trick. Oscar Wilde was the making of Morley. The producer, Gilbert Miller, came over from New York and arranged its New York transfer. The play never had the chance of commercial success in Britain because the Lord Chamberlain refused to relax his ban upon its public performance.

After the Second World War it was performed in 1945 at another club theatre, the Boltons, and Sir Terence Nugent, the Lord Chamberlain's comptroller, wrote 'It is undoubtedly a good play but I do not recommend you to pass it. It is entirely about perverts, and . . . this subject is taboo as a dramatic theme.' By 1958 the Lord Chamberlain was prepared to relax his ban, but the play's aspirant producer, Arnold Taylor, was told that *Oscar Wilde* would only be licensed if Wilde's son did not object. Vyvyan Holland did. He wrote a letter to Lord Scarborough, the new Lord Chamberlain, saying that he found the play 'in very bad taste', and liable to give the public 'an entirely wrong impression of the whole wretched business'. But his objection to the play's public performance rested on his assertion that if presented 'it would certainly cause distress to my wife and son'.[37] The Lord Chamberlain obliged Holland, without seeking to enquire whether there was any truth in Holland's assertion that the play was either distasteful or inaccurate. In fact the play depends largely upon known fact, and the sexually explicit is avoided.

The Stokes brothers argued that it was not Wilde's homosexuality that ruined him but his recklessness. Wilde, in this play, refuses to skulk in the sexual shadows, keeping homosexuality to the closets of discretion. Instead, he shows a homosexual face to the world, or at least to the highest society in which he mixes with his working-class pick-ups.

The play, in its purportedly moral resolution, leaves Wilde claimed by nemesis in his Parisian exile, impoverished, drunken and generally ostracised. He is the picture of the mighty, mightily fallen, dependent upon the kindness of strangers. Audiences are asked to pity rather than to condemn him. The Stokes brothers kept their Wilde close to the gay original, garbed him in wavy hair, a large green scarf, a prominent ring upon his finger and drenched him in a charm that verged on smarm. Wilde was restored to theatrical life as a flagrant hedonist and aesthete. But Wilde's capacity and eagerness to shock by show, and word of mouth, with paradoxical epigram, and by irony is simplified. In the play he subscribes to a moral rebellion; in life he challenged moral orthodoxies. The playwrights laid the greatest stress upon the man's failure to heed the disquiet of his friends who arraigned him for offending social, not sexual, convention. 'If Oscar chose all his friends from the pages of Debrett it would not matter so much,' one of them observes. 'One can hardly blame people when they see him treating a stable lad to champagne at the Café Royal, for thinking it a little odd' (1.ii.34). Such behaviour, in what an admonitory Frank Harris describes as the 'native land of the hypocrite' (1.ii.47), characterises the Wilde of the play's first phase.

In this Wilde world the rich likes of him can take their pleasures where they choose, if they pay for them. 'I like people with no principles better than anything else in the whole world,' he proclaims (1.ii.41). Hedonism is placed on a pedestal and worshipped manfully in an Algerian hotel.

The theatrical portrait is not a particularly attractive one. The select use of Wildean epigram is calculated to establish him as a rampant, self-absorbed egotist who sees little further than the end of his own penis, or someone else's, particularly if it belongs to a working-class youth. The humiliations of the court hearings enacted verbatim, and Wilde's sexual interest in young men, disguised as a grandiloquent, spiritual platonism, do not much ruffle the fabulous composure. The spending of too much sexual energy in the wrong sexual places leads him to the kind of abasement that, the authors imply, is inevitable and proper, but also piteous.

The London theatre critics responded to this version of Wilde's downfall with predictable displays of embarrassment. The *Daily Telegraph* critic left the theatre 'with a slight unpleasant taste in the mouth', while *The Times*, in disdainful tones, dismissed the play as a piece which 'merely relates what were best forgotten'.[38] This public discussion of homosexual desire infringed the convention of silence. When it arrived there two years later the New York critics, outspoken where their British counterparts had been reticent, suggested the extent to which homosexuality was still construed as a medical condition. They resorted to such words as 'psychopath', 'perverted', 'disease' and 'pathological infirmities' in their periphrastic attempts to describe homosexuality. In terms recalling the shocked language that greeted the English and American premières of Ibsen's *Ghosts* in the late nineteenth century, Brooks Atkinson of the *New York Times* referred to Wilde's court hearing as 'unsavoury . . . a malodorous scandal and a ghastly case'.[39] He was deaf to the play's pleas. He was in the majority.

The camouflaging procedures employed by Keith Winter and Shairp to disguise their real concerns were scorned by two playwrights of the 1930s who dared to deal with the discovery of homosexual attachments, and with family response to such revelations. Both of them suggest that the homosexual youth should be either encouraged to be himself or simply accepted as he is. In *Whiteoaks*, seen at London's Little Theatre in 1936 and at the Hudson Theatre, New York, in 1938 adapted by Mazo de la Roche from her novel, and *The Good* by Chester Erskine, on Broadway, the same year, the two homosexual adolescents are identified by the tell-tale signs of effeteness. Their intellectual and artistic interests are regarded as symptoms of homosexuality.

The two youths are described almost identically in the stage directions. Finch in *Whiteoaks* is 'a lanky youth of eighteen, very sensitive and nervy', an aspirant musician who cannot do the usual masculine thing of riding a horse or training a dog (1.i.1). At the climactic moment of the play he collapses in unmanly sobs on the piano seat, something which his well-built, rather aggressive, brother would never do (3.66 and 1.i.1). His nervousness, his sensitivity, his slimness are obviously intended as signifiers of homosexuality; his musicianship is pointedly contrasted with his sporting brother's aggression. But in the conventional play of the time – and *Whiteoaks* is one of the most unconventional – the aggression, the roughness and plain-speaking of Finch's brother would be regarded as admirable aspects of masculinity; here they are not. Howard, in *The Good*, is not 'lanky' but 'slender.' He is 'sensitive' rather than 'very sensitive', 'emotional' rather than 'nervy', 'sincere' – which is daringly neutral in this context – and 'gentle' as befits a youth who recites poetry and likes flower-arranging.[40]

Whiteoaks is not quite a play about homosexuality in the sense that I have characterised the genre. *The Good* deals in sporadic melodrama. It describes American parents obliged to face the facts of their adolescent son's homosexual love affair with a man twice his age. But Finch, it has been noticed, is the first – the only – homosexual character in pre-war Anglo-American theatre to be specifically 'rewarded' although he is gay. His musicianship and unconventionality are here approved and applauded. Howard is also given his chance of happiness at the expense of his enraged parents.

The Good, which unsurprisingly lasted just a few nights on Broadway in 1938, is set in typical period theatrical territory, a grand home on Hudson Point. Howard's requited passion for the local choirmaster, a man in his thirties, springs the play's crisis of hysteria and accusation. And it induces domestic collapse when the adolescent unbelievably reveals his secret to the family doctor. It is this doctor who promptly brings the news to where it supposedly belongs, in the bosom of the boy's family. But *The Good* rejects the typical resolution of plays of this genre. It does not destroy the passion that is the cause of crisis. Howard's affair inspires an outburst of familial problems. Erskine refuses to imbue his homosexual hero with guilt or shame. In terms astonishing for the American stage of 1938 he suggests that a sexual relationship between a homosexual adolescent and a man in his thirties is not inherently depraving, exploitative or wicked. And although Howard's lover is a choirmaster, and therefore presumed to be a stereotype of homosexuality, he is, remarkably, 'well-built and lacking the flamboyance to be expected in men of this type' (1.38). Furthermore it is the unhappy 16-year-old who makes all the running, to escape from his family; the choirmaster urges Howard to remain with his parents.

The play was presented at a time when the Broadway theatre still believed in sexual innocence, when the idea of adolescent sexuality scarcely reared a demanding, urgent head. The nature and extent of that innocence is beautifully suggested in the play's initial dialogue between the local vicar and the boy's mother. It is typical of a long-ago American society where homosexuality is so remote from mind or expectation that the discovery of its existence is rude and painful:

> MRS ELDRED. I don't see terribly much of him myself these days. He's all wrapped up in your choirmaster. They're inseparable. Spent last night with him. In fact I haven't seen him since.
> VICAR. Oh, Duncan. You don't say. Now that's very good. I'm glad to hear that. Francis is a fine fellow. Very decent. Excellent musician too. Splendid organist. So they've hit if off . . . now that's nice.
> MRS ELDRED. Must be rather a bore for Mr Duncan. He's twice Howard's age.
> VICAR. It's a tribute to the boy.
> MRS ELDRED. Well I don't really object. If Mr Duncan gets tired of him, he'll put a stop to it himself.
>
> (1.25)

Such parental lack of awareness imparts to the subsequent scene of sexual revelation a pathos that it would not otherwise attain. What Erskine shows, therefore, is a successful process in which a very young homosexual sets himself and his life in defiance of the codes by which the heterosexual majority live. Medicine, church, school and family offer Howard nothing but admonitory negatives and condemnation of the sexuality on which his happiness and sense of well-being depend. No reviewer of the play appeared to understand the nature of Howard's bravery or the challenge to received standards that the play offered. Yet in the scene of sexual revelation homosexuality is still interpreted as a profound family catastrophe. The family doctor reveals the facts of Howard's homosexuality as if he were telling the family their son was fatally ill. 'It's hard to tell you this. He's not well. There's nothing I can do about it. He's not a normal boy. His instincts are not normal' (2.38). Still, the play is so organised that Howard appears a notably self-adjusted, self-accepting young man in a society that does not wish him to carry such self-esteem.

Mazo de la Roche's *Whiteoaks* offered a complementary study of homosexual youth, equally at odds and out-of-place in a conventional upper-middle-class Canadian family in Toronto of the 1930s, where she places men mainly astride horses or doing manly things with sporting dogs. Ostensibly the play depends upon the clash and clamour of a large family, all of them seeking to acquire the inheritance of a 102-year-old grandmother who has, unbelievably, yet to make her will.

The play depends on the relationship forged between the ancient woman, forever railing against hypocrisy and family humbug, and her homosexual 18-year-old grandson, Finch. The grandmother is the outspoken enemy of those conventions on which her family depends, and Finch is as much an outsider as she is, a fact that brings them together in mutual sympathy. Finch's homosexual attachment is revealed in a device worthy of Sardou or Scribe, when a letter drops from his pocket and is found to be written by a male who has dared to address the youth as his 'Darling Finch'. No other details are supplied, though the warning given to the embarrassed Finch, by his middle-aged, unmarried brother, is couched in terms of outraged extremity: better an 18-year-old man frequent a brothel than be in love with a man, he rages, flinging the letter into the fire.

The effect of this revelation and of Finch's ashamed silence would, in a conventional play of the period, serve to ruin the youth's chances of being a beneficiary of his grandmother's will. But although Finch, unlike Howard, is invested with a conventional view of homosexuality, being rich in self-loathing, there is no such certainty. 'I'm no good,' he tells his grandmother in the midst of a veiled sexual confession, whose significance she does not miss. 'You're a queer boy, but I like you, yes, I like you very much,' she replies (1.ii.27). The effect is sensational. Nothing is said directly, but the use of the word 'queer' indicates that she knows just what he is admitting.

At the play's close, when the old woman's will is read, and Finch is revealed as her beneficiary, his confession and the fact of his homosexuality acquires renewed importance. De la Roche rejects the ruling fiction that the artistic and possibly effeminate young homosexual should be treated as a pariah. Instead, she suggests that he should be supported and encouraged in the daunting business of being true to himself. And as if to reaffirm the force of this, Finch's tormenting older brother recognises him as 'the strangest, the sanest' of them all (3.66). In some sense Finch's 'queerness' has been accepted, even approved.

The theatre critics, on either side of the Atlantic, either intentionally or wilfully, ignored de la Roche's sensational apology for the homosexual. The critic of *The Times* described him merely as 'a musical alien' and 'clumsy, shy, tautly strung'. On Broadway they were more outspoken. *Variety* condemned Finch to the status of the diseased, as 'almost a pathological case'.[41] Both plays used the traditions and conventions of the commercial play: Ethel Barrymore, a 1930s star, bestrode *Whiteoaks* as if a popular player could make popular what de la Roche was showing. *Whiteoaks* and *The Good* are, in a sense, Ibsenite liberation plays. But there is no disguising the fact that the Freudian analysis of homosexuality fell mainly upon deaf ears. The theatres' perception of homosexuality remained both negative and malign. The atavistic myth by which homosexuality was characterised continued to flourish on the stage.

3

THE ENEMY WITHIN: 1949–1958

DEFINING THE DANGER

Every night in the autumn of 1953, from Monday to Saturday, the actress, Deborah Kerr, who was appearing in Robert Anderson's *Tea and Sympathy*, would stand on the stage of the Ethel Barrymore Theatre in New York, wearing a well-worn look of suffering. Every night she would be told that a woman simply did not know what a man always knew. 'All right,' her irritated stage husband, a housemaster and queer-stalking former athlete, would berate her. 'So a woman doesn't notice these things. But a man knows a queer when he sees one' (1.46). There was no missing the sense of panic in his accusation, a panic related to the theatre from the world beyond the stage.

What the housemaster claimed with such authority was, however, untrue. For the rigour and intensity of that part of the Cold War campaign devoted to removing homosexuals from the public service and the military was inspired by the belief that it was very hard to recognise homosexuals at a glance. There was a new conviction that the iconography and the stereotyping by which the homosexual was supposedly recognised were not, after all, reliable guides.

Newsweek had warned in 1949 that 'scores of inverts' had managed to penetrate the ranks of the armed services in America. 'Some are deceptive to the uninitiated,' warned the book *Washington Confidential* in its chapter entitled 'A Garden of Pansies'.[1] But it was important to try to recognise him at first glance, for by 1950 the homosexual was being endowed with a fresh identity, as a potential traitor and spy. Senator Joe McCarthy and Republican National Chairman, Guy George

49

Gabrielson, were warning Republicans in particular and America in general that homosexuals or 'sexual perverts' – there was believed to be no distinction – were perhaps as dangerous as the actual communists who have infiltrated our government in recent years.' Homosexuals in the public service, McCarthy argued, were susceptible to blackmail since they ran in fear of being exposed. Homosexuals, therefore, constituted a security risk. They were unseen corruptors of the body politic.[2]

McCarthy, whose accusatory techniques depended upon 'the innuendo, the reckless charge, the big lie', worked through 'character assassination, guilt by association and trial by publicity.'[3] He helped to foster an anxiety that public and indeed private morality had declined and that homosexuality was a cause of this falling-off. He was also quick to suggest that homosexuality was inextricably bound up with communism. As communism was construed as the threatening archetypal enemy without, so was homosexuality construed as the enemy within.

The danger that the homosexual was said to pose for America was accentuated by a fictitious conception of the nature of homosexual desire and an idealised notion of its heterosexual correlative. Homosexuality was a form of addiction. Homosexuals were proselytisers trying to persuade malleable heterosexual males into succumbing to that most dangerous of sexual cocktails. Implicit in this myth-making process was a strange sense of the sexual instability of the male heterosexual, as if he were easily seduceable. And, interestingly, psychiatrists of the 1950s argued that the vehement persecutors of homosexuality tended to be men who were unconsciously projecting their own homoerotic desires upon others. Heterosexuality, by contrast, when safely practised in the haven of marriage, was said to put sex in its place as one component in a relationship whose matrix was the family.[4] The potency of these myths lay in their relative imperviousness to evidence that limited their validity.

By December 1950 the tenor of McCarthy's character-assassination was validated by a Senate sub-committee. The homosexual, the committee reported, was defined by his 'lack of emotional stability', the weakness of his 'moral fibre' and his capacity for seducing heterosexuals. His vulnerability to blackmail made him even more dangerous.[5] The dread of the betrayer and the spy was a reaction to the Cold War which had risen like a sinister phoenix from the ashes of Soviet–American co-operation between 1942 and 1945. The satellite regimes installed by the Russians in Eastern European states and the insurgent Communist movements in Asia were interpreted as the signs of a brutal and expansionist Soviet Union.

The defections of Guy Burgess and Donald Maclean, British diplomats who vanished to Russia in 1951, the execution of Julius and Ethel Rosenberg for spying, and the betrayal of America's nuclear secrets by Alan Nunn May, exacerbated a pervasive fear of treachery. The defection of Burgess and Maclean corroborated what had been asserted about the security risk posed by homosexuals. Burgess scarcely concealed his desires. Maclean, although married, was known by the security services to succumb to homosexual acts when sufficiently drunk. He drank a lot.[6]

The Kinsey report of 1948 played its role in fostering homophobia as well. Kinsey in an apt metaphor had 'mapped the unsurveyed sexual landscape of the nation'.[7] Kinsey's statistics also reinforced the idea that heterosexuals could be enticed into homosexuality and the report indicated homosexuality was not an all-or-nothing condition. The findings suggested that 50 per cent of males admitted erotic responses, at some stage of their life, to their own sex and that 37 per cent had 'at least one post adolescent homosexual experience leading to orgasm'.[8] If male sexual desire was no more fixed than the pendulum of a clock, then homosexuality could be said to pose an undreamed-of threat to the family life, and to heterosexuality.

The reactive witch-hunts in the American public service, the FBI and the military to seek out and expel homosexuals were thus responses to the political anxieties of the Cold War. The American fears that Britain was similarly affected led to 'strong US advice to weed out homosexuals as hopeless security risks, from important jobs'.[9] One of Scotland Yard's senior officers was reported to have spent three months in America 'while working on a plan to march to war against vice'.[10] The British Home Secretary, Sir David Maxwell-Fyfe, the Metropolitan Police Commissioner, and the Director of Public Prosecutions, all men of rampant homophobic persuasion, shaped and executed the policy.

The homosexual was now demonised, cast as the archetype of

danger, the epitome of the decadent and the corrupt. There was, however, a countervailing process which sparked rebellion. Some of the adolescents of the 1950s, children of the new consumer and materialist society, were to become 1960s countercultural revolutionaries. This new generation was encouraged by the new modes of advertising, and by the advent of television, to spend its way to happiness and to self-satisfaction. It was targeted as a world-wide new constituency. It boasted its own new music, its records, its films, its non-conformist fashions. The beatnik and the teddy boy were variously cast as the rebels in orthodoxy's world.

The most notable symptom of this new tendency was theatrical. Kenneth Tynan, the most influential and radical theatre critic on either side of the Atlantic, described the West End of the 1950s as both a 'dust bowl' and a 'waste land, owing its aridity to improvident speculators' with the same arthritic speculators controlling it 'as they did the other means of communication'.[11] Its plays were principally bounded by landed drawing rooms, whose plots and characters made but 'superficial contact with reality'. Broadway, with its more eclectic traditions, had spawned the American Group theatre, with Lee Strasberg, Elia Kazan and Harold Clurman. It had achieved a school of political and social realism that Arthur Miller and Tennessee Williams would extend. Yet it was in London that the new wave broke upon the shores of the old.

One May evening in 1956, at the Royal Court Theatre, John Osborne's *Look Back in Anger* burst like a bolt from the blue. To judge by the uproar that the first night inspired you would think that he had declared civil war upon the West End theatre. And in a sense he had. The modern theatre movement had arrived. Here, according to Tynan, was 'post war youth as it really is'.[12] This youth looked back in anger and blazed with fury about the likely future and the disreputable present. 'A dandy with a machine gun', was Tynan's jubilant description of Osborne whom he pictured sniping in the trenches of the class and sex war.[13] The lower-middle classes in the young, left-wing iconoclastic shape of Jimmy Porter had taken over the stage. A full-scale tirade was delivered against the ruling establishment and its social and sexual conformities.

Look Back in Anger, with its invective against the torpors and complacencies of an antique Britain, dependent for self-esteem upon dreams of imperial glory, served as a rallying cry for a new generation. The play was not just a single shot in the dark. It emerged as the second play in the English Stage Company, founded by George Devine, the 46-year-old actor-director, whose heart had long been set on an alternative, writers', theatre with 'the right to fail'. He believed the English stage had 'reached the point of complete dissociation' from the world beyond and he wanted to heal that breach. So he accused and explained his mission.

> Had we not seen six million Jews murdered? Were we not seeing McCarthyism in the United States, the emergence of the coloured races? . . . There had been drastic political and social changes all around us; the new prosperity state was more than suspect. Both political parties looked the same. No man or woman of feeling who was not wearing blinkers could not but feel profoundly disturbed.[14]

The minor revolution, for which Devine called, addressed social and political issues that the English theatre ignored, and was symptomatic of cultural rebellion and of dissent. These minor rebels – for their rebelliousness was not usually enduring – were a loosely cohesive group, young, principally male, often lower-middle-class. Their signatures were scrawled across the new Free Cinema movement, a *declassé*, new literature, with a proletarian hero hurrying on up. Since Osborne's play coincided with the publication of Colin Wilson's *The Outsider*, Wilson's philosophical brooding and Osborne's social invective came to be regarded as the protesting sounds of a new generation. The Royal Court press officer provided an easy card of identity by which the media could characterise a new protest generation when he described Osborne as 'an angry young man'.[15]

But the Royal Court did break into the kitchens and backrooms of life. It gave voice to the classes below stairs. The process was an inspiration to New York's new theatrical generation: off-Broadway, created down-town, became a network of little studio spaces, away from commercial demands and devoted to productions of new European drama. Off-off-Broadway, one more stage away from the conventional, would supply the real challenge to the values of Broadway in the next decade.

THE HETEROSEXUAL AS A GAY VICTIM

The commercial theatre, obedient to the political and social orthodoxies that the Cold War had instilled, still cast homosexuality as archetypically dangerous as well as evil. Two commercially popular plays of the period, *Tea and Sympathy* and Philip King's *Serious Charge*, are muted and ambivalent rebukes to homosexual witch-hunting, so timid that they criticise the techniques of McCarthyism, as applied in a private American boarding school for boys and an English country village, by showing up the anguish suffered by two heterosexuals falsely accused of being homosexual on the basis of circumstantial evidence. Both plays concur in reflecting the governing sense of panic about homosexuality engendered by politicians, doctors and clerics. Orthodox discourse about homosexuality is of a threat to nationhood, an epidemic and a dangerous addiction. The words of one British High Court judge in 1955 at Buckinghamshire Assizes express this idea most powerfully:

> Wherever I go I find the same ugly story . . . I don't know what is happening to this nation. The percentage of cases of this class which we have to try today is absolutely terrifying. If this evil is allowed to spread, it will corrupt the men of the nation.[16]

And a senior government minister, Lord Hailsham, warned in terms redolent of the dangers of plague and drug-taking: 'Homosexual practices are . . . contagious, incurable . . . Homosexuality is . . . as much a moral and social issue as heroin addiction.'[17]

Virtually no theatre critic, reviewing either the New York or the London production, alluded to the way in which *Tea and Sympathy* was a veiled critique of McCarthyism. The Lord Chamberlain would not give the play a licence for public performance in Britain, and the powerful producer, Binkie Beaumont, responded by presenting it for members of the theatre club which he and two other impresarios had formed to circumvent the ban upon Tennessee Williams's *Cat on a Hot Tin Roof* (Plate 2) and Arthur Miller's *A View from the Bridge*. A lofty review in *The Times* merely noted that the play's shock value turned out 'to be more formal than real', and found little except the 'relentlessly sentimental' within it.[18] The American reviewers, four years earlier in 1953, similarly failed to note or respond to Anderson's covert sexual and political nuances: 'A play that catches a group of characters in a complicated web of hostilities and sympathies and looks deep into the hearts of its principal people', Brooks Atkinson wrote in a superficial notice in the *New York Times*.[19] It was a typical review of the production.

Keith Baxter, who was a 23-year-old actor in 1957, played one of the sporty youths in the London production. 'It was the most fragile play, but in its own way it appealed against bigotry.' He suggests that neither in London nor on Broadway did the play pose problems for actors. 'Tony Perkins took over the leading role on Broadway, and his career flourished.'[20]

Mid-century playwrights who wished to deal frankly with the subject of homosexuality, and in terms rejecting the idea that such sexuality was commensurate with evil and danger, were deterred by the rigid fact of stage censorship and by conservative producers. Terence Rattigan, a dramatist at the height of his popularity in the 1950s, illustrates the difficulty. His non-conformist and liberal sympathies for the outcast and the unconventional, his dislike of specifically British forms of hypocrisy, were always qualified by his need for the acceptance and approval of an upper-middle class which he also despised.

His earliest play, *First Episode* (1934), written with Philip Heimann, while they were both Oxford undergraduates, audaciously concealed homoerotic feeling by giving each of the principal young men, Tony and David, a girl-friend. The play has never been revived nor has it been published, but no one reading it today will miss the governing emotion of David, as he schemes to break up his friend's relationship with an actress of a most uncertain age. 'You're just a filthy degenerate,' the actress rages at him, in case the ambiguous point is missed in the veiled obliquities of Rattigan's writing (2.ii.33).

Rattigan never dared as greatly after that. The reviewers either did not choose to mention or did not appreciate the significance of the young men's relationship. But the dilemma of the actress in *First Episode*, driven by a passion that is wanly reciprocated became a characteristic leitmotiv in his plays where characters were often driven by sexual or emotional desire. The objects of that desire lack the capacity or the will to return the feeling in kind. Although these plays were concerned with heterosexual situations, it looks as if Rattigan, who found creative stimulus from the circumstances of his own life, transposed homosexual relations and placed them in conventional sexual guise.

The Deep Blue Sea (1952), in which a judge's wife, Hester Collyer, suffers through an affair with a vacuous but sexy Battle of Britain hero, was acclaimed as an exposé of doomed erotic passion. According to Rattigan's friend, the theatre critic B.A. Young, the first version of the play dealt with a homosexual affair, and was directly inspired by Rattigan's own relationship with Kenneth Morgan, a young man who left him and subsequently committed suicide. Rattigan showed this version to Hugh Beaumont, the managing director of the omnipotent production-company H.M. Tennent, who told him that he would have to 'take his story and cast it in more acceptable form' if Tennent's were to produce it. Rattigan agreed and rewrote the play.[21] His only, minor concession to the original idea was to imply that the foreign doctor who saved Hester's life has been struck off the medical register for a homosexual offence. But even in this detail Rattigan lacked courage. By the third draft of the play the original imputation of homosexuality to the doctor had been excised.[22]

Even when the Lord Chamberlain's veto upon the discussion of homosexuality had been rescinded Rattigan continued to play the role of pussy-footer. When the much-derided *Variation on a Theme* was presented at the Globe Theatre, in 1958, several critics accused him of concealing a play about homosexuality in heterosexuality's guise. 'Are things what they seem?' asked the headline to Harold Hobson's review in the *Sunday Times*. Kenneth Tynan woundingly suggested that Rattigan was pandering to the Lord Chamberlain and the playwright's mythical creation, a totem of suburban middle-class conventionality, Aunt Edna, by masking the play's true sexual subject.[23] Rattigan had certainly given the critics some grounds for their accusations. *Variation on a Theme* concerned the affair of a rich middle-aged divorcée and a young man, who was not only that most sexually suspect thing, a ballet dancer, but also sported a homosexual manager in tow. Similar accusations were levelled by critics when Rattigan's *Man and Boy* was staged at the Haymarket in 1963, with the cinema's superannuated matinee idol, Charles Boyer. Both the *Sunday Times* and *Observer* reviewers suggested that father and son were in reality homosexual lovers.[24] Yet when Rattigan did deal with a form of homosexual desire in *Ross* (1960), a play about Lawrence of Arabia, his psychologically astute interpretation of the reasons for Lawrence's retreat into anonymity, and the concealment of his true identity, became a mere aside in the play's development. Rattigan's suggestion that Lawrence, played by Alec Guinness, had been rent asunder by his discovery that he enjoyed being beaten and buggered, was expressed in most periphrastic terms. That was essential, if only to avoid the Lord Chamberlain's censorship. But Rattigan simply allowed audiences to infer the impact of this event upon Lawrence's life.

Having dealt so often with 'the struggle of frightened, damaged people to find self-expression and fulfillment in a society whose moral codes inhibited them' Rattigan appears to have been awed and controlled by those codes, even as he realised their limitations and defects.[25] It was characteristic of him, therefore, that the original stimulus for *Table Number Seven*, the second play in his double bill *Separate Tables* (1954), should have been set aside when he came to write it. In the autumn of 1953 one of Britain's most famous actors, who was also a close friend of Rattigan's, was found guilty of persistently importuning for an immoral purpose in a public lavatory. It looked for a while as if the actor faced professional ruin; a report of the offence was published on the front page of the *Daily Telegraph*. Rattigan was greatly moved by his friend's courage and grace in adversity. He determined that the offence for which a bogus Major in *Table Number Seven* was at first ostracised should be a homosexual one. But in the end he decided that the Major's offence should be that of touching women in cinemas. Rattigan tried to justify this change in the most disingenuous terms: 'If I had written the man as a homosexual the play might have been construed as a thesis drama, begging for tolerance specifically of the homosexual. Instead it is a plea for understanding everyone,' he said.[26]

Rattigan did, of course, want to find the courage to write what he called a 'thesis' drama about homosexuality. And although his principal biographers, Michael Darlow and Gillian Hodson, argued that he would have been prevented from doing so by the Lord Chamberlain, their contention fails to pass muster.[27] Rattigan was a master of the oblique. His play could have been organised both to avoid the Chamberlain's blue pencil and to make an incisive comment upon the period's persecution of homosexuals. The impact of such a play, coming from such a playwright, might have been very strong. Rattigan funked it. He was, his biographers apologised, terrified his mother might finally realise that her forty-three-year-old unmarried son was homosexual. He was so fearful of being associated with homosexuality that when a defendant in a major homosexual case being tried at the Old Bailey, in 1954, came to Rattigan, seeking 'refuge from the hounding of the press' Rattigan showed him the door.[28] The pathetic incident was of a sort that might have inspired a Rattigan play. But Terence Rattigan, a man who concealed and hated the fact of his homosexuality, would never have dared to write it.

Other playwrights suffered as well. Rodney Ackland, his contemporary, and a far better playwright – ranked alone in his generation as the theatre's equal of Greene, Auden and Waugh by some critics[29] – had to censor his vision of the real, depressed spirit of London in 1945, as reflected in his play *The Pink Room*, which was seen briefly in London in 1952. He was unable to include within this canvas a portrayal of a homosexual relationship and had to make do with a heterosexual version of it. Even so, the play's scathing serious satire was not appreciated. Binkie Beaumont even described it as a 'libel on the English people'[30].

The more popular plays about homosexuals preferred to conform to sexual myths and sensationalism. 'A grave drama about abnormality' was the *New York Post*'s alluring headline for its review of a 1954 adaptation of André Gide's *The Immoralist*, that confession of forbidden desire, despair and blackmail, performed at Broadway's Royale Theatre.[31] Meyer Levin's *Compulsion* seen in the same period at Broadway's Ambassador Theatre, based upon the trial of two psychopathic homosexual murderers of the 1920s, could not have been better pitched to pander to the idea of homosexuality as elemental danger.

Typically, *Tea and Sympathy*, filmed in a sexually chastened version in 1956, with Deborah Kerr providing a friendly bosom on which the tormented youth, Tom, was invited to do more than lean, to save him from the dangerous possibility of homosexuality turned out to be one of the most popular American plays of the decade.

The real value of *Tea and Sympathy* is, however, the extent to which it defies orthodoxy. Anderson impugns the crude and popular mode of accepting a man as heterosexual if he manifests archetypically male characteristics. He suggests that the man who appears the model of masculinity could still be homosexual. Conversely, the play implies, a man or youth should not be categorised as homosexual on the basis of stereotypical gay signs or effeminacy, since he might well be heterosexual. Further, through his heroine, Laura, the housemaster's wife, Anderson derogates the American worship of the masculine archetype: the true, mature and most valued males are those, she argues, who incorporate aspects of the female archetype instead of suppressing them: 'Manliness is not all swagger and swearing and mountain climbing, manliness is also tenderness, gentleness and consideration' (3.152).

Her language caricatures the theory, but the meaning is clear. The archetypically masculine housemaster, Bill, all pipe-smoking and mountaineering with the boys, is accused by his wife of latent homosexuality, and of imputing to Tom those very sexual desires that he fears in himself. Shadow Projection, that system by which the despised characteristic in one's self is projected onto an enemy, stands revealed as the hallmark of the play's McCarthyite accuser. When the curtain falls, Tom is posed to prove himself a real 'man' in the hands of the housemaster's wife, with whom he has long been infatuated. There she stands, having given him tea and sympathy, and now prepared to induct him into the joys of heterosexuality.

But Anderson's play, for all its criticism of gender stereo-typing, does not suggest that it is cruel or morally wrong to persecute and ostracise those who *are* homosexual. The play exploits the period's obsession with homosexuality, while making an appeal for the supposedly oppressed heterosexual. Real homosexuals, audiences were left to conclude, should expect to suffer the very oppression that Anderson condemns when meted out to heterosexuals.

Homosexuality, as refracted through the eyes and minds of Tom's accusatory school-mates, is a fearful abnormality from which young men go running scared, as if it were sexually transmitted at a glance. The imputation of homosexuality causes such intense problems, induces such bewilderment and suicidal despair, that suicide beckons as the best way out for the anti-hero. Tom himself exhibits a set of stereotypical homosexual characteristics which are his undoing. He is depicted as a natural outsider, of the social as well the sexual sort. His interests are unmanly. He sits in his room playing his guitar, instead of joining in the rough, manly stuff of sport, and when he does go in for tennis he resorts to the tricks of 'a cut artist', redolent of female guile rather than the 'hard drives and cannon ball swerves', indicative of brute, male force (1.56). Worse, he likes the feminine pursuit of acting and appears in the school plays. Worst of all, he is cast in the female parts of Lady Teazle and Lady Macbeth. His appearance is also against him. He sports long hair rather than a masculine crew-cut which, one of his room-mates feels, would disarm nagging suspicion, suspicion born of the fact that he lacks the style of the 1950s macho 18-year-old.

Anderson never quite dispels lurking suspicions about Tom's true sexuality, if only because the incident that precipitates his hero's crisis invites them. Tom is seen 'bare-arsed' on the beach, alone with a young schoolmaster, who abruptly hands in his notice as a result of this sighting. Harris, the man in question, sent down and out by circumstantial evidence and rumour, is the play's first victim of McCarthyism. But in his case Anderson hints that there may be a basis for the smearing rumour. 'Why didn't you keep your mouth shut? . . . I never touched you, did I? . . . Did you say to the Dean I touched you?' asks the schoolmaster (1.33). And in a last goodbye to Tom he intensifies suspicion rather than disarms it: 'I should have been more discreet' (1.34).

True to the McCarthyite 1950s, Anderson shows the way in which you were expected, when accusing someone of homosexuality, to express a sense of outrage that people harboured such desires. 'Just to think about it is disgusting' Bill says of the 'bare-arsed incident'; 'if he's kicked out maybe it'll bring him to his senses. But he won't change if nothing's been done' (1.14). Homosexual desire, according to this suggestion, when manifested in adolescence, may be banished through strong talk and firm action. This is the first of the sexual myths which *Tea and Sympathy* retails and perhaps mocks. There are others.

Tom's father, summoned to the scene of shame, is prepared to accept the charges levelled against his son on the basis of the sighting on the beach, and of the youth's failure to play 'hard drives and cannon-ball serves' (1.56). Tom's room-mate, Al, similarly succumbs: 'He does act sort of queer. He sort of walks lightly . . . sometimes the way he moves – the things he talks about – long-hair music all the time' (2.82). In other words a man's musical tastes, as much as his body movements, are indices of sexual orientation. And in a comic microcosm of 1950s theorising on masculinity, and homosexual departures from it, Tom receives instructions in the art of walking tall and manly. He fails in the exercise. Indeed, when both he and his room-mate try to walk like men, feminine self-consciousness, the antithesis of male spontaneity, characterises their gait. Tom laments 'Now I'm not going to be able to walk any more. Everything I've been doing all my life makes me look like a fairy' (2.91). This is a useful, if pathetic, comment on the way we are judged by what we seem and not by what we are. 'I don't know the reason for these things,' Al says helplessly. 'It's just the way things are' (2.90). The importance of not only being but also seeming straight is affirmed as a young man's first duty. In fact, it is as important to seem heterosexual as to be it.

Yet this test of judging a man by his walk was, and perhaps still is, considered by some American psychiatrists to be both a test of masculinity and a reliable guide to the nature of the walker's sexual desire. 'A masculine walk', the American psychotherapist C.A. Tripp wrote in his most influential monograph on homosexuality, interpreting it as an average and non-contagious mode of sexual expression, 'is straightforward, energetic and contains large, sharp-edged movements, as opposed to small hesitant or soft motions'. Tripp stresses that effeminacy although found, for whatever reasons, more frequently in homosexuals, is 'relatively rare' even among gay men: 'It would not require as much attention as it does, if it were not that, in the minds of many people, it characterises the whole group.'[32] So Tom, characterised on the basis of myth, incites such anxiety that when he is in the showers everyone rushes out at the sight of him, as if to show he is regarded as a sexual predator.

Vito Russo, in *The Celluloid Closet*, makes a trenchant comment on Anderson's real intentions as observed in the cinematic version of the play: '*Tea and Sympathy* is the ultimate sissy film. It confirms what the creators and portrayers of sissies have always sought to deny, that the iconography for sissies and for sexual deviates is the same.'[33] Just so. However misleading and inaccurate that correlation may be, Anderson was echoing a generally accepted view that sissies really were deviants. Furthermore, his subversive assault upon the practice of worshipping the male archetype is prevented from becoming any defence of sissies by the play's countervailing horror of authentic homosexuals.

The sexual sympathy Laura lavishes upon Tom is regarded as the consolatory due of the latently heterosexual youth accused of homosexuality. Laura exposes the limitations and deficiencies of reverencing the archetypical male. But while she has been prepared to suffer her husband's latent homosexuality, the idea that Tom has similar sexual desire appals her. 'But Bill you don't think, I mean you don't think Tom is –,' she says, as if the very word 'homosexual' would sully her lips (1.43). Tom's attitude is similarly horrified: 'You mean – d'you mean, you think I'm whatever you call it?' (1.67). 'Homosexuality' is the play's taboo word.

Tom, in the scene of his sexual rescue, also conforms to a popular medical myth of the 1950s. 'The shy man inclines to run away from women,' judged a psychotherapist. Tom certainly does that. Then, in an attempt to prove with the local prostitute that the slurs upon his sexuality are untrue, he fails to rise to the occasion, and rushes away to try to kill himself with a kitchen knife. 'A predominantly homosexual youth', the psychotherapist consoles, 'may sometimes overcome his inhibitions, provided they are not too greatly ingrained, through an experience with a sympathetic but not too demanding woman.'[34]

Anderson's *Tea and Sympathy* feeds upon the myths engulfing homosexuality, while rejecting those that characterise heterosexual males. It depends, therefore, upon a form of sexual apartheid. Homosexuals are pariahs, while the sensitive, atypical heterosexual youth is rewarded with love and satisfaction.

By so suggesting, *Tea and Sympathy* is a play ultimately in harmony with its own nasty times.

In 1958 the Arts theatre club, in London, which had long specialised in a repertoire of experimental work, new writing and non-commercial work, presented *Quaint Honour*, a play by Roger Gellert. It too dealt with an outbreak of homosexuality in a private school for young men; but it was conceived in terms radically different from those of *Tea and Sympathy*. *Quaint Honour* is unremembered, unfilmed and uncelebrated, existing now as a theatrical footnote. Yet when the play was recently republished, Gellert wrote that it had been 'considered dynamite in its time'. And an epigraph by Lady Warnock, the heterosexual mistress of Girton College, Cambridge, puts *Quaint Honour* in a positive context from which Anderson would have recoiled: 'Homosexuality', she says 'is not bad and, especially at school, may be positively good.'[35]

For *Quaint Honour* departed from the convention of its times by seeking to validate adolescent homosexuality as uncorrupting and beneficial to consenting adolescent parties. A homosexual relationship between a prefect and a 14-year-old youth is discovered, causing a confrontation with the angry housemaster. The crisis is resolved with the offending prefect's expulsion. Yet although the 18-year-old's future prospects may be adversely affected by this dismissal, *Quaint Honour* still depicts him as a young man whose homosexual activities cause him neither guilt nor shame, and who justifies his sexual behaviour with impenitent self-confidence. A special case is being pleaded. The British traditionally regard the homosexual activities of middle-class and upper-middle-class adolescents, at sexually segregated private schools for the affluent, as a passing phase and not an authentic sign of sexual orientation.

Homosexuality is therefore deprived of its negative myths. Tully, the 18-year-old homosexual hero, is sporting, athletic and confident. And Turner, a teenage *agent provocateur*, actually incites the play's hero to turn his sexual attentions upon an innocent 14-year-old, as if homosexuality were all a game. The aura of corruption and degeneracy is discarded. No wonder the play failed.

Philip King's *Serious Charge*, presented at St Martin's Theatre in London in 1955, is the British correlate for *Tea and Sympathy*. It deals with a man displaying some characteristics that are regarded as signs of homosexuality. And here too a man is threatened with ruin on the basis of a trumped-up charge. But where Anderson depended upon circumstantial evidence to show how the uproar of accusation would be heeded in heterosexual society, King suggested that the malign and blackmailing accuser is unhesitatingly believed, because the accuser confirms what stereotypical signs of homosexuality suggest. Yet the play, presented with Patrick McGoohan in the leading role and subsequently filmed with Anthony Quayle, never mentions the word 'homosexual'. As soon as it comes to matters of sexuality, people speak in innuendo and circumlocution. When a 30-year-old vicar, Howard Philips, is accused by Larry, an 'angelic-looking' 17-year-old, of attempted sexual assault, it does not matter that this angel of darkness has already been sacked from the church choir for the crime of 'pouring absolute filth' into the receptive ears of the two youngest choir boys (2.ii.51). King also schematically stacks all the odds against the cleric. Larry's accusation is couched in the terms of innuendo to ensure that the Lord Chamberlain's blue pencil was not deployed: 'I – I don't know how to tell you. He tried to, tried to . . .' (2.i.40). His complaint falls upon receptive ears because Howard invites sexual suspicion. He may be archetypically masculine in appearance and manner, with a pipe in hand (that 1950s icon of quintessential maleness). But he is over 30, unmarried, has no apparent interest in women, lives with his widowed mother, and is in a profession vaguely associated with homosexuality. Most significant of all, he shows a disconcerting ability as an amateur interior-designer. Male ballet-dancers, hairdressers, antique-dealers and interior designers had long been classified as homosexual, victims of the idea that the artistic, creative, decorative and expressive talents required in such occupations were essentially feminine. Britain of the 1950s had achieved a zenith of gender stereotyping in which the female was downgraded and all forms of male physical prowess exalted. So, it was suggested, 'secure family life' was the best antidote to homosexuality, this security being induced by an 'understanding, tolerant, but virile and decisive father' and a mother manifesting 'the gentleness, patience and passivity usually associated with womanhood'.[36]

To read *Serious Charge* now is to visit a vanished form of theatre, in which sexual suspicion and sexual passion cannot be expressed, only conveyed by hesitant allusion. 'He really has quite a flair for interior decorations,' says Howard's mother to a 30-year-old spinster Hester, who has been besotted by Howard at first glance. Her response nudges a dim-witted audience towards suspicion. 'One would never think it meeting him. One usually thinks of artistic men as being rather – well, you know what I mean' (1.i.3). And if we do not know, King is quick to explain that the room is decorated and furnished in 'beautiful taste' (1.i.1). And 'taste', Hester usefully explains, means not the 'usual stuffy browns and dark greens one finds in so many bachelor's rooms', but something 'artistic . . . what you might call a real woman's room' (1.i.1).

The visiting schoolmaster, Granger, male to his fingertips, is portrayed as a stereotype of the 1950s male. He can appreciate interior design but cannot manage to achieve such artistry himself:

GRANGER. I'd like my wife to see this. Do her good. Not much imagination when it comes to furnishing a room and her colour schemes are a nightmare. Your mother's obviously got flair.

HOWARD. My mother . . . Oh! Mother had nothing to do with this. I'm afraid I'm responsible.

GRANGER . . . Good lord . . . [*uneasily*] Oh yes, yes. Most contemporary. But I can't get over you . . . Good lord.

(2.ii.46)

This is comic in its preposterousness; Howard is circumstantially accused. 'Those three facts that I am a person, a bachelor and have what you call artistic flair – add up to the one big fact that I must be a pervert. Is that it?' The Schoolmaster virtually assents: 'I'm just telling you what will be in people's minds' (2.ii.53).

The play's conclusion, in which Larry's accusation is discredited, restores the priest to his penitent flock. The vicar, his mother urges, has work to do in battling against evil. But what is the evil that King diagnoses? Surely it is the state of law that then enabled a street-wise heterosexual youth to blackmail a heterosexual who was presumed to be homosexual. The casting and the performance of two ostentatiously masculine actors, Patrick McGoohan and Anthony Quayle, in the theatre and film version, ensured that such was the production's aim. King was therefore principally exploiting the period attraction of homosexuality and titillating prominent audiences. He was doing nothing more valuable or daring than that.

'BUT NOT FOR LONG TO HOLD EACH DESPERATE CHOICE'

Until the furore of an astonishing first night at the Aldwych Theatre, on 12 October 1949, female sexuality was more approved in theory than displayed upon the twentieth-century West End stage. Celia Johnson in Noël Coward's *Brief Encounter*, that celluloid tribute of 1945 to a woman's stiff upper lip and firmly crossed knees, was as far as the British cinema or theatre was permitted to go. Miss Johnson, it was true, had been adulterously kissed, though in respectable long-shot. But no sexual passion had been spent, no clothes shed and the actress had ended up in her husband's arms, virtue triumphant over vice, the sanctity of middle-class married life affirmed, after a small diversion.

On the Aldwych stage, that October night, there was Vivien Leigh, in a new play by a little-known American playwright. She was gazing at the revealed torso of Bonar Colleano, playing Stanley Kowalski to her Blanche du Bois in Tennessee Williams's *A Streetcar Named Desire*. Her gaze suggested that a woman could actually be excited by the half-naked male body. The West End stage was daring greatly. The Lord Chamberlain had closely scrutinised the text and only allowed the play a licence on condition the producer, H.M. Tennent, excised the words 'that had two people in it' – a reference to Blanche du Bois's recollection of how she discovered her 17-year-old husband in a room, clearly up to no good, with a man.

The huge crowds outside the theatre, the film stars and politicians in the auditorium, the fourteen curtain calls were indices of a rare excitement that was only exacerbated by the critics' vituperative reviews. 'The spirit of daring', wrote the *Sunday Times* theatre critic, Harold Hobson, which he [Williams] introduced into the London drama was in many quarters received with a venomous opposition, unparalleled since Clement Scott's denunciation of Ibsen. Like *Ghosts*, it [*Streetcar*] was widely spoken of as 'a nasty and vulgar play,' and many theatre goers walked out of the performance in noisy disgust . . . The reaction was sheer, half-witted moral horror.[37]

'Unrelieved sordidness,' said the *Daily Herald*. 'It is sordid, sexual . . . geared to bring out as much sexual detail as is permissible on the stage,' accused the *Daily Express*. 'A messy little anecdote that somehow took the fancy of New York', the *Observer* loftily observed, alluding to the way in which New York had taken to the play, garlanding it with awards. Over there almost every theatre critic had applauded Williams's new play. 'Williams is certainly the Eugene O'Neill of the present period . . . a savagely arresting tragedy,' Howard Barnes had written, in a comment that was typical of the New York response; 'For those who find excitement in lust and brutality', sneered the *Evening Standard*, by comparison.[38] Moral outrage spread in London after that first night. Lady Ravensdale, daughter of the Marquis of Curzon, demanded that the Public Morality Council lobby for the play to be banned. 'Lewd and salacious,' the Council duly warned. 'Low and repugnant,' judged an MP, raising the subject of *Streetcar* in the House of Commons.[39]

The 'spirit of daring' to which Harold Hobson referred has long been forgotten. But the impact of that daring has to be remembered when assessing the way in which Williams managed to depict sexuality, particularly female sexuality, on stage, and also how he portrayed young men as clear objects of desire. He dealt with the wild cards of sexuality, when such desiring was not to be mentioned on the stage. He had no specific social or political interests, but he allied himself, after O'Neill and with Miller, against the American cult of materialism and success. His plays are devoted to those for whom the good news does not arrive, the sexual and social outsiders, the misfits, the fugitives, the downcast and down-at-heel – the people whose lives had so rarely occupied the stages of Broadway and the West End. The family unit is a battle-ground. He was the bohemian outsider looking back at what he had left behind. It was in these ways that Williams's developed homosexual sensibility brought him into alliance with the nonconformists. For he believed that his occupation as writer, and involuntary vocation as homosexual, allied him with those seeking freedom to be themselves. 'If you can't be yourself, what's the point of being anything at all?' he asked.[40] The tone recalls that of the Beat generation to which he did not belong – he lacked the Beats' extravagant gusto and sexual candour.

His plays and those of Miller were thus quite out of sympathy with the prevailing spirit of materialism and orthodoxy. 'The new model citizen of the period', it was being said, 'made a virtue of submerging his identity in the team ... [he was] a conformist prepared to trade independence of mind and spirit for immunity from social pressure.'[41] Williams – not, it might have been thought, a naturally courageous man – had the true courage of the fearful; of those who refused to go against conscience and who are prepared to face whatever their paranoid imaginings suggest they may suffer as a result. Joe Orton, a post-Gay Liberation biographer suggests, regarded Williams as sexually closeted, though of course Orton risked nothing in his life by his play-writing; Williams did. When the first Eisenhower administration was equating the spy, the communist and the homosexual as equal threats to the state, Williams in *Cat on a Hot Tin Roof* dared to suggest that an icon of American masculinity, an archetypal American hero, a former football champion, might be homosexual, and his friendship with his best buddy (another football hero) homoerotic at best.

But if Williams's sensibility inspired major plays, written from the perspective of the outsider, if his sensibility inspired an empathy with women sexually wracked by inadequate males, the drama was not achieved without cost and regret. 'Most of you', he wrote in the late sprawl of his *Memoirs*,

> belong to something that offers a stabilising influence: a family unit, a defined social position, employment, in an organisation, a more secure habit of existence. I live like a gypsy. I am a fugitive. No place seems tenable to me for long any more, not even my own skin.

The sadness and the alienated sense of exclusion of that self-description, are characteristic of the beliefs and experiences of some mid-century homosexuals – and of bohemians. 'My place in society then [1949] and possibly always since then, has been in Bohemia,' he said. 'I love to visit the other side now and then. But on my social passport Bohemia is indelibly stamped, without regret on my part.'[42]

There are also pronounced associations between Williams's own unhappy early life and his dramatic fictions. That early life supplied the stimulus for flight, for dissociation from the world of fixtures and fittings. The garrulous mother at angry odds with her wandering, often absent, husband, the disturbed sister withdrawing into silence, the feminine, little boy tormented at home and abroad – 'called a sissy by neighbourhood kids and Miss Nancy by my father' – re-emerged, transmuted in his plays. 'I draw all characters from myself,' Williams acknowledged. 'I can't draw a character unless I know it within myself.' Elia Kazan, his principal director, amplified: 'Blanche du Bois the woman is Williams.'[43] Some critics argue that the playwright betrayed women in the process, that his plays were often costume dramas of a special kind, in which the playwright transcended a veto upon homosexuality by an artful transvestism. The likes of Blanche du Bois and the Princess in *Sweet Bird of Youth*, according to this accusation, were 'baroquely transvestised fantasies', symptoms of the 'palpable fear and self-pity, guts and bravura of the ageing homosexual'. The use of the word 'baroquely' serves to suggest that there is something inauthentic in Williams' heroines, that they are excessive, cross-dressed versions of the playwright. Molly Haskell, the American film critic, who makes this accusation, argues it was Williams's habit to cast himself as a masochist *femme fatale*, suffering at the hands and the restricted minds of sexy 'brutes and beachboys'. Even the gay film critic Jack Babuscio goes some way towards accepting the truth of this charge, believing that Williams used women to his 'advantage' and that his 'crypto gayness found relief in the form of female guise'.[44]

There is a crude and reductionist element to these charges. There are both powerful and heterosexual women who dread ageing and the loss of their desirability. Heterosexual men, appreciative of the fact that many women are not simply attracted by physicality, do not suffer as their female counterparts. Homosexual men and heterosexual women are liable, therefore, to be subject to the same anxieties. Williams responded to and exploited the fact of these affinities. Actresses – and not just those attracted to baroque characters – have for forty years discovered Williams's heroines as authentic and not as drag queens.

But this is not to make light of Williams's unresolved guilt about his homosexual desires and the forms in which those guilts were projected. In *Small Craft Warnings*, seen in 1973, a young man, fearful that his sex-appeal is fading, defines all homosexuals in terms that the homophobes of the 1950s had made their accusatory own. Homosexuals, the young man says, are addicts to a futile sexual process which resembles the 'jabbing of a hypodermic needle' and leaves them coarsened by the 'quick and hard and brutal acts' (1.214). That dismissive and puritan aversion to homosexual pleasure owes much to his own early struggle to discover his sexuality.

He was 26 when he finally succumbed to his true desires. And ever after he was running scared of the time that would put paid to his sexual desirability. His heterosexual young men betray a particularly homosexual dread of ageing and a fear that they are about to lose allure. For Williams's sex-life, as if in reaction to these phobias, was characterised by what looks like a compulsive but joyless process of brief encounters on a daily basis. He tended to consume young men almost at the rate that he popped pills and swallowed quantities of alcohol. Yet these transactions rarely brought him content. According to his great friend Paul Bigelow, the playwright's promiscuity derived from an

> essential inability to accept the fact that he was the object of someone's commitment. Friendship he could accept, but sex he distrusted ... perhaps because he ordinarily disconnected it from affection in his own life. He never accepted that he was sexually loved ... Physical intimacy he tended to distrust even as he needed it constantly.[45]

This disconnection explains his termination of the successful relationship with his long-term lover, Frank Merlo, who, from all accounts, gave him the very commitment of which he was suspicious. For Williams, sex was thus the mechanistic distraction of the moment, not the long-term fix for which he hankered. The moth-like compulsion for the brief lights of eros left him fluttering in the wrong places, looking for what he craved – a secure and lasting commitment. When found it was discarded. Yet the self-destructive responses to puritan guilt and familial insecurities inspired one of the great post-war sequences of modern theatre. And the Wanderer and the Fugitive, those figures whom Roger Boxill described as the recurrent, star-crossed archetypes in Williams's work, are creative responses to Williams's sense of the impossibility of lasting love in a cruel country, in a violent, materialist society.[46]

In *Cat on a Hot Tin Roof* and *Suddenly Last Summer*, homosexual desire is cast as the prime agent of catastrophe. Both plays are true to the spirit of the times. In both to be accused of homosexuality strikes as much panic in the family as it did in an America fearfully purging the military and the public service. But although the two plays were written and performed within the space of five years, their view of homosexuality is radically different. *Suddenly Last Summer* might be reckoned a gothic elaboration upon the theme of *Cat on a Hot Tin Roof*, but it is more than that. It marks the zenith of a tradition in which the theatre conveyed the sense of homosexuality as a force of evil. The difference in attitude may have been caused by altered circumstances. Williams wrote *Cat* while deep in a depression, which was mitigated by mixed cocktails of alcohol and drugs. *Suddenly Last Summer* was conceived and completed when his state of mind had deteriorated and he was undergoing intense psychotherapy.[47] But neither play is simply about reactions to homosexual desire in a society outraged by it. The need to deny the existence of such sexual desires in *Cat* or to suppress the evidence of homosexual activity in *Suddenly Last Summer* is subsumed within a larger frame of reference. Williams harks back to Ibsen and O'Neill and the dialectic of people evading and concealing truth, who prefer the pipe dreams and balms of illusion.

Williams himself was conscious of the metaphoric role he assigned to homosexuality and why he did so. 'You still want to know why I don't write a gay play,' he asked in a 1976 interview he had requested with a gay journal:

I don't find it necessary. I could express what I wanted to express through other means . . . I would be narrowing my audience a great deal [if I wrote for a gay audience alone]. I wish to have a broad audience because the major thrust of my work is not sexual orientation, it's social.

Williams seems unaware of a distinction between a gay play and a play about homosexuality; his response to the question skirts the fact that he never chose to write about the new conceptions of gay desire and relationship in the post-Liberation period. But Williams's early life shaped his view of human relations. And according to his closest friends he never really advanced beyond the stage of hating homosexuals while being homosexual himself.[48]

Cat on a Hot Tin Roof is staged within the heaving bosom of a *nouveau riche* American family whose acquisitiveness and materialism are a mirror of America's governing spirit: this America and its microcosm, a family in the deep south with the cotton plantation as support, believe that the worthwhile existence is achieved through the getting of material things. This is the first life-lie of the play; it is matched by a form of 'mendacity', to use a key word of the play, that controls the forms of relationship in it. *Cat on a Hot Tin Roof* stages a series of contests between those who proclaim themselves truth-seekers but who are self-deceivers.

Williams does not deplore the pursuit of material things. He regrets that school of belief that puts false store upon them and overvalues their significances. It is revealing that the play's elaborate notes for the stage design ask that 'a monumental monstrosity peculiar to our times – a huge console combination of radio, phonograph . . . TV set and liquor cabinet' be emphasised. 'This piece of furniture . . . is a very complete and compact little shrine to virtually all the comforts and illusions behind which we hide from such things as the characters in the play are faced with' (1.14). The vulgar symbols of wealth are substitutes for religion, supports for that illusion of well-being that Williams will penetrate and lay bare.

Family life and relations in *Cat on a Hot Tin Roof* are hypocritical, loveless and unsatisfactory. The overarching family concern is a battle for the inheritance of Big Daddy's estate. It is a contest mainly conducted by Big Daddy's two daughters-in-law, girls who have married above themselves and intend to continue the upwardly mobile journey. Here the ties of marriage and of blood are loose. Heterosexual relations are fraily observed and preserved. Big Daddy looks back across the decades upon a marriage of inconvenience, founded upon enduring repulsion: 'I haven't been able to stand the sight, sound or smell of that woman for forty years now – even when I laid her! regular as a piston' (2.72). For his older son he has little more affection: 'I hate Gooper and Mae an' know that they hate me' (2.73). 'He loves his family, he loves to have them around him', Big Mamma, shimmering in 'half a million flashy gems', insists (3.85). The 'system of mendacity', as Williams terms it, is also conveyed through the family's response to Big Daddy's illness, in Maggie's belief in her husband's heterosexuality, and in Brick's alcoholism. Big Daddy's terminal cancer is dismissed soothingly as no more than a spastic colon. Death and homosexuality become the two dread unspeakables, the high fear of which inspire father and son to tell truths they cannot bear to contemplate.

Brick, the lost hero of the football field, is never characterised as a simple closet homosexual. Yet the man's alcoholism, his broken ankle and the crutches propelling him, are the symbolic and literal signs of someone who is running scared. That scare, although given peculiar significance in the sexual witch-hunt years, is characteristic of that new age of sexual doubt and awareness that Kinsey had proclaimed. Brick's latent homosexual desire is so thoroughly sublimated that he can only see in it the very kind of truth and purity elsewhere absent in his life. His refusal or inability to rise to the marital occasion and provide his wife with the progeny that will secure the inheritance hints at this truth. So the dilemma, which relates Brick's latent homosexuality and Big Daddy's need to make his last will and testament, causes Williams to challenge the period's stereotypical notion of homosexuality. Brick is the modern American theatre idea of the perfect male hero. He is the embodiment of all that masculinity is supposed to entail. He is not damned with the tell-tale signs of artistry, sensitivity or nervousness. The frail-looking Ben Gazzara, who created the role on the New York stage, may not have dynamically proclaimed the fact of Brick's athletic, masculine status, but Paul Newman in the 1958 film version did. And Newman's sexy performance gave fresh dynamism to Williams's act of sabotage and challenge. For not only does the play dare to suggest that homosexual desire may lurk unacknowledged in the body of a hot, heavily male sex-object, it questions the all-American dream of male bonding which Brick celebrates with such over-emphatic fervour: 'Exceptional friendship, *real, real, deep, deep* friendship' (2.78).

Williams is thus indicating that sexual identity cannot necessarily be gleaned by signs or even by behaviour. The inner subconscious life, it becomes grimly apparent in the play's wrenching central act, may have designs of which the conscious is dimly aware or even ignorant. Between the repressed desire and fulfilment has come the censorious superego which manifests itself in Brick's puritanism and his conventionality. His alcoholic need and his withdrawal from heterosexuality suggest the body's sense of crisis.

Cat on a Hot Tin Roof thus becomes the first truly modern play about homosexual desire and the most important one. It relates the demands of the public world to private lives. It questions the idea of fixed or unchanging sexual identity and the complex tension of the conscious and unconscious mind. As Big Daddy refuses to admit his imminent death, so both Maggie and Brick, however much characterised as seekers after truth, will refuse to contemplate the idea of latent homosexual desire. Williams, in interviews and in stage directions, adopted an attitude of studied ambivalence in relation to Brick's sexuality: 'His sexual nature was not innately "normal",' he said, at once qualifying the observation, 'but Brick's overt sexual adjustment was, and must always remain, a heterosexual one.'[49] In the instructions for Brick's outbreak of rage and fear when accused of homosexuality he demands that some 'mystery should be left in the revelation of character in a play' (2.75).

Yet there could be no more flamboyant innuendo than that which Williams arranged for the play's central encounter. 'Brick's detachment is at last broken through. His heart is accelerated; his forehead sweat-beaded; his breath becomes more rapid and his voice hoarse' (2.73). It is a description that keys with a contemporary, medical description of the latent homosexual who was also often characterised as alcoholic, caught off-guard:

> Pressures from repressed homosexual inclinations often produce acute or chronic anxiety neurosis. Analysts report that anxiety states, palpitations, sweats, phobias and the like frequently turn out to be caused by unconscious homosexual tendencies which, when they threaten to break forth into full consciousness produce feelings of acute fear and tension.[50]

The moment when Brick jumps to the false conclusion that his father is accusing him of 'sodomy' is preceded by a melodramatic but appropriate stage direction: 'Brick is transformed as if a quiet mountain blew suddenly up in flame' (2.77). It is this violent change of demeanour that signals the play's momentous unveiling, when father and son force each other to face up to what they have most feared in secret.

Brick, true to 1950s type, believes that there is but one stereotype of homosexuality, a single construct. It is that of the effeminate sissy. In his accusatory volley of epithets and tags of abuse, homosexuals are 'queers', 'old sisters', 'fairies' and 'dirty old men' (2.72-8). Big Daddy, he assumes, is comparing his 'true friendship' with the two old homosexual lovers who employed his father and bequeathed him the estate. Williams establishes these dead lovers as the model of a happy, fruitful relationship, which has bequeathed the family its basis of material security: a positive homosexual form of life.

But the violence of Brick's denunciation of homosexuals, and his eagerness to proclaim how he and Skipper persecuted one of their college fraternity when they caught him in the forbidden act, sabotage the protestation of his own normalcy. Brick's comic-pathetic avowal of the 'clean true' perfection of his friendship with Skipper is betrayed by the stress upon its lack of physicality – no more than a little, mutual touching of shoulders, and hands solemnly shaken when extended across the space separating the bedrooms they shared, while touring as professional footballers (2.79). That recollected iconography of sexless attachment in the hotel room, expressed in a ritual of formality, invites the very audience suspicion to which Williams has systematically pandered. And Brick's chronic unhappiness is made to seem more than guilt for abandoning a best friend who confessed he was in love with him.

The superannuated footballer emerges as one of Williams's guilt-struck wanderer-fugitives, whose days of sporting glory are over and who cannot face the tedium of average life with its professional and married responsibilities. 'Time just outran me,' he says (2.74). His greatest wish has been to prolong forever the athletic days of football, to remain forever young with Skipper. The *puer aeternus*, the man who continues to show the characteristics of the free-spirited adolescent in later life, is not necessarily homosexual, but Williams surely envisages Brick's commitment to the dream of post-adolescent male-bonding as a symptom of suppressed homosexual desires. The unlived life is what torments the footballer.

At the end of the play, in the first and better version which Williams preferred to the optimistic finale that Elia Kazan demanded, Maggie is poised by the bed, prepared to seduce or inveigle her husband into that sexual act which would bring them a child, the inheritance and the commitment she craves. Since she has already spread the lie of her pregnancy, it is urgent that she should achieve this success. But, as written, there is absolutely no sign that Maggie's lie will be converted to truth or that Brick will assist her in a process he abhors.

The National Theatre production of 1988, in London, brought out the play's overwhelming sense of homosexual desolation as it can never have been evoked before. Ian Charleson, who played Brick in the greatest performance of a career cut short by AIDS, was a man who found it hard to come to terms with his own homosexuality. He brought to *Cat on a Hot Tin Roof* his finest acting. He had the pained, icy demeanour and diction of a man who could not give voice or form to great passion which longed for expression. His Brick, in the second act, finally blazes into terrible fury, terrible because it shows that fury has become his only allowed form of high emotion. And at the play's end he basks in a resigned melancholia, cut off entirely from both wife and family; a grim, small smile plays upon his face. There was a sense that his sexual disaster was only about to begin, that Brick's latent homosexuality would be forever latent and his life-lie maintained to the end.

When the play was first produced in New York in 1955, most critics ignored its concern with sexual motives and disguises.

No critic alluded to the way in which Williams had discarded the stereotypical stage homosexual for a new model. The New York reviewers, as much as the characters on whom they lavished their scorching criticism, preferred to be evasive and mendacious. 'The truth invariably terrifies them. That is the one thing they cannot face or speak,' wrote Brooks Atkinson in the *New York Times*. 'They can find comfort in each other only by falling back on lies.' But then Mr Atkinson himself did not seem exactly anxious to speak of the mendacity that Williams had exposed. In his review there was not a single reference to Brick's dilemma or to his relationship with Skipper.[51] John McClain, in the *New York Journal American*, at least acknowledged, if in illiterate fashion, the nature of the accusation levelled against Brick. 'There is the implication, at least, that the most motivation in the play derives from an unnatural relationship,' he wrote. But he referred to the fact only to deplore the way in which the unacceptable face of sexuality had dared to show itself within the walls of a fine, upstanding American theatre. 'This may be life, to be sure, but how stark and unremitting can you get?' Walter Kerr in the *New York Herald Tribune* took a contrary view. Scarcely daring to specify the cause of Brick's alcoholism and dejection, except as something 'unnatural', he objected mightily to 'a tantalising reluctance . . . to let the play blurt out its promised secret'. Yet the secret could not have been clearer for those who wished to see it.[52]

When *Cat on a Hot Tin Roof* was presented in London in 1958 (for club audiences only, since the Lord Chamberlain refused a public licence for the play on the grounds of its homosexual references) the responses were similar. The drama critic of *The Times* found himself unable to summon up sympathy for Williams's characters. This was not, he assured his readers, because the play happened 'to turn . . . on accusations of homosexuality', but because Williams's people were like 'ferocious animals, rather than human beings'.[53]

In both countries reviewers selected and emphasised those aspects of the play that were conventional and unexceptionable. The homosexual aspects were virtually ignored, except by implication. The critic of the *New York Daily Mirror* who briefly alluded to 'an unnatural relationship', had seen members of the public queuing for the first performance. 'We trust their stomachs are stronger than ours,' he concluded.[54] But it was the minds not the stomachs that mattered. No critic was strong-minded enough to see or comment upon Williams's questioning of the restrictive codes of sexual orthodoxy and of the damaging impact of that orthodoxy. Even Kenneth Tynan concentrated upon mendacity and ignored homosexuality.

'The critics were not helpful, they were rather cautious,' says Peter Hall, who was a very young director aiming high at the time when he took on the first London production. 'Only Kenneth Tynan and Harold Hobson were well adjusted to the situation. It seemed then a fundamentally shocking thing that life could be so restricted, that artists, dramatists could not write about the full spectrum of life.'[55]

Suddenly Last Summer was staged both in New York and London in such humble circumstances that it looked as if Williams was on the verge of losing his box-office appeal, or so producers reckoned. In New York *Garden District*, the double bill of which *Suddenly Last Summer* constituted the larger, sensational, part was presented in 1958 at the York Theatre. The York was one of the first off-Broadway studio theatres, devoted to staging the work of the new and the unknown rather than the famous and familiar. For the first time in Williams's theatrical career a play of his was arriving in New York without a single star player.

In London, the play's subject-matter would have meant that it could only be staged in club conditions, had not the Lord Chamberlain just relaxed his ban on plays about homosexuality. Yet the play was only presented at the small Arts theatre club, directed by Herbert Machiz, who had also staged the play in New York. The principal roles of the cousin and the mother were at least taken by Patricia Neal, the former film star, and Beatrix Lehmann, one of the principal classical actresses of her generation, with a particular facility for conveying elements of the sinister-grotesque in which her part as the mother abounded. The producers' diffidence may have been inspired by the conviction that the play's horrifying homosexual Grand Guignol and its expressionistic frame, staged in a Victorian Gothic Garden, would prove too much for traditional audiences.

Yet the play garnered superlatives from the critics both in London and New York. For despite the play's shock tactics, its climactic revelations of cannibalism and stratagems for a dangerous lobotomy, *Suddenly Last Summer* was construed as a shocking but highly moral fable. It handed out exemplary, fatal punishment for Sebastian, a homosexual writer whom Williams had conceived of as a monstrous aberration of nature. It is as if Williams were disavowing what he had professed about homosexuality.

In the lurid here and now of *Suddenly Last Summer*, homosexual desire is conceived in terms of lust – not pure lust even, but rather as a predatory, pitiless form of exploitation in which Sebastian, rich American in the Third World, has sexually colonised the starving youth of Acbeza de Lobo, and masochistically submitted to their punishment in a style that recalls the submission of the saint whose name he bears. 'I tried to save him doctor . . . [from] completing ! – [a] sort of! – image! – he had of! – sacrifice to a! – terrible sort of a – God,' his cousin Catharine pants (4.170). The masochistic impulses imputed to Sebastian run in parallel to a form of manipulation and exploitation of his close female relatives, his mother and his cousin, for both are used to procure youths whom Sebastian is too shy to recruit himself.

It is as if Williams's ideas about homosexuality had been subverted, as if he had been converted to the idea that homosexuals were liable to be the sexually voracious monsters of nature. 'Conversion' seems to be the right word. Williams was in the midst of intensive Freudian analysis when he wrote the play. All the unfinished business of his past, some of the guilts and griefs of his adolescence must have been coming back to him. And his analyst, he explained later, was urging him to break with his lover, Frank Merlo, and 'to attempt a heterosexual life'. Thus at a time of pervasive depression, when his doubts about his powers as a dramatist were heightened by the adverse reception of one of his major plays, *Orpheus Descending*, he was being told that homosexuality was his great undoing.[56]

But *Suddenly Last Summer* cannot be written off as an obedient act of self-repudiation in which Williams's *alter ego*, the dandy poet with a damaged heart, is picked to death, his flesh consumed as suitable punishment for his sexual appetite. The play is a more subtle and supple form of transmuted biography, a rite of confession and accusation, in which Williams draws up a table of charges against his mother, on whom Mrs Venable is clearly based, and himself, for supposedly wrecking the life of his sister, Rose.

The play's environment and the behaviour of its people are violent and unnatural. The garden in which the play is staged is luridly scarred with images of contorted and hideous vegetation. It is more jungle than back-yard. It teems with 'massive tree flowers that suggest organs of a body torn out, glistening with undried blood'. Its riven contours are symbolic analogues to the shredded condition in which Sebastian was found at the point of death. The cries and whispers in this place are not those of the benign-natural but 'beasts, serpents and birds, all of savage nature' (1.37). This sinister landscape, from which the natural, the beautiful and the benign have been taken, matches the people who move within the garden.

'I have followed the developing tension and anger and violence of the world and the time that I lived in through my own steadily increasing tension as a writer and person,' Williams wrote at the time.[57] The reference to the way in which world tension matched his own developing anxiety seems most pointed. *Suddenly Last Summer*, reined just away from the B horror movie, is a vision of society reduced to violent fundamentals, possessed by the lusts of greed and sexual rapaciousness. These drives are concealed behind façades of decorum and the glosses of civility. Truth finally catches up with and overwhelms Sebastian's mother and wrecks the false reputation she has posthumously cultivated for him. But Catharine, the truth-bringer, wanders out of the play damaged for life: the trauma of watching her cousin eaten alive has done for her.

Homosexuality, as made manifest in the desires and designs of Sebastian, emerges as the precipitating cause of this catastrophe, but it takes Catharine's revelation to show it as such. Williams organises the play in two opposing processes. As Mrs Venable creates a fiction of her son's sexual life and his demise, so Catharine reveals the truth about it: she confesses the truth about the murder of Sebastian. Mrs Venable has the power of money to induce an experimenting doctor to perform the lobotomy which will 'cut' Catharine's 'hideous story out of her brain', a plan which recalls the lobotomy inflicted upon Rose Williams (4.188). And Catharine's mother and brother, eager to secure the pending inheritance from

Sebastian's estate, are quite prepared for Mrs Venable's lie to prevail over any truth.

Mrs Venable's fiction recreates the dead Sebastian as the model of the exquisite artist, whose supposedly sexless existence is devoted to the rare pursuit of his own sensibility and its expression, in a single poem each year. But Williams, through the mouthpiece of the mother, mocks Sebastian's preciousness as he endows him with the negative attributes of the stereotypical homosexual. Sebastian is a caricature of Williams's sexual and artistic personality. He is chronically weak from rheumatic fever, forever popping pills; he writes just one exquisite poem a year. And in Mrs Venable's enchanted, comically unselfconscious recall he is locked with her in bonds of unnatural closeness; her husband has been exiled to the perimeter of her life while she has travelled the world with Sebastian. She is a modern Jocasta who has never bedded her son but relished their bizarre togetherness. 'We were a famous couple. People didn't speak of Sebastian and his mother . . . they said Sebastian and Violet' (1.148).

In Catharine's revaluation of Sebastian, the charm, the sensitivity and attentiveness of the man prove to be surface decoration. Sebastian is transformed into a neo-Victorian construct, the homosexual predator whose evil designs are belied by his suave exterior. As Sebastian made use of his mother until she lost her looks, to make 'contacts' for him in smart places, so Catharine in the first summer of his middle-age was used, in her transparent bathing dress, as bait for third-world boys. This process of use and dependence parodies grotesquely the ties and transactions of family attachment.

On the sexual hunt Sebastian has dehumanised his sexual choices, seeing them as items in a meat market, succulent pieces of flesh to be consumed. 'Cousin Sebastian said he was famished for blonds. That's how he talked about people, as if they were items on a menu. That one's delicious looking, that one's appetising' (2.156). For this lusting Williams awards Sebastian the final punishment. The rich American consumer is consumed by the poor third world. As, in sexual terms he has eaten, so in literal terms is he eaten: the lust has become a drive so dangerous, so all-consuming, that it is careless of the threats from rough trade youths. The words of the play's title reverberate. They do not refer to the fact of Sebastian's

sudden death but to the abrupt appearance of that insidious
enemy in almost all the plays of Tennessee Williams – time.
'Suddenly, last summer,' Catharine recalls, 'he wasn't young
any more' (4.178). *Suddenly Last Summer*'s sense is of a world
where both nature and human nature are everywhere savage,
where God is cruelty incarnate, where love is a matter of use
and abuse, where Sebastian's homosexual desiring is only one
symptom of this lapsed society. That view is communicated with
thrilling, expressionistic flair. But the way in which Catharine's
traumatised condition is attributed to Sebastian's lusting – and
indeed the form of these lusts – imparts a factitious melodrama
to the play. Sebastian, and his arid, empty life, becomes a form
of self-accusing, a self-punishing for using young men in a
form of trading. The play's struggle involves a battle to impose
conformity, rather than to resist it. *Suddenly Last Summer* is
Williams's one play that resists liberation, or finds in liberation
that depravity which the orthodox of the 1950s believed was
synonymous with homosexuality.

Yet Williams's sense of alienation and dissociation was spur
and stimulus to his homosexual sensibility; his is the first
post-war example of homosexual sensibility employed in the
making of plays for the American theatre, and achieving a vital
form of drama.

THE CURE

The Cold War dread of homosexuality inspired a medical and
social effort to 'cure homosexuals'. And *The Small Hours* by
Leueen MacGrath, the actress, and her husband, George S.
Kaufman, is a theatrical witness to the popularity of this
fairy-tale notion, which reached its dangerous zenith with
aversion therapy. The play also conforms to the belief in
homosexuality as a form of deviancy, inducing a whole array of
symptoms. In *The Small Hours*, presented on Broadway in 1951,
a young man is shown heading for breakdown and addiction
to the 'depraving drug', cannabis, because of his fight to ward
off homosexual desires.

Peter, the play's 23-year-old example of well-repressed homosexual longing, is not only artistic, but hankers for a holiday
alone on an island in Greece. When seen loitering outside 'a
disreputable door in a disreputable neighbourhood', the worst

Plate 1 1933. Henry Hewitt as Trump, Frank Vosper as Mr Dulcimer, Hugh Williams as Julian and Catherine Lacey as Leonora in *The Green Bay Tree*, Mordaunt Shairp. (Photo by Houston Rogers from the collections of the Theatre Museum. By courtesy of the Board of Trustees of the Victoria and Albert Museum)

Plate 2 1958. Ben Gazzara and Barbara del Geddes in *Cat on a Hot Tin Roof*, Tennessee Williams. (Photo by T. Armstrong Jones (Lord Snowdon) and Tony Sim, from the collections of the Theatre Museum. By courtesy of the Board of Trustees of the Victoria and Albert Museum)

Plate 3 1964. Beryl Reid and Malcolm McDowell in *Entertaining Mr Sloane*, Joe Orton. (Photo by courtesy of John Haynes)

Plate 4 1966. Noël Coward, Irene Worth and Lilli Palmer in *A Song at Twilight*, Noël Coward. (Photo by Angus McBean from the collections of the Theatre Museum. By courtesy of the Board of Trustees of the Victoria and Albert Museum)

Plate 5 1968. *The Boys in the Band,* Mart Crowley. (Photo by Houston Rogers from the collections of the Theatre Museum. By courtesy of the Board of Trustees of the Victoria and Albert Museum)

Plate 6 1979. Tom Bell and Ian McKellen in *Bent*, Martin Sherman.
(Photo by courtesy of John Haynes)

Plate 7 1985. Antony Sher in *Torch Song Trilogy*, Harvey Fierstein.
(Photo by courtesy of John Haynes)

Plate 8 1986. Martin Sheen in *The Normal Heart*, Larry Kramer.
(Photo by courtesy of John Haynes)

is anticipated, and rightly (4.13). Peter, caught in the act by the police, is attempting to buy cannabis, a drug which the authors clearly regard as a recipe for utter ruin. And his father's response to the news of his son's arrest suggests that the parents of the 1950s equated an addiction to drugs with sexual deviation. 'He's just doped. Your son is a drug fiend,' the father announces, 'He is a weak, self-pitying sissy who kept seeing himself in poetic terms' (16.47). His mother can only plead in retaliatory defence that Peter is 'sensitive' (16.47). Worse still, Peter succumbs to what the stage homosexual was always expected to succumb to – a flood of tears. He emerges from prison, where he has been sent for his attempt to buy cannabis, born again. Latent homosexuals, you might think, would emerge from incarceration as homosexually proficient and practised rather than still fixed in the latent stage. But in this silly fairy-tale he emerges as the dramatic proof that your homosexual son can be sexually transformed by a term in prison and a helpful prison doctor.

'You know why I've been such a stinker and why I took dope and why I can't get on with anybody?' he asks. 'No matter how I say it, it's going to upset and shock you. I wish I could have shielded you from this, but my own need for help is too great. I'm a latent homosexual, that's what's wrong with me' (16.69). This confession, the first open homosexual confession made upon the English or American stage since another 'drug addict' announced himself to be homosexual in Mae West's *The Drag*, opened up first lines of communication between parent and son. The mother's response suggested that she would support her son but then he was trying to convert to heterosexuality.

Since the 1940s, there had been a school of psychiatric opinion contending that the homosexual might be a suitable candidate for 'cure', and that homosexuality itself was an acquired abnormality. Beset with rather dangerous drug treatments as well as conventional psychotherapy, the willing and sometimes the unwilling homosexual became the profession's guinea-pigs. In the 1950s, aversion therapy, a form of medical terrorism, achieved temporary and specious cures. The patient, sometimes against his will, would be injected with drugs that caused acute nausea or the terrifying sensation of being unable to breathe. He would then be shown pictures of sexually attractive young men, and come to associate his sexual desires with nausea or difficulty in breathing. It was a therapy that sometimes worked, but not for long and never indefinitely. The medical establishment tended to approve this sort of therapeutic effort. 'No doctor should advise a young person to rest content with a homosexual orientation, without first giving a grave warning about the frustration and the tragedy inherent in this mode of life.'[58]

Such a sense of panic over homosexuality flares up in Arthur Miller's *A View from the Bridge*, where a malicious, sexual slur, imputing homosexual desire to an obviously heterosexual young man, directly precipitates death and the break-up of a family. Eddie Cabone, a middle-aged dockworker, incestuously hankering for his teenage niece, plants an insulting kiss upon the lips of his rival, the young man who loves the girl. Eddie's intention is to suggest by this insulting action that the young man is in reality homosexual. And for the young man the kiss is the grossest possible insult. It impugns his virility, his manhood and his identity. The kiss, in the end, precipitates murder and the break-up of a family.

It was because of this kiss that the Lord Chamberlain refused to allow the play to be publicly performed. And Anthony Quayle had to take the leading role in a private 1956 production, at the Comedy Theatre, which was converted into a private club for members. The depiction on stage of such forms of desire, even in terms that disparaged and caricatured homosexual feeling, was thought too shocking to meet the naked eye in public. In these circumstances it was inevitable that homosexuality was exiled from the London stage except when presented in club performances. A young playwright, Jeremy Kingston, was one of the last victims of this veto. His play, *No Concern of Mine*, was presented at the Westminster theatre in 1958. He had originally attempted to write about homosexual desire, with a young male drama student longing to be in those male arms that held his sister. But his producer, Robin Fox, instructed him to eliminate all traces of this unrequited passion to ensure that the play was licensed. Kingston, now a theatre reviewer for *The Times*, had to agree to the fundamental alterations, or forfeit the chance of a production. He remembers the circumstances clearly.

It's perhaps scarcely possible now to appreciate how fidgety the times were in the 1950s. There was the increasing call for changes in the law to do with homosexuality, but oddly enough there was a feeling that censorship and self-censorship was actually stricter than before.[59]

As a result the motives of the play's principal characters were quite inscrutable, and the reviews of the production reflected a sense of bewilderment.

Yet on the very day that Kingston's play was first performed, there was announced a decision which marked a change of heart and mind. A slight change in the climate occurred and a slight liberal breeze at last stirred in orthodox and establishment minds. The absolute veto that outlawed all discussion of homosexuality upon the British stage was rescinded. In less than ten years the closet doors would be unbarred. And instead of skeletons within, ordinary human beings would be found. The homosexual, the decade's archetype of danger and of depravity, was soon to be placed in front of the audience.

4

OUT OF BONDAGE
TOWARDS BEING: 1958–1969

WHERE THE DIFFERENCE BEGINS

The British and American theatre's twentieth-century prefer-
ence for lagging behind the times, rather than surging ahead
of them, was abruptly broken down in the reactive aftermath of
the Cold War. The ideas of consensus and orthodoxy to which
the mainstream theatre subscribed, and by which it had been
controlled, were steadily eroded by the impact of the 1960s'
Counter Culture. The very conception of the theatre's role, its
function and its constituencies began to be challenged.

In Britain the gradual, nation-wide development of state
subsidy for the performing arts through the Arts Council,
and in America, through its puny equivalent, the National
Endowment, encouraged a theatre whose imperative was not
triumph at the box office. The new off-off-Broadway troupes,
the radical, socially motivated companies formed in American
universities and outside them, and in London the outburst of
the fringe were controlled by directors, writers and performers
who would rank themselves with the Counter Culture rather
than its precursor, the Old Uniformity.

Before the Second World War it would have been possible
to argue that there were governing myths about homosexuality, which the theatre retailed. By the 1960s the theatre began to echo with the noises of dissonance, of the
clash between a new culture and the old. There could be
no better way of appreciating this change than by comparing
two plays written within two years of each other in the
1960s. Both were concerned, directly or covertly, with homosexuality. Noël Coward's *A Song at Twilight* (Plate 4), was

presented amidst much fabricated hullabaloo at the Queen's Theatre, London, in 1966 with the misnamed Master in his last theatrical role, and, sadly, looking not far from being on his last legs. Two years earlier Joe Orton had introduced himself to the London theatre with *Entertaining Mr Sloane* (Plate 3).

The two plays might, however, have been written in two different centuries for all their similarities. *A Song at Twilight* looked back to Pinero in form, technique and values. Coward's style of camp depended upon languid affectation. Here it had become so decrepit and listless that it could not even aspire to artificiality. Homosexuality, in his twilight dramatising, is the cause of guilt, concealment and evasion. It is the cause of blackmail by virtue of reveal-all letters. *Entertaining Mr Sloane*, by contrast, is the sight and the sound of the future before it occurs. Homosexuality loses its old gloss. The stereotypes vanish. The accretions of negative myths and fictions are discarded – a few years before the designation 'gay' replaces homosexual and begins to be taken as an identifying badge of pride. A great cultural change is coming on and *Entertaining Mr Sloane* is a faint premonition of the changing of consciousness.

Those transformations, by which gay men and lesbians began to see themselves as a specific, oppressed minority with its own identity and culture, were not isolated phenomena. Gay Liberation was only one sign of the times, of the dissent from orthodoxy, of the culture of protest. The post-war period had been marked by a drift from a 'patrist' or patriarchal system, with its close observance of hierarchies, controls and rules, to a 'matrist' system, which limits its observance of tradition, and of the rights of hierarchy to control individual behaviour and conduct. Matrism approved personal freedom and individual choice.

The Counter Culture, with its hippiedom, the rebirth of feminism and the associated rejection of the male conception of what constituted female role and duty, and the dawning of Gay Liberation, were all matrist in orientation. Similarly, the hippie rejection of marriage and the family, of the mass systems of production and distribution, exalted the self and self-discovery against the range of conformities. Pleasure and self-fulfilment were matrism's lode-stars.

The feminist movement was a clear correlative of Gay Liberation, which sought for analogous departures from orthodoxy. 'Feminism's attack upon traditional sex roles', John D'Emilio, the American historian of the Gay movement wrote 'and the affirmation of a non-reproductive sexuality . . . paved a smoother road for lesbians and homosexuals, who were . . . championing an eroticism that, by its nature, did not lead to procreation.'[1] The principle of sexual pleasure without procreation was, in practical terms, assisted by the liberating development of contraceptive techniques.

From the later 1950s the Gay Rights Movement began to contemplate, and then to adopt the techniques of aggressive militancy. By the mid-1960s, in a new climate of community and fellow-feeling, gay groups in both the east and west were arguing that the homosexuals' conception of themselves as constituting a 'problem' was really a question of 'prejudice and discrimination'.[2] The Gay Movement came to emulate the confrontational tactics of both the new Left protest movements and of Black Power. 'Black is beautiful' and 'Gay is good' were comparable affirmations, the second inspired by the first. Gay Liberationists were defining themselves as a distinct cultural minority. The Stonewall riot, which erupted in June 1969 in New York, was not, therefore, just the first gay uprising in America; it was a signal that gay militancy was not theoretical but practical. The rioters had something to fight for. Within months there were Gay Liberation cells all over the country.

BREAKING CENSORSHIP'S BONDS

Another sign of matrism's new ascendancy was observable in that process by which both Britain and America began to relax their systems of literary censorship. In America, from 1957, the American Supreme Court had begun to reinterpret the definition of obscenity, increasingly permitting the publication of material that would earlier have been declared obscene. In the atmosphere of developing sexual candour homosexuality began to be described. It was no longer something unspoken in between the lines. Allen Ginsberg's *Howl* broke with convention in its homosexual affirmation and candour. Hubert Selby's *Last Exit to Brooklyn*, William Burroughs's *Naked Lunch*,

John Rechy's *City of Night* and Gore Vidal's revised and more optimistic 1964 edition of his earlier *The City and the Pillar* do not constitute a genre. While Vidal's blithe humanism, his sense of gay desire as the simple sign of taste, has no ideological contact with Selby's yoking of suppressed homosexuality with degradation, both novels transcend the old taboo upon the discussion of homosexuality.

Britain's Obscene Publications Acts of 1959 and 1964, with their complex definition of obscenity and the 'public good' defence, allowing obscenity where it could be justified in terms of a value that invalidated or transcended obscene elements, engendered a similar liberalising process. And it was this liberalising fervour that helped to lay the foundation for Britain's version of a permissive society. Laws making divorce and abortion easier to obtain and homosexual acts between two consenting adult males legal were represented as magnificent extensions to the boundaries of freedom.

American theatre, which had not been subject to such stringent systems of censorship, still profited somewhat from the new relaxations. In 1965 the New York State's ban upon the depiction of homosexuality was lifted: it was a ban whose efficacy had been more observed in the breach than the observance, but the Broadway audiences and managers were so alike in their conformist ideologies and their homophobia that there had been scant incitement to venture into the territory. In Britain there was a far more momentous change. Within the space of a little more than eleven years the ban upon homosexuality – which, as far as the stage was concerned had been the unspeakable, unshowable aspect of sexuality – was lifted. First, in 1958, the Lord Chamberlain bowed to the enquiring spirit of the times and relaxed his absolute veto upon the discussion of homosexuality on stage. In 1946 and 1957 he had consulted 'A wide circle of persons prominent in clerical, legal, scholastic, medical, governmental, judicial and artistic circles' to advise whether to maintain the absolute ban. The 'wide circle' was sufficiently narrow-minded, on both occasions, to give him a resounding 'yes'.[3] But, inexplicably, one year later he had changed his mind. It may be that he had finally been embarrassed by the tactics of two West End producers who had converted the Comedy into a theatre club for three famous productions of plays by Miller, Williams and

Anderson. 'The subject', the Lord Chamberlain announced in a sort of proclamation of intent to Mr Charles Killick, Chairman of the Theatre's National Committee, 'is now so widely debated, written about and talked over that its complete exclusion from the stage can no longer be regarded as justifiable.' 'Complete' was the operative word. Now the Lord Chamberlain was prepared to allow what he called 'serious references' to homosexuality, as opposed to the sniggering innuendos, the camping of male chorus boys and jokes in revues which he had allowed to slip through his net. But anything that smacked of the 'salacious' or the 'offensive' would still be proscribed. 'Embraces' of the homosexual kind or, worse, 'practical demonstrations of love' (as he called them) 'between homosexuals' would still be outlawed. As a final concession, he solemnly announced 'We will allow the word "pansy" but not "bugger".' One of his Examiners subsequently took advantage of this relaxation to tell the Lord Chamberlain in his report on *A Patriot for Me* that it was 'The Pansies' Charter of Freedom'.[4]

Not that many dramatists took advantage of the Lord Chamberlain's relaxation; or, if they did, they could find no producer who wished to challenge the sexual status quo. Even the Royal Court did not present a single play about homosexuality until *A Patriot for Me* (1965). And not until the passing of The Theatres Act of 1968, which did away with the Lord Chamberlain's theatrical powers and gave the stage safeguards similar to those provided by the Obscene Publications Act, did playwrights become free to discuss and depict what the censor would not tolerate.

So despite the shock of the new, the prevailing and popular conception of homosexuality as it emerged upon the mainstream stages in the 1960s was only a moderated refinement of traditional views. Traces of compassion for the homosexual, revealed as a life-victim rather than a threat, triumphed over the 1950s conception of him as archetypically dangerous. He was no longer the epitome of evil either, but he remained an object of contempt. A play like Shelagh Delaney's *A Taste of Honey*, first seen at Joan Littlewood's Stratford East in 1958, is a key to understanding the changing perspective. But ranged against Delaney's portrayal of the young gay man, equivocally seen as the ideal, altruistic but pathetic friend

is, say, Peter Shaffer's *Black Comedy*, with the predatory stereotype of the flaunting queen. And Christopher Hampton's
When Did You Last See My Mother?, a play performed at the
Royal Court in 1966 and written when he was still in his
teens, provides the old familiar equation of homosexuality and
life-alienation.

Mart Crowley's play, *The Boys in the Band* (Plate 5), which
graduated from off-off-Broadway to Broadway itself, in the late
1960s, is the true transition drama. For it straddles two worlds:
it exists fretfully in the old dispensation of homosexual guilt and
despair; it looks, as that word 'band' in the title suggests, to a
new one where signs of community, of sexual self-confidence
also exist, and where an alternative to heterosexual modes
of living and expectations is approvingly and affirmatively
provided. The theatrical evolution from Delaney to Crowley
is, therefore, remarkable.

KICKS AND SCREAMS

In his summing up of the theatrical year of 1959, Kenneth Tynan
joyfully celebrated the way in which, across the space of the
previous four years, 'the English theatre had been dragged . . .
kicking and screaming into the twentieth century'.[5] One of the
signs of the new theatrical times created at the Royal Court,
he noted, was the way in which 'the poor', who had been
excluded from the life of the typical, luxuriant drawing-room
comedy, 'murder melodrama' or 'barrack room farce', were
now allowed a leading role. In the past, if they were allowed on
stage, they stumbled on briefly, 'clutching cloth caps', before
being condescendingly sent back to the car, the garden, the
estate or penury. By 1959, the Royal Court theatre had begun to
deal with social issues and people in whom the West End had
shown scant interest.

But even the Royal Court had not inflicted such a 'damaging dent in the West End structure', Tynan judged, as
Joan Littlewood with her Theatre Workshop Company out
at Stratford East.[6] Her decades-old ambition had been for
'a people's theatre outside the West End', yet by the end of
1959 two of her productions were being fêted in the heart of
West End playhouses. One of them, written by a 19-year-old,
was the first modern British play to depict a working-class

homosexual. Shelagh Delaney's *A Taste of Honey* is set in the midst of impoverished, deprived tenement life in working-class Liverpool, where a dejected, homosexual art student, evicted from his rented room for the 'crime' of being homosexual, finds a modest welcome in the home of another outsider. She is Jo, a pregnant teenage girl, who has been deserted both by her black boyfriend and her mother, an ageing good-time girl.

They achieve content and provide mutual support in the domestic ménage they create together. Yet Delaney's attitude to the homosexual is ambivalent and interesting. In Geof she created what appears to be a stereotypical homosexual. He is effeminate, shy, gentle, artistic. He lacks assertiveness, confidence and power. And Jo mocks his effeminacy remorselessly. Yet the play suggests that in him she has discovered a surrogate mother-figure, whose domestic skills and maternal compassion help her through a lonely pregnancy. Those very facets of Geof's character that Jo derides as stereotypically homosexual are also those that bring the heroine comfort, happiness and security. The pregnant and unmarried teenage girl, regarded in the 1950s as an emblem of flagrant immorality, finds common cause with the epitome of supposed degeneracy. Geof proves a far more altruistic and valuable mother-figure than the woman who has deserted her daughter in her months of need. A feminine man is thus approved, in qualified terms, for being 'feminine'. No heterosexual lover and no real mother help Jo out. And Jo's mother only returns when she needs to.

As originally played by Murray Melvin, both on stage and on film, Geof emerges in stereotypical form. Jo has scarcely befriended him when he is seen 'cutting out a baby's gown', as though to justify her mocking if affectionate comment 'You're just like a big sister to me' (2.i.54 and 55). Jo's taunts all depend upon Geof's effeminacy, and his failure to live up to the conventional notions of manhood: 'You'd make somebody a lovely wife' (2.i.57), or 'You're just like an old woman really' (11.ii.74); and, finally, 'You don't show much sign of coming fatherhood' (2.i.59). So insistent are these criticisms that it seems as if they are there to make a homophobic point. But, significantly, the Lord Chamberlain's Examiner was disgusted by these references and the homosexual elements had to be reduced.[7]

Geof is being both applauded and mocked, as if Jo cannot fathom or approve the reasons for which a man can assume a supposedly female role. Geof is also described as a social outcast, a misfit without a single friend, even though Liverpool has traditionally been one of those cities more accepting of homosexuality. 'I'd sooner be dead than away from you,' he warns Jo. 'Before I met you I didn't care one way or another whether I lived or died' (2.i.59). In the real world, Delaney implies, Geof's notable effeminacy, rather than the homosexuality of which it may be an expression, leaves him lacking in self-esteem and self-confidence. 'You've no confidence in yourself, have you?' Jo taunts him. 'You're afraid the girls might laugh' (2.i.56). No wonder, then, that he puts up no fight, makes no response and slinks out when Helen, Jo's returning mother, shows him the door with jubilant good riddance: 'You can clear off, take your simpering little face out of it' (2.i.63). The 'arty little freak' (2.i.63) does not even achieve Jo's support or gratitude.

Yet Geof emerges from the play and Delaney's pen as the one authentically good person within it; the exception to a prevailing selfishness, and the odd man out in situations where everyone is struggling to achieve what they want, or what they feel they need. 'You're a funny little man', Jo says in her tribute to him. 'I mean that. You're unique' (2.ii.76). Delaney had thus written the first major British play in which a gay and effeminate man is both ridiculed and approved, derided and accepted. Geof has the strength of mind to be himself, to fight against orthodoxy.

Jo, the voice of a new generation, or at least a representative working-class girl, accepts, if only for a brief time, a homosexual man as her best friend and mate. No cold shoulders are turned. The homosexual is humanised and brought in from the cold. It is a new departure. The revolt against the conventional forms of relationship and for a personal liberation is about to begin. The positive form of this struggle against orthodoxy occurs in the plays of Joe Orton, the negative in John Osborne's *Look Back in Anger*. The comparison reveals the opposing perceptions of a homosexual-despising heterosexual and a heterosexual-mocking homosexual. But there is more to this distinction than that.

THE IMPORTANCE OF HAVING BEEN ORTON

On 4 May 1964, W. A. Darlington, the 74-year-old critic of the *Daily Telegraph*, who had been that paper's principal reviewer for forty-four years of unbroken service, attended a first play by an unknown playwright, presented at that antecedent of the fringe, the Arts. He responded in terms reminiscent of the disgust and outrage of his predecessor, Clement Scott, when reviewing Ibsen's *Ghosts* in 1891. Of all the plays Darlington had seen in his reviewing life, this was the one he disliked more than any. 'I feel', he confessed, 'as if snakes had been writhing around my feet.'[8]

Joe Orton's *Entertaining Mr Sloane* does not mark the birth of a movement. But Orton's importance in the history of the theatre's treatment of homosexual politics is vital. Orton is where the difference begins as far as the theatre is concerned. Orton, in his modern way, is the theatre's first homosexual revolutionary, before the times were gay. He rejected all the controlling assumptions about homosexuality. He was the first playwright in Britain – indeed one of the first writers in either Britain or America – to reject the dominant myth of homosexuality as sickness and sin and to live without the oppression of guilt. *Entertaining Mr Sloane* stands somewhat apart from the majority of plays considered in this study, since in *Sloane* (as in the rest of Orton's small œuvre) homosexual desire poses no problem or crisis. But Orton has such a crucial function and significance that, even though he does not seem to fit within this survey, he set the kind of terms and sexual agenda with which the next generation of dramatists would engage. Orton sought to deprive sex of its mystique; furthermore he showed up cherished emblems of respectability and authority, the family unit, the policeman, the psychiatrist as sources of sexual and moral irregularity. And the sexy, bisexual youth emerged as the victim of all these in his plays.

The sharp divorce between the old order of dramatists and a new generation is best revealed in a comparison between extracts from Tennessee Williams's *Memoirs* of 1976 and Orton's *Diaries*, written nine years earlier. It is the difference between the realist and the neurotic romantic puritan. 'Get yourself fucked if you want to,' Orton quotes himself, advising his sexually suppressed and often miserable friend, the actor Kenneth Williams, 'Get yourself anything you like. Reject all the values of society. And enjoy sex. When you're dead you'll regret not having fun with your genital organs.'[9] 'I have known many gays,' Tennessee Williams wrote, 'who live just for the [sex] act, that "rebellious hell" persisting into middle-life and later, and it is graven in their faces and even refracted from their wolfish eyes.'[10] The description says more about Williams's hatred of his own sexuality than of any promiscuous homosexual.

Both these writers went in hot and constant pursuit of sex. Williams took to homosexual guilt as a pig to truffles, seeing himself dragged involuntarily to some lower depths. However much he proclaimed a Lawrentian belief in sex as liberation and fulfilment, 'deviant satyriasis' was the accusatory phrase he used to describe his own sexual activities as a young man, thereby rating his sexual desires with the bestial and demonic. Sexual rebellion was hell for him. For Orton sexual rebellion was (or would be) victory against a society of hypocritical conformists. 'It's the only way to smash the wretched civilisation,' he mused.[11] Williams's archetypal characters, the ageing young man, and the fading belle, both of them in fear of time, are creative projections of a particular homosexual sensibility: love is lost or never to be kept. Orton's archetype is the sexy boy on the make.

Homosexuality posed no problem for Orton. In stating this, I will, I suppose, be accused of ignoring the fact that Orton ended up battered to death by his lover, Kenneth Halliwell. This fact has been made central to interpretations of Orton's life; it is, however, far from being crucially relevant. First, Orton's biographer, John Lahr, interprets the playwright's life and demise as some form of morality play, doom suitably waiting to spring upon the sinful couple. 'The spectre of death lurked behind his own pursuit of pleasure,' he writes of Orton, in the tone of a character from a Joe Orton play, 'Promiscuity was a ... flirtation with death'. He considers Orton's sexual forays in public lavatories to have been sheer danger.[12] But in the age before AIDS, Orton's sexual pursuits were not death-bringing: gay-bashing had not then become the grimly familiar occurrence it is today. In public lavatories Orton would have been susceptible to sexually transmitted disease and police entrapment; but his reputation would not have been ruined by a court appearance since he did not set store by conventional standards.

Second, Orton's death is interpreted as suitable punishment for his promiscuity, killed because of those two supposed components of the homosexual stereotype, jealousy and acute crapulousness. Simon Shepherd, writing a post-Gay Liberationist interpretation of Orton's life and sexuality, suggests that the pair were murdered by 'a polite version of the fascism and the heterosexism they hated'.[13] But this is almost as perverse a reading of the life as Lahr's. Shepherd, whose book totally eclipses Lahr's, and sharply places the playwright in sexual and social context, emphasises Orton's sense of freedom achieved in promiscuity, and of his enjoyment of sex without commitment. But he also interprets all Orton's jaunty screwing as a solution to his necessary dependence upon middle-class society, whose pruderies he hated. And this promiscuity, he concludes, only became a problem when Halliwell, 'forced by Orton's new career and friends into his role of wife-at-home, started moralistically to limit that "freedom"'. Shepherd suggests the lovers' sex-life together had been basically good. 'What was making them tense was also destroying their love.'[14] But any close reading of the diaries suggests quite otherwise. Orton's relationship with Halliwell was not primarily sexual at all. They wanted different sexual things and Orton could not, did not, want them from Halliwell or with him. Incompatibility loomed. Halliwell wanted a homosexual version of heterosexual marriage, with faithfulness over all. Orton did not. Promiscuity was sexual necessity for him; it also gave him the sense of freedom he craved.

Halliwell, although snubbed by some actors, was not forced into the role of wife by the theatre world. Halliwell did win some help and some understanding from Orton's actor and actress friends. But the wretchedly despairing Halliwell, lacking self-esteem or purpose in life in 1967, was also showing symptoms of mental disturbance. It is impossible to deduce why Orton failed to interpret or respond to these danger signs. But it may be that the isolated, almost hermetic, life that the men had led for so long meant that Orton had no real, long-standing friends who would sound any alarm that he would regard as serious or significant. They were locked in an exclusion zone, which they had created as a barrier to a world they detested.

Instead of interpreting Orton's sexual escapades as escapist activities, I believe it is wiser to see them as aspects of his homosexual identity. His devotion to Halliwell, which lasted until the last phase of their lives, came principally to depend upon domestic companionship, shared beliefs and emotional ties. But Orton believed in a feast of sexual plenty and not in romantic love. He was also attracted sexually to adolescents and had no pangs about these highly illegal desires. His sense of homosexual identity affects and characterises his plays. A dissociation between sexual pleasure and erotic love emerges. Mr Sloane is the British theatre's most unabashed male sex-object. Sex is his commodity, his first asset, and he will trade in it. And the family, as pictured in *Entertaining Mr Sloane* and *What the Butler Saw* is a source of power, but of power selfishly, hypocritically, irregularly used. The family is not celebrated, it is dissected. Orton's assault upon the probity of family relations is thus made years before that of the Flower Power generation.

Kath and Ed, the middle-aged brother and sister in *Entertaining Mr Sloane*, condone the murder of their father, that they may both enjoy the 18-year-old Sloane in the ever-after. In *What the Butler Saw* the forces of order and harmony are restored, but only to reveal that mother has unwittingly had sex with her adolescent son and the father has lusted after the girl who is, unknown to him, his own daughter. 'Orton's terrible obsession with perversion', wrote Harold Hobson, who had been *Entertaining Mr Sloane*'s most eloquent enthusiast, 'which is regarded as having brought his life to an end, and choked his very high talent, poisons the atmosphere of the play. And what should have been a piece of gaily irresponsible nonsense becomes impregnated with evil.'[15] But Orton did not, of course, aspire to gay nonsense; what Hobson interprets as the 'poison' of the play is its sabotaging of male authority, of the systems which it operates. The dangerous but sexy hooligans of the play, as Shepherd vividly shows, are, if not bedfellows of the non-conformist rockers and mods of the times, at least fellow outsiders.

The diction of his characters, which has been for so long labelled 'Ortonesque', is one further and organising sign of his sensibility. The diction of his characters is camp, a camp that in its relish of the shocking paradox and formalised artificiality recalls Oscar Wilde. But it is Wilde's diction taken, as the critic Ronald Bryden observed, from the ranks of the high-born and reordered to become redolent of welfare-state gentility.[16] It is a diction of large pretension, which relies on artificiality and unnaturalness, in which official and formal language, the style of the official form, of bureaucracy, of newspaper headlines and advertising copy is married to common-place speech. Both their content and their expression are inspired by homosexual sensibility.

Entertaining Mr Sloane is a fantasy of sexual versatility and abundance, a saturnalia during which lip-service is paid to traditional sexual morality, decorum and family love, while in practice these cherished shibboleths are betrayed. Orton jubilantly plots the downfall of the British family and its respectability. *Entertaining Mr Sloane* creates a family where the ties of blood are betrayed by the nagging insistence of lust. Mr Sloane, the cocky young hero of Orton's imagining and, probably, his sexual fantasising, accepts himself as a bisexual object of desire and exploits the fact. The essence of amorality is to feel no guilt as a result of behaviour that is either anti-social or immoral. Sloane, whose conscience has gone missing, presumed dead, may be a psychopath. He feels no flickers of remorse for having killed one man, and in the course of the play, he kills another, who recognises him as the murderer. And this killing troubles him not a wit. But Sloane's sexual versatility and desirability, his willingness to cater both to the demands of the middle-aged Kath and her homosexual brother, Ed, prove his salvation. Here the critics' sense of outrage and revulsion begins. For the play signals its lack of a moral view, or at least a view of the sort that conventional critics demanded. Neither Kath nor Ed care a jot that they are besotted by their father's brutal murderer. The action presses towards a solution by which Sloane will be shared on equal terms by the smitten brother and sister. That will be his punishment for kicking their father to death. But the punishment is accidental, incidental. As symbols of the British tendency to humbuggery Kath and Ed neither admit nor refer to Sloane's murder. Conscienceless and lustful, their amorality resembles Sloane's. Kath wishes to be mother/lover to Sloane while Ed, whose relationship with his father has been torpedoed by years of feuding silence, wants him as his lover/son.

A parody of the happy ending is arranged. Lust is all. A compromise, promising sexual content for some short time for the brother and sister, is predicted. Sloane, the passive object of desire who comes to hand with the resignation of the youth who knows no other way out, is absorbed into the new family circle. His sexual power is overwhelmed by their social power. The paradigm of the old sexual morality, with its guilts and conventions, is discarded. Sloane is a 'transmitter of a genuinely erotic male sexuality'. Such a youth was far from the homosexual stereotype. He was one of masculinity's alluring new youth-models, offering a ride into a new world of opportunities, expressing homosexuals' affinity with other oppressed outsiders.[17]

The figure of the sexy hooligan is Orton's shadow, a projection by which he becomes the free, conscienceless subverter of morality, the begetter of sexual anarchy. For all Orton's jubilant sex-games in lavatories, and casual pick-ups, despite the Arab teenagers who willingly came to hand on his last holiday in Marrakesh, he was not himself a transmitter of such freedom in real life. He had been the obedient mother's boy in adolescence and when mature, despite his rages over upper-and middle-class hypocrisies and rudeness, remained the socially adaptable, well-mannered young man about town. He was always curious to observe the middle-class fashionables in their habitats.

'I'd like to meet you. When? Do give me a ring. I don't think we'll see eye to eye on drama,' he wrote to Peter Cadbury, Head of the London ticket agency Keith Prowse, who led an attack upon *Entertaining Mr Sloane* when it reached the West End.[18] And in ordinary society he practised what was, even for the later 1960s, a charmingly oblique form of sexual seduction.

> I can't just ring up and suggest coming over for sex . . .
> I mean – even for me that's a bit crude. I've got to wrap
> it up a bit. I've got to at least meet him on his own for a
> couple of hours,

he wrote, when intending to secure some new young chap for sex.[19] The sexy hooligan became, therefore, one of Orton's ways of escape from functioning as the well-mannered and charming young playwright, risen from the lower-middle class. He could not become such a hooligan, but he could identify with the cocksure, homosexual outsider. That was his chosen identity.

Lahr, predictably, fails to understand the fact. He is quite unable to appreciate that Orton's 'unvarying outfit – National Assistance boots, high-cuffed blue jeans, white T-shirt and leather jacket' were not, as he suggests, part of Orton's 'personality' but the new emblems of the homosexual, the code and badge of identity. It was an identity disguised: Hal and Dennis, as played by Simon Ward and Kenneth Cranham in the 1966 production of *Loot* that Charles Marowitz mounted at his experimental theatre outpost, the Cochrane, looked rather like smart young mods. Orton's own stipulations for the actors playing these roles were similar to those he had demanded for Mr Sloane. 'I don't want there to be anything queer or odd or camp about the relationship of Hal and Dennis,' he instructed, 'They must be perfectly ordinary boys who happen to be fucking each other. Nothing could be more natural.'[20] The rigid lines of sexual demarcation were being scrambled so that the sexuality of the boys was resistant to category. Nick, the page boy in *What the Butler Saw*, looks similarly available, a youth whose sexual sophistication recalls Mr Sloane and that hooligan's lack of qualms over selling his body. These youths blur sexual distinctions.

Ed, the hankerer for Mr Sloane, is the true example of an Ortonian homosexual. Masculine, assertive, determined and controlling, he lacks some of the old negative aspects. But he is also sinister, dangerous and hypocritical. Both the hooligans, and Ed himself, anticipate one of the controlling assertions of the Gay Liberation movement. Gay Liberators sought to remove the rusty shackles of self-oppression by refusing to accept society's estimate of them. In Orton's fictive world the transcendent importance given to personal satisfaction ensures that guilt's strait-jacket will never be worn.

'Complete sexual licence . . . Sex is the only way to infuriate them,' Orton confessed optimistically to his diary.[21] And the sexual anarchy that breaks out in *What the Butler Saw* reflects Orton's obedience to his own instruction. Homosexual desire and performance was but one symptom, in his imagining, of healthiness breaking out in a screwed-up Britain. John Rechy in his remarkable fusion of fiction and autobiography, *The Sexual Outlaw*, would take Orton's estimate of homosexuality's disruptive potential further, in the 1970s, by arguing romantically that the 'promiscuous homosexual' was nothing less than 'a sexual revolutionary'. The pressures of ostracism and persecution produced in him, Rechy wrote hopefully, a brilliant defiance, a form of emergency existentialism. 'Knowing that each second his freedom may be ripped away arbitrarily, he lives fully at the brink.'[22]

Entertaining Mr Sloane, and indeed Orton, did not aspire so greatly. But in his attempt to normalise and make natural those sexual drives that were outlawed, Orton was doing something quite radical. It was one thing, in the 1960s, for homosexuals to ask for pity and understanding but something far more daring to demand that homosexuality be deprived of its aura of awfulness. 'In Sloane,' said Orton in a revelatory 1967 interview,

> I wrote about a man who was interested in having sex with boys. I wanted him played as if he was the most ordinary man in the world. And not as if the moment you had sex with boys, you had to put on earrings and scent. This is very bad and I hope that now that homosexuality is allowed people aren't going to continue doing the conventional portraits there have been in the past.[23]

Orton was talking at a time when the Sexual Offences Bill, exempting certain homosexual acts in private from prosecution, had not become law. He was drawing attention to the way in which he wished to see the homosexual on stage deprived of his stereotypical aspects and how as a dramatist he wishes to assist in this process.

In the first production at the Arts Theatre, Dudley Sutton, whom the director Patrick Dromgoole miscast as Sloane, looked the angelic part but did not act it. He was costumed in respectability rather than in the erotic leather gear that Malcolm McDowell wore for Lindsay Anderson's 1975 revival at the Royal Court. And, of course, Orton's sexual enthusiasm for the teenage male could not be stressed. Yet the play's sexual formula emerged with the force of a cold shower on a hot day. Mr Sloane faces up to Ed. All the old signs and codes are discarded. A new convention is being achieved. No homosexual or bisexual is sensitive, artistic, nervous or emotional in Orton's plays. Indeed, Halliwell reproached Orton utterly for his refusal to acknowledge sensitivity.

An entire sequence of homosexual proposition and response is also conveyed through a system of new signs, allusion and nuances in the play. The subtext, the concealed action, describes a homosexual transaction negotiated at some speed. Yet to the naïve or the innocent this dialogue seems to approve the idea

of male athleticism and conventional morality. It is a new mode
of signifying:

> ED. I . . . well, well [*Breathless*] A little body builder are you?
> I bet you are . . . [*slowly*] . . . Do you . . . [*shy*] exercise
> regular?
>
> SLOANE. As clockwork.
>
> ED. Good, good. Stripped?
>
> SLOANE. Fully.
>
> ED. Complete [*striding to the window*] How invigorating.
>
> SLOANE. And I box. I'm a bit of a boxer.
>
> ED. Ever done any wrestling?
>
> SLOANE. On occasions.
>
> ED. So, so.
>
> SLOANE. I've got a full chest. Narrow hips. My biceps are –
>
> ED. Do you wear leather . . . next to the skin? Leather jeans,
> say? Without . . . aah
>
> SLOANE. Pants?
>
> ED. Get away! [*pause*] The question is are you clean living?
> You may as well know I set great store by morals.
>
> (1.22)

The Lord Chamberlain's Assistant Comptroller in 1965, John
Johnston, who has since revealed that he believed Orton's
plays were examples of the Artaudian Theatre of Cruelty, was
quite out of his depth.[24] The Lord Chamberlain required
few deletions from this or any other homoerotic scenes in
Entertaining Mr Sloane, though one of his staff found the
'homosexual aspect . . . filthy'. It was the so-called explicit
heterosexual activities which he would not allow to be depicted:
Kath's breasts could not be fondled. There could be no naughty,
simulated copulation when Sloane rolled on top of her. The
play's homosexual elements, relayed in language of code and
innuendo, were scarcely criticised until Emile Littler, a powerful
impresario, chiefly known for his presentation of pantomimes,
attacked Orton's play as 'absolutely filthy'. Littler was not
very adept, except at making money, and he included in his
indictment not only Orton but also the Royal Shakespeare
Company's production of Harold Pinter's *The Birthday Party*,
Samuel Beckett's *Endgame*, David Rudkin's *Afore Night Come*,
and Peter Weiss's *Marat/Sade*. It was the morality of Orton's
play to which he objected. Yet though some of the London

reviewers disliked *Entertaining Mr Sloane*, only Darlington was vehement in disapproval and Harold Hobson, barking up the wrong tree, approved its 'vision of total evil'.[25]

On Broadway *Entertaining Mr Sloane* was staged at the Lyceum theatre, with Sheila Hancock replacing Madge Ryan's bland London performance and providing rank, middle-aged sexiness. Orton was there to watch and judge the effect of the new production. 'As Eddie [Lee Montague] is being played right, the audience are very worried that this attractive masculine man should be a power and threat to them,' he wrote back to Halliwell, of Alan Schneider's production.[26] The play's sexual animus was now more strongly projected. And most of the New York reviewers responded with the kind of affronted anger and uproar that had characterised Darlington's London review. 'A medieval cesspool,' accused the *World Telegram and Sun*. Howard Taubman's notice in the *New York Times* condemned Orton for using characters 'so sunk in dirt and degradation that his point is vitiated almost before he has begun'. And the use to which Orton put the person of Kath was 'an object lesson in how to demean a play', bringing, perhaps, 'a smirk to the lips of a theatre-goer of debased tastes'. But what most enraged Taubman was his belief that he had detected a covert homosexual agenda in the play. The scenes involving Kath's pursuit of Sloane 'might secretly delight those epicenes who look upon the public humiliation of women as grand sport', he wrote, 'But it is repugnant to anyone who believes that even a foil in black comedy deserves to be something juster than nasty, vulgar patronising.'[27]

Taubman's suggestion that some homosexuals enjoy the sight of sexually eager women subjected to humiliation is curious, since it ignores the notorious and misogynistic heterosexual impulse that Leslie Fiedler diagnosed in more than a century of American fiction. In real life, also, it is heterosexual males, not homosexual men who pre-eminently murder, assault and brutalise women. But Orton, who used to refer disparagingly to Tennessee Williams's heroines as 'drag queens',[28] did create, after Williams, a line of frankly libidinous and slightly grotesque females. In *Entertaining Mr Sloane* Kath does suffer for her desire in a way that Ed does not. Shepherd, while accepting that Orton was a misogynist, argues that such attitudes are derivative of the controlling heterosexual male majority. But he blames Orton, and homosexuals generally, of dislike of female 'power' and suggests that Orton disliked 'camp' because it ran in opposition to his own cult of 'homosexual masculinity'.[29] Shepherd's unexplained definition of 'camp' seems to be caricatured femininity. Homosexuals, in this reading and in Orton's, are identified as a variant upon the heterosexual male supremacist. Such a reading does not diminish the fact of Orton's misogyny as it is manifest in *Entertaining Mr Sloane*, even as it explains it. Yet Taubman's assertion that homosexuals relish the public spectacle of female humiliation seems a curious inference to be taken from the play. First, Orton is far from typical among homosexual playwrights in derogating women, though there are undercurrents of heterophobia in homosexual literature of the period. Kath's physical unattractiveness is a symptom of such a phobia, but she is generally depicted in terms more sympathetic and favourable than those allowed to Ed or Sloane. She may be ugly and childlike; but she is neither vicious nor cruel.

Taubman's own concealed agenda was far more morally disreputable than Orton's. Writing in the tradition of homophobia that had marked a line of American theatrical reviewers from George Jean Nathan to Brooks Atkinson, Taubman was the first of a 1960s generation of reviewers to claim that homosexual dramatists were contaminating the theatre by demeaning heterosexual relations and derogating the female. In 1963, to help audiences discover the homosexual dramatists' conspiracy, Taubman had written a preposterous article for the *Sunday New York Times* suggesting that plays where conflicts between the sexes existed might be a sign of a dramatist's homosexuality.[30] But if such signs were taken as indication of homosexuality few major dramatists would have emerged as heterosexual. Chekhov and Ibsen would certainly have been deprived of their sexual identity.

Orton's homosexual sensibility was the motor of his activity as a dramatist; it inspired his theatrical acts of social and sexual subversion. It also robbed homosexuality of its melodramatising force upon the stage. Yet Lahr and other critics have attempted to argue, as we have seen, that his sexuality was also his undoing. The homophobic Lahr, writing in 1978, interpreted homosexuality in general as a pseudo-psychiatric dilemma. 'Geraldine's predicament', he wrote in his assessment of *What the Butler Saw* 'displaces in laughter the schizoid bind of the homosexual from which Orton tried to extricate himself.' Even in the 1960s, however, homosexuals were not necessarily schizoid at all.[31] Orton was battered to death. It was not a crime committed by a lover enraged that Orton kept visiting lavatories for sexual relief; it was murder while the balance of Halliwell's mind was disturbed.

At the time Halliwell was going out of his mind during that last summer of their lives, Orton was realising their relationship ought to end. He wanted it to. He even asked the writer Penelope Gilliatt to effect the divorce. But Orton – and here an essential decency shines through – was anxious about the break. He intuited that Halliwell would not survive the rupture. His lover was involved in a symbiotic relationship with him; without Orton, Halliwell would be left with no one to sustain him. Part of Orton cherished Halliwell for all that Halliwell had helped him become. So he was trapped, wanting freedom; perhaps being on the verge of taking the great step. In the meantime he stayed, and resented. He knew Halliwell read his diaries – indeed, Halliwell in his suicide note explained that the diaries provided the explanation for murder. These diaries can only have incited the poor fellow's jealousies and resentments. Orton was both punishing Halliwell by living a free sexual life and at the same time suffering the man's dependence, despair and depressions. 'It was me that got Joe to write', he told the actress Sheila Ballantine, who was appearing in *Loot*,[32] days before he murdered Orton. It was a domestic tragedy, one of the kind that sometimes befalls heterosexual marriages too. The end does not detract from the worth of the plays nor limit their power. Orton's flight from the orthodoxies and towards liberation, his subversive conception of the lusts and hypocrisies powering family life, caused him to create a theatre of provocation and dissent. Homosexuality becomes a weapon of outrage in a new kind of war in his plays.

SCANDAL AND CONCERN

It is John Osborne who most trenchantly characterises the prevailing sexual attitudes of the time. John Osborne's *A Patriot for Me* was the English theatre's great homosexual *cause célèbre* of the 1960s and one of those plays that assisted the Royal

Court in their guerrilla war to rid the professional theatre of censorship by the Lord Chamberlain. The Lord Chamberlain's correspondence, and papers relating to the administration of the censorship from 1901 to 1968, have only just been placed in the public domain. And the thick file on *A Patriot for Me* confirms what has long been believed.[33] The Lord Chamberlain was remarkably eager to see the Royal Court prosecuted for circumventing his veto upon the play by subterfuge and by presenting it for 'club' members when no real club appeared to exist.[34] But the government's law officers refused to allow the Director of Public Prosecutions (DPP) to proceed with a case against the theatre, because the play had 'attracted a great deal of public interest and a good deal of public support and has been running for some time'.[35]

In other words, the critics' response to the play and that of the public was so positive that a prosecution could not be allowed. The papers also reveal that the Lord Chamberlain's staff were opposed to the production and the play because they believed it constituted an incitement to homosexuality. An assistant secretary in the Lord Chamberlain's office, R. Hill, based his justification for the ban upon assertions contained in the British Medical Association Report on Homosexuality published in 1955, which had warned that you could 'acquire' homosexuality through 'seduction' or because of 'aspirations': 'Some people adopt homosexual practices because they think such activity denotes superiority of mind.' But Hill's chief fear was that the play's transvestite ball, 'by presenting homosexuals in their most attractive guise, dressed as pretty women, will to some degree cause the congregation of homosexuals and provide the means whereby the vice may be acquired'.[36] This pathetic, deluded notion that a collection of drag queens would turn the men of England gay at a stroke would be laughable had it not been taken seriously. It was a view that held the frightened old military fogeys of the Chamberlain's office in a vice-like grip, as if homosexuality had some special potency, rather than outlaw status.

The play itself conformed to that decade's authoritative view of homosexuals, as the theatre expressed it. Osborne's homosexual anti-hero is viewed ambivalently with contempt and pity. His desires are overwhelming impulses that ruin his life and bring him little but pain and regret. In a debate in the House of Lords, the historian and Provost of University College, London, Lord Annan, suitably commented three years later, 'I cannot conceive of any play less sentimental towards homosexuality, more cold-eyed and ruthless in its exposure of the horror of life of a particular kind of homosexuality and less likely to induce anyone to get into this practice.'[37] Osborne shared the same contempt for homosexuals that the Lord Chamberlain's office displayed; but office and author were old adversaries and could not see how close they were.

Osborne had fought with the tooth and the nail of his invective prose against the censor, ever since *Look Back in Anger* had been sent back to the Royal Court in 1956 with a long list of unacceptable passages and words. By 1966, out of ten Osborne plays staged in London 'only one was licensed without any requests for cuts and changes.' The Lord Chamberlain's office had collected a virtual dictionary of profane words to which the rebellious Osborne had resorted, from 'camp' and 'pouff' to 'crumpet', 'queer' and 'fairy'.[38] In Osborne's musical, *The World of Paul Slickey*, a 'queer' Income Tax Inspector had been banished and the 'Honourable Penelope Cumming, always worth a few inches', had been similarly treated. Osborne had also had a foretaste of the Lord Chamberlain's attitude to dramatists who presumed to write about homosexuality when his 1955 play, *Personal Enemy*, written with Anthony Creighton, was being produced at the Opera House, Harrogate. Its inspiration, like that of *A Patriot for Me*, was political, and in the words of the play's producer, Patrick Desmond, 'dealt with a McCarthy-type witch hunt in Canada and the two young men accused of being "commies" (i.e. liberals) were also smeared with the homosexual brush'.[39]

Four days before opening night Desmond and Osborne were summoned to St James's Palace. They were informed by 'a gentleman whom I understood to be the Lord Chamberlain's head reader' that the Lord Chamberlain 'would not tolerate perversion'. After the excisions demanded by the Lord Chamberlain *Personal Enemy* emerged as a 'largely unintelligible play', which was no doubt just what was wanted.[40] Although Osborne did not write about homosexuality in direct terms again until *A Patriot for Me* was produced, it had remained a ghostly presence shuffling between the lines. And the drama critic of *The Times*, Irving Wardle, aptly noted in his review of *A Patriot for Me* that a 'preoccupation' with homosexuality had 'haunted' Osborne's work since the days of *Look Back in Anger*.[41]

The playwright's ambivalent and sometimes irrational attitude to homosexuals had been expressed in a remarkable polemic he contributed to the *Daily Express* in 1959. Osborne was responding to an article in which a journalist named John Deane Potter had launched an attack on the 'unpleasant free-masonry' in London's theatre.[42] Potter believed the West End was firmly in the grip of homosexuals, who favoured homosexual actors when casting. Such 'evil men', he urged, should be 'driven from their positions of theatrical power'. Potter's attack was a veiled assault upon the probity of Binkie Beaumont, the most powerful London producer of the mid-1950s.

Osborne's response is significant for what it reveals about his own attitudes to homosexuality and the kind of homosexuals he loathed. 'A man or woman's sexual preferences are his own concern until he tries to force or impose them on others,' he wrote. A world without homosexuals 'would have been a poorer place, and art, philosophy and literature would have suffered most of all'.[43] Osborne similarly recoiled from the 'detestable' idea of driving homosexuals from the theatre. Yet, Osborne revealed, ever since he had started to work in the industry he had attempted 'to attack the dominance of homosexuals in all its fields'. His animus was directed against a 'homosexual art' which was, or had become, 'over-traditional, conservative, narrow, parochial, self-congratulatory, narcissistic'. It had infested the West End theatre, he said, slyly alluding to what were the Binkie Beaumont hall-marks, with 'unreal, chintzy plays, gorgeous decor and a glamorous selection of theatrical lords and ladies glittering over all'. It was 'bad'. It was 'boring'. It was 'unadventurous'. What could be done? Osborne seemed uncertain. If heterosexual art existed, and he did not know that it did, let it be produced. But, he asked, who had encouraged and demanded 'this Queers' theatre'? Who but the public, 'slavishly encouraged by the critics'? He imputed to homosexuals in theatre both a function and power that they lacked. And, in depicting Colonel Redl's downfall, *A Patriot for Me* was placing trumped-up homosexuals in their place as lowly, pathetic men. The unhappy Redl, reeking of self-hatred, cursed with a love-life that always went wrong and by nagging sexual desire, was for Osborne, the epitome of the homosexual.

The process that led the Royal Court to turn itself into a club theatre to present Osborne's play, after it had become clear that the Lord Chamberlain wanted to destroy the heart of its matter, was protracted and arduous. Lieutenant Colonel John Johnston, the Lord Chamberlain's Assistant Comptroller, whom the play's director, Anthony Page, recalls as 'desiccated and very poker faced, with no humour or flexibility',[44] told the Royal Court that the play could not be licensed since it intended to 'exploit homosexuality in a manner that may tend to have corrupting influences'.[45] The Lord Chamberlain, 'cannot', wrote Johnston without a hint of a smile between the lines,

> allow such scenes as a homosexual ball at which some of the men are dressed as women (including one who portrays Lady Godiva dressed in a gold lamé jockstrap) and others in which men embrace each other and are seen in bed together.

'It was a terribly funny letter,' Page recalls.

> We went to see Johnston and told him the play was a serious exploration of character. We got a few things allowed, but we were up against an impasse. We had gone through the bureaucracy of the time. The play could not be done except in club conditions. But there were no cold feet.

It was almost a year, however, before the Royal Court took the decision to mount the club production. The play went into production with high hopes and with great difficulties in casting the leading role. Osborne was in his prime as a writer. Laurence Olivier had taken the lead in *The Entertainer* and Nicol Williamson in *Inadmissible Evidence*. Albert Finney had been his Luther. The Court, relishing the controversy engendered by *A Patriot for Me* wanted, therefore, a major actor to play Redl. Here, after all, was the first major homosexual character to be created for the English stage by a leading dramatist in the twentieth century. Surely actors, star actors, would queue for the chance of playing the part. It was not so.

'No one wanted to play the part,' Page recalls.

We just drew blanks. I remember going to talk to Brando.
He read it. He didn't object to the play or the theme. But
he didn't do it. We tried O'Toole ... We just couldn't
get an English actor of the right sort. They were probably
frightened for their career. Then Christopher Plummer
showed an interest. But his wife said that there should
be scenes showing that Redl was very good with women.
If that was done then he would be much more willing
to take the part. John [Osborne] had quite a good laugh
over that.

The reluctance of major actors was attributable to shrewd and
simple calculation. To be seen playing the role of a homosexual
would be liable to lead to the whispers of sexual insinuation.
Famous actors who were homosexual had to conceal the fact. A
career or a reputation could be lost, actors must have felt, if they
took on the part. The English theatre, whose liberal credo was
qualified by a certain conservatism and canny diplomacy, did
not then look favourably on sexual daring. The witch-hunt years
had scarcely passed. In the circumstances it is not surprising
that a heterosexual actor, and a foreign one, finally agreed to
play Redl. Maximillian Schell, a dour, introverted, Viennese
actor, agreed to take the part of Redl. 'But having got into it
Max had certain inhibitions,' Page remembers. 'He would not
go to bed naked. He wore long johns. And this theory that Redl
was heterosexual, that his unfortunate affair with a woman had
made him gay, kept coming up from him.'

Helen Montagu, now a theatre producer, was hired as
casting director by Page. An Australian girl, who had studied
at the Central School of Speech and Drama with Vanessa
Redgrave and Judi Dench, she came to the play brimming
with enthusiasm. 'When I got to the scene with the two men
in bed I thought I'd never read anything more daring in my
life. I'd been brought up on censorship.' She was entrusted
with the business of casting the other roles. It was not only
Redl who was difficult to cast. So too was the pivotal role
of the drag-queen Baroness who gives the scandalising drag
party of the second act. Michael MacLiammoir was among
a grand list of thirty actors (including Gielgud and Coward)
who would not take the opportunity, despite Page's advocacy

of this role's significance. George Devine, the English Stage
Company's heterosexual artistic director, who was also an
interesting occasional actor, was happy to do what the homosexual MacLiammoir would not. 'I didn't realise how good he
would be,' Page says. 'George loved getting dressed up. He'd
come through dressed in his costume with his cigar,' Helen
Montagu remembers, 'and he'd go into the ladies loo. He liked
going through in front of all the students wearing his gown.'
The smaller roles, even the homosexual ones, were far easier
to cast. Younger actors, desperate for work and opportunity,
were not so particular, though Devine's biographer, Irving
Wardle, insists that most young performers were scared of
playing 'bum-boys'.[46]

Devine himself called a press conference to announce the
Royal Court's decision to perform the play in club conditions.
He begged reporters not to make the Lord Chamberlain's deci-
sion to ban the play for public performance seem ridiculous.

> I just want it to be seen. Anything you lot do to make the
> Lord Chamberlain look absurd will be detrimental to us.
> If he is challenged by this action it could be very, very
> harmful to the job of getting this important play on.[47]

On this occasion the reporters duly obliged.

The first night was fraught with an unusual sense of anticipation and anxiety. 'All the actors were very nervous,' Helen
Montagu recalls. 'They were stepping into the unknown. And
everyone was worried about how the ball-scene would go.
Men dressing up as women and singing and dancing wasn't
exactly usual in the London theatre.' But the first-night audience
responded with an outburst of applause. The commercial omens
were also promising. By the beginning of June, just four weeks
before the opening, membership of The English Stage Company,
which was required to attend a performance of *A Patriot for Me*,
had leapt from 1,600 to almost 4,000. 'Thanks to the censor,'
Wardle commented later, 'there was no need for salesmanship.
The scent of a possible clash with the authorities had aroused
the English blood-sport instinct.'[48]

The morning after the first night, the Royal Court realised
the gamble was set to pay off: the reviews, although not
uniformly admiring, were uniformly respectable. In *The Times*
Wardle, while noting that the play depended upon the standard

Osborne theme – 'the relationship between the community and the outsiders' – found in it a fresh concern with the 'reluctant rebel', rather than the happy one.[49] And the homosexual scenes were despatched 'with a passion that by-passes all the defensive mockery with which we habitually try to insulate the homosexual from society'. Harold Hobson, writing in the *Sunday Times*, went further. 'If I did not know it to be untrue I should think that the Lord Chamberlain was mad,'[50] he said, referring to the reported decision to ban the play from public performance.

A Patriot for Me's close scrutiny of an intelligence officer in the Austro-Hungarian army before the First World War, is a pseudo-psychological account of the homosexual outsider impelled to betray his country in an effort to save his reputation. The play functions as a critique of the homosexual in a heterosexual world, and to sabotage the idea that homosexual love endures. Osborne is imbued with all the negative myths about homosexuals, imbued with the tales he must have been told in childhood of homosexual treachery, narcissism, bitchiness and cruelty, of the homosexual's inability to make lasting commitment to anything much, of his habitual stresses and strains. Once Redl gives himself up to homosexual life everything goes virtually from bed to bedlam. Young male lovers who flaunt their expensive tastes and constant demands inspire him to operatic disgust. One of them goes out of his mind. The transvestite ball, which Redl reluctantly attends, is a grand parade of men who strip themselves emotionally bare to reveal the guilt and rejections that homosexuality has entailed, burdens they endure with nonchalant flippancy.

A Patriot for Me, is however, somewhat more complex than this analysis suggests. Osborne also views homosexuality and his homosexual characters in socio-cultural rather than exclusively in personal terms. Private lives are not completely extrapolated from the political circumstances in which they are conducted and by which they are affected and influenced. The play spans a late phase of the Austro-Hungarian Empire, from 1890 until a year before the First World War. That Empire, class-conscious, complacent, snobbish and anti-semitic is, as filtered through Osborne's mind, a metaphor for the Britain of the early 1960s. Redl himself who is a triple outsider, lower-class, Jewish and homosexual, takes only a reluctant stand against conformity. He does not battle against orthodoxy. He wants to be its vehicle, and Osborne subtly gives him a personality that helps him in this respect. He seems the model of conventional masculinity, and both Schell, and Alan Bates in a revival at Chichester Festival Theatre played him so. With his male lovers, when all defences are down, he expresses himself in shows of masculine assertiveness and power.

Yet this does not detract from the extremity of the personal sexual battle he has to wage. Osborne conceives him as a man struggling to achieve a faithful constant lover, in a homosexual milieu where constancy does not exist and sexual treachery prevails. The viciousness of this homosexual *demi-monde*, the voraciousness of Redl's sexual desire and the constant ruin of his emotional life are made to seem inherent aspects of homosexual existence, rather than behaviour that society and an institution outlawing homosexuals have helped to form. Osborne is thus suggesting that homosexuals are habitually reckless in their pursuit of sexual pleasure, which they put before all loyalties, and prepared to surrender to blackmail rather than to risk exposure. At the same time, he implies that a law that gives power to the blackmailer, whether it be an individual or an enemy state, is not an admirable one. Even the *New Statesman*'s critic, noting that Redl 'betrays his country for himself', did not impugn Osborne's characterisation of homosexuals as inherently unreliable.[51]

Mary McCarthy, the one critic who mounted an efficient attack upon the play's central argument at the time of its première, expressed her reservations trenchantly. 'It cannot be that he [Osborne] intended to show that a homosexual, in or without a duelling helmet, is always a security risk. The play at the very least must have aimed to be fair to homosexuals.'[52] But why, it has to be asked, should anyone assume that Osborne, of all people, should renounce the habit of a decade, and opt for fairness and dispassion? And homosexuality, it was, and still is, believed, makes of man a security risk, even if the man in question is known to be a homosexual. McCarthy almost concedes the fact that Osborne does not aspire to fairness. 'Incidental scenes reveal that homosexuality can lead not only to espionage but to madness and general loss of moral tone. You get to hate yourself.'

Even if it is conceded that Osborne's characterisation of

homosexuality seems largely simplistic and sensational, the author's treatment of Redl's crucial decision not to yield to blackmail is curious in its perfunctory nature. Whether by omission or intention he suggests that Redl agrees to spy for Russia and betray his own country without hesitation, conflict or struggle. Oblensky, the blackmailer, puts the possibilities for Redl starkly, and it is in the shadow of these polarised alternatives that the play is subsequently conducted. 'What can you do? Change your way of life? It's getting desperate already, isn't it?' Oblensky says.

> You don't know which way to turn, you're up to your eyeballs in debts. What would you do? Get thrown out? Exposed for everything you are, or what the world would say you are . . . What would you do at your age, go back to base as a waiter or a washer-up, sit all alone in cafes?
>
> (2.iii.80)

The words strike home. Osborne's Redl is the model of the promiscuous homosexual. He beds eight young men in six weeks, after he has lost his own male lover to the countess who once hankered for him. His vulnerability to blackmail is increased, therefore, by an emotional isolation and desperation that are made to seem typical of homosexual life in the Empire. But the conclusion to which Redl comes seems less persuasive than the journey taking him there.

Osborne sends Redl out on a slow voyage of sexual discovery in terms mirroring a process experienced by some young homosexuals of Osborne's time. Redl's façade is exemplarily composed. Stiff, correct and withdrawn, he seems a perfect military gentleman. But from the very first scene there are undertones of unease, of something unspoken. At the close of the first scene Redl 'cradles in his arms' the bloodied body of a handsome young officer, killed in a duel and for whom he has acted as second (1.i.20). The relationship is correct and conventional, but it is also replete with homoerotic undertones.

Seventeen scenes later Redl takes a young Lieutenant, whom he loves, in his arms. The transition is complete. Redl has moved in the time and years between from seeming heterosexual to being homosexual. The play describes the nature of that journey, and depends at first upon a series of signs to suggest the interior drama in which Redl is engaged. Siczynski, the handsome young Lieutenant who is killed in the first scene, is Redl's mirror image. Like Redl he is a Jewish outsider. Unlike Redl he is accused of being homosexual.

Redl's dream, which he describes immediately before the duel, is emblematic of this sexual struggle. What is repressed in him, exists, transmuted, in the form of the dream, with its vision of a court martial, and Redl arrested for speaking through 'wire-netting' to a friend who he knows will be found guilty (1.i.19). The crime is, of course, a homosexual one, and Redl's contact through 'wire-netting' suggests his involuntary and guilty attraction to what is forbidden. In the course of the first act, the dream becomes reality. But Redl continues to play a heterosexual role while longing for a homosexual one. That function is typical of both the nineteenth and twentieth century. It depends upon the denial of identity.

Running in counterpoint to these scenes of sexual dissimulation are those that show the Russian secret service beginning surveillance of Redl's life, to see if he may manifest any weakness that renders him suitable for blackmail. Osborne arranges the ten scenes in groups of two, the second antiphonically showing up the deceits of the first. Redl fulfils his role as a heterosexual soldier, and then suffers the sexual strains to which his role-playing subjects him. But what is repressed will not be denied. It insists on expression. 'All this incessant, silly weeping. It only happens, it creeps up on me when I'm asleep,' Redl tells the Countess (1.vii.47).

Redl's first experience of homosexual passion is an extreme version of the shocks, the disillusion and the dissatisfaction he will suffer through the course of his sexual career. The young private he has bedded pockets Redl's valuables and the gold crucifix which proclaims the religion he had adopted, while four other soldiers beat him up. 'Don't be too upset, love, you'll get used to it' remarks the private (1.x.58). It is a very 1950s scene: to give way to homosexual desire invites violence and humiliation. And the scene as played in Anthony Page's production was very casual, very vicious and very shocking.

The play's drag ball in wintry Vienna of 1902 offered a complementary sense of outrage. 'Osborne's ball scene', Ronald Bryden wrote in his review, is the play's 'centre, its validation, the image from which all else takes perspective and completeness. It is funny, compassionate, grotesque, humane and defiant.'[53] Yes. But this crucial scene does more than inspire compassionate, affectionate responses. The ball allows a night of pleasure when homosexuals in Vienna can abandon lives of subterfuge. Their habitual role-play gives way to another form of acting. They caricature and mock femininity and female behaviour. George Devine's performance as the Baron who gives the party was a case in point. Attired in 'pompadour feathers, a pearl and diamond choker and a beautiful fan', as specified by Osborne, and 'elbow-length gloves and an upswept red-gold wig set off by a sparkling coronet', Devine had reincarnated Queen Alexandra in a show of hyper-camp. Homosexuals taunted for being mock women become the mockery of what women are. 'This', says the Baron who gives the party, 'is the celebration of the individual against the rest' (2.i.64).

But these images of supposed homosexual liberation, the jubilations in dark times, are no such thing. Osborne particularises the guests at the drag-ball in terms that betray his own seething revulsion and disgust. The male prostitutes are 'paid bum-boys'. There are 'rich discreet queens', 'grotesques', and 'whores' (2.i.6). Redl, significantly, is almost alone in refusing to step out in drag. Instead, he wears the emblems of heterosexuality and conformity. His masculine companion, Lieutenant Kovacs, 'is fixed in a mixture of embarrassment and amusement', as if to indicate that he too is discomfited by the versions of homosexuality that dance before them. But once he becomes drunk Redl abandons his lover and is caught 'giggling helplessly' with the Baron's effete boyfriend, Ferdy. 'He's just being himself for once,' the Baron notices (2.i.69). In other words, Redl also has an undignified sexual self which is concealed until drink dispels inhibitions. But at last Redl lashes out at Ferdy, and with this violent gesture brings the evening of homosexual abandon to a shuddering halt. For Ferdy is that image of homosexuality by which Redl is both attracted and repelled.

The homosexual, as Osborne depicts him, is not just flippant, shallow and sexually obsessed. The party-goers despise the conventional forms of Empire, marriage, family life and religious faith. They lack loyalty to anything except their own desires. These men incarnate Redl's worst fear that he too may become like them. And Osborne, as if to confirm that Redl

116

has succumbed, or will, provides an epilogue to the ball, in the form of a lecture on homosexuality by a Viennese Freudian Dr Schoepper, who turns out to be homosexual himself. This epilogue confirms what the drag scene suggests. The party-goers, with their pleasure-prone joviality, far from being refugees in a hostile world, are simply people 'enjoying the physical sensations of the body without any reference to the responsibilities involved in the relationship' (2.ii.77). This verdict is prefaced to the scene of Redl's entrapment by the Russians, and his almost instantaneous decision to yield to blackmail. He has shed his responsibilities and abandoned his loyalty to his country, just as the party-goers betrayed them in jest. The process is complete. But before Redl is exposed and successfully urged to commit suicide, Osborne dramatises what Dr Schoepper has asserted. It is a paradigm of the 1950s myths about homosexual life. Redl becomes the stereotypical ageing homosexual, the lines of self-hatred fiercely drawn. He rains down the blows of Osbornian invective upon his lover, but is really expressing his fear of becoming the pathetic, absurd, old homosexual of 1950s demonology.

> You little painted toy, you puppet, you poor duffer, you'll be, with your disease and paunch and silliness, and curlers and dyed whispy hair, and long legs and varicose veins, like bunches of grapes, and prostate and thick waist, and rolling thighs and big bottom, that's where we all go . . . and you can't mistake it. Everyone'll see it.
>
> (3.v.98)

The tether, at the end of which Redl is now stranded, is made to seem the natural last halting place of the homosexual. The equation by which homosexuality and blackmail have led to treachery is complete. The pity that Osborne seeks to arouse by the soldier's decline is qualified by the sense that you must expect homosexuals to betray their country.

A Patriot for Me is best interpreted as a post-Wolfenden morality play imbued with the views of a puritan 1950s liberal. Homosexuals in A Patriot for Me are thus comic-pathetic Peter Pans, forever in flight to a never-never land of their own making. They are at once sad and preposterous, comic and dangerous. There is no consistent strong sense that his homosexual characters are socially conditioned – merely a delicate balance between a great contempt and a mediating sense of pity. Osborne, albeit attracted by the allure of overweening rebels, would not give his Redl the elements of courage and positive consciousness that he had imparted to his other fighters against convention.

Colonel Johnston, later Sir John, claims that after the play went in to production the Lord Chamberlain, Lord Cobbold, continued to keep something that all the evidence suggests he never possessed – 'an open mind'.[54] So when the Royal Court told Sir John of its decision to present the play as a 'club' production for members of the English Stage Company, the Assistant Comptroller retaliated by informing the DPP of what was about to occur.

The tone of Sir John's letter to the DPP, written on Cobbold's instructions, was calculated to persuade the DPP to prosecute:

> The Lord Chamberlain would also wish to emphasise that he has no desire to interfere with the operations of genuine theatre clubs. He is solely concerned to avoid a position where the law can be brought into disrepute by what is no more than a subterfuge.

But Lord Cobbold, who two years later nearly banned the Royal Shakespeare Company's production of Peter Brook's *US* on the grounds that it was 'beastly, anti-American and left wing',[55] found that he lacked support from the Labour government and its law officers. Lord Cobbold had lost the battle, but he ensured that the play was not produced for public performance.

The Royal Court needed to transfer the play to the West End to recoup some of the large costs. And Anthony Page went to see Sir John in August 1965 to ask that Cobbold reconsider his decision not to allow the play a licence, arguing that the play's homosexual aspect had caused no outrage. But Sir John stalled. He sent Page a letter saying simply 'There are aspects of this play other than those raised in your letter, and these, as well as the evident merits of the piece, will have to weigh with the Lord Chamberlain when making his decision.'[56]

Cobbold refused to revoke his veto. Significant pleaders put their case. He ignored them all. Lord Goodman, then Chairman of the Arts Council, asked Cobbold to reconsider. Cobbold would not. Lord Harewood was similarly repulsed. So too was Laurence Olivier, when as Director of the National

Theatre he told Cobbold in 1966 that he wished to revive the play. However, Sir John reveals that Lord Cobbold asked the actress Irene Worth for her view of the play, though he does not explain why.[57] Sir John quotes her as saying in a letter dated 8 August 1985 'I really didn't think it needed to be limited to a subscription audience. It seemed to me to be written with seriousness, dignity, humanity and to be impartial.' Only the first noun is accurate; of humanity there is a scant sign.

PITY FOR PERVERTS

Beyond the worlds of homosexuality conveyed by Osborne and Orton, and before *The Boys in the Band* broke the mould, there were predictable vistas of homosexuals suffering not quite manfully, and inspiring a limited, superior form of pity from disapproving audiences. Strangely it was the commercial West End stage, and not the Royal Court theatre, that took advantage of the Lord Chamberlain's modest relaxation of the total ban on plays about homosexuality. Joan Henry had already written a screenplay *Yield for the Night*, in which Diana Dors had been elevated from sex symbol to play a thinly disguised version of Ruth Ellis, the last woman to be hanged for murder in Britain. Henry's script left no doubt that her sympathies were ranged with the wretched Ellis and not the Home Secretary who doomed her to the gallows. *Look on Tempests* was fired by a similar, socially motivated concern, and its attention was again focused upon an acutely suffering young woman. Presented at the Comedy theatre, where the New Watergate club had produced its members-only season of banned homosexual plays in the 1950s, *Look on Tempests* cast a highly popular veteran, the former chorus girl, Hollywood supporting player and West End star, Gladys Cooper, opposite the young, untested Vanessa Redgrave, in her first major role. The play deserved to win a coterie following at least. It did not. In the springtime of 1960 it ran just a few weeks. We need to see why.

Look on Tempests faces up to a young woman's discovery of her husband's love-affair with a young Italian, of his appearance at the Old Bailey, and of a mother's refusal to accept the facts of her son's sexual identity. But the play's revelation of upper-middle-class England facing up to the public exposure of homosexuality in the family is secondary to Henry's critique

119

of the 1950s police witch-hunts that brought men to court. The
political and the personal are brought into true relationship.

The homosexual affair has only been discovered by an unfortunate accident, through that familiar theatrical method of
sexual exposure, the secret love-letter – discovered in this
instance believably by customs officers searching the baggage
of the Italian. The play reflects the new attitude to homosexuals,
regarding them as unfortunate victims of desire rather than as
essentially dangerous or evil. Miss Henry, through Rose, the
desolate young wife, dares to suggest that the husband, far
from being condemned like a pariah of the suburbs, should be
accepted, understood and forgiven. 'I believe it was love he's
to be punished for,' Rose tells her mother-in-law, Mrs Vincent,
a woman who would rank homosexuality as one of the seven
deadlier sins, while they wait for news of the verdict at his Old
Bailey trial (3.ii.30).[58]

The problems with which Henry deals are quite complex. The homosexual passion, which disrupts and threatens
a marriage, and may ruin a comfortable and secure middle-
class professional life, is true to the demands and standards
of its time. The husband's homosexual love-affair has been
furtive, entirely secret, unacknowledged; Rose, the wife, in
an awkward retrospect, describes the dilemma of being a
woman who falls in love with a man whom she believes to
be predominantly homosexual, but with whom she cannot
discuss her sexual doubts. The conventions of the time do
not allow it. The play, conforming to the West End theatre
conventions, is staged in the plush heights of Knightsbridge,
with a loyal and ageing servant, in life-long service, attending
to the family's whims and needs. The environment and the
manners are those of the upper-middle-class play on which
the new theatrical movement has turned its back. The effect is
rather disturbing. Here they are, the conservative, complacent,
narrow-minded rulers and administrators of England, the last
children of Empire, the caste on which E.M. Forster had set
his accusatory sights in *Howard's End*, being forced not only to
suffer Philip's trial, but to question their faith in that morality
and that law which has brought him to the Old Bailey. They –
who lack imagination and empathy, who are accustomed to
have the world in their pockets, who have found that money
buys all they need – are now forced to stretch their minds,

to find capacity for imagination and projection, and to realise that life is neither bought for money nor, in all circumstances, controlled by it. Homosexual desire has done for their security and their esteem. They will never be the same again. They have had their illumination.

Mrs Vincent, Philip's mother, is a British period-piece, a paradigm of her class's essential introversion, its moral rigidity and its lack of imagination. 'What', she asks in the play's first, truth-finding exercise, 'was he [her married son] thinking of, inviting an Italian boy, that he hardly knew, to come to this country?' (1.i.27). A clash between two generations is arranged, and between two opposing moralities. Mrs Vincent is required, by necessity, to accept the existence of emotions, desires and, worst, sexual actions that she has been schooled to find disgusting. 'How can you stand here and talk about beautiful love letters from one man to another?' she asks (1.i.27). 'It is possible', Rose answers, 'for a man to form a passionate attachment for a person – other wives have had to face it' (1.i.27).

Rose hopes for the ability to accept the variable nature of sexual desire in her husband. Mrs Vincent's attempt to induce a 1950s sense of shame in her daughter-in-law fails, because Rose is able to interpret the sexual acts that will end in her husband's imprisonment as symptoms of love not lust. Hers is a different way of seeing, since it concentrates upon the emotion that instigates the sexual activity rather than the activity itself.

Philip, the cause of the anguish, is a Freudian and very 1950s example of homosexual desire, unsuccessfully repressed in conformity's cause and through marriage. He is the son of a dominant mother and of a father who lacked salience, was absent often, died early and showed signs of that supposedly unfailing symptom of homosexual feeling, sensitivity. 'He couldn't stand unpleasantness,' Mrs Vincent recalls, 'Why he even fainted once, when I was having my ears pierced' (1.i.27). Rose uses the same suspicion-inducing adjective – 'sensitive' – to describe Philip. For although he proved 'brave' on RAF service, 'he always felt too sick to eat' when he came back from night-time operations (1.i.27). The clear implication is that a fine, upstanding heterosexual would have enjoyed a three-course air-force dinner.

But even heterosexuals are changing a little. Rose mentions

the disgust that she had noticed on the face of Philip's step-father, Clive, when told of the homosexual charges laid against Philip – 'the revulsion that any normal man feels towards things of this kind,' she says (2.ii.27). Those old theories of sexuality and desire were being challenged, and in *Look on Tempests* even Clive gladly acknowledges and accepts the fact: 'There's never been any tape-measure to assess what is normal and what is not,' he responds. 'Our standards are based on the many – not the few. If I ever appeared revolted, it's because I don't pretend to understand some things' (2.ii.27). It is a useful development.

By the end of the of play Mrs Vincent has made an important concession, as if she has come to recognise the inadequacy of her religious and moral codes as a means of dealing with the complexities of sexual desire. 'Could it be', she asks, kneeling down to comfort the stricken daughter-in-law, whom she has neither admired nor liked, 'that "circumstances", that "life" which you were so afraid of, have handed me a pair of spectacles which until now I've always been too vain to use?' (3.i.30). The point is made in terms calculated to be understood by the very best upper-middle-class audiences who would have sympathised with Mrs Vincent's original condemnation of homosexuals.

Look on Tempests, therefore, offers a fresh perspective upon the laws forbidding homosexuality, by depicting the wretched consequences of homosexual passion, without directly presenting the values, views and feelings of the man condemned by these laws in the witch-hunting 1950s. The play was undervalued, misunderstood and dismissed in 1960, for it asked traditional West End audiences to consider that homosexuality existed in its families and its marriages, and that this fact of life should be accepted rather than resisted. Most successful plays about homosexuality in the 1960s traded in discretion rather than liberation, and oppression rather than revolt. Noël Coward's *A Song at Twilight* and Charles Dyer's *Staircase* show the way.

COWARD'S WAY OUT

There is a certain appropriateness in the fact that Noël Coward, who had successfully concealed his homosexuality from the

curious public eye for four decades, should have been the last
playwright to write a play that endorsed the old orthodoxy about
homosexuality. His play may take advantage of the relative new
freedoms of the 1960s, before the Lord Chamberlain lost his
control of the theatre, but the view Coward has of homosexual
desire is distinctly *déjà vu*. He asks for pity and understanding
for the famous and gay likes of him, people who have put
conventionality and fame before authenticity. His last play,
A Song at Twilight (Plate 4), presented by the ageing Binkie
Beaumont, with Irene Worth and Lilli Palmer, was one of the
West End's last old-fashioned displays of star-power: even the
seat-prices at the Queen's Theatre were increased. And no
one could doubt that the lure was the chance, for play-goers
of a reactionary frame of mind, to see the master's theatrical
swan-song.

The irony of this is that when Coward was still young, and not
writing directly about homosexual relations, his best plays were
vividly informed by a homosexual sensibility. The diction of his
pre-war characters, the techniques and strategies of disguise,
and an apparent empathy with outsiders from the conventional
family unit were the signs of this sensibility. Coward-speak,
that terse, artificial lingo where sentences were clipped to
near-baldness, was a form of period camp; and this jargon,
with its sophisticated use of innuendo and suppression of
feeling, conveyed more than it expressed. *The Vortex, Design
for Living* and pre-eminently *Point Valaine* – rescued from
fifty years' undeserved oblivion in a revelatory production at
Chichester Festival's studio theatre in 1991 – are all dressed in a
series of suave disguises and codes. None of them engages with
specific homosexual matters, but all contend with outcasting
and the sense of being outcast.

Point Valaine, dismissed when presented on Broadway with
Alfred Lunt and Lynne Fontanne in 1934, was condemned for
its concern with 'ugly lust' of the heterosexual sort. But there
turns out to have been more than met the Broadway eyes of 1934
or those of Liverpool, when the play was presented there by an
evacuated Old Vic company in 1944, with one of Ivor Novello's
favourite leading ladies, Mary Ellis, taking on Fontanne's role.

Coward's account in *Point Valaine* of the impact of that
typical 1930s hero-figure, the daring young aviator, upon a
middle-aged widow and a Maugham-like novelist, is powered

by a particular realisation of the woman's predicament: it is the predicament of an English woman living far from England, guiltily defying British social and sexual conventions as they then applied to females of her age and class. Not only has she dared to rank sex before love, and pleasure before respectability, she has presumed to conduct an affair for several years with the Russian head waiter at her West Indian island hotel. In abandoning the Russian for the aviator, another much younger and equally unsuitable object of desire, she merely varies the form of her sexual-emotional life. Her dilemma and her behaviour has something in common with the experience of some homosexuals who also leap the barriers of class and status in their sexual relations, who also ignore the obstacles that may attend a relationship where one partner is almost twice the age of the other. A series of coded parallels are thus established between the social unacceptability, in the 1930s, of some heterosexual relations and all homosexual ones. A similar form of coding is employed in *The Vortex*, where young Nicky Lancaster's cocaine addiction serves as a metaphor for homosexuality and in *Design for Living*, where the *ménage à trois* is deprived of some of its negative aspects and portrayed as a conceivable alternative to the family conventions. Coward preferred thematic ambivalence to head-on argument. Disguise is his form.

However, by the time he came to write *A Song at Twilight* Coward's younger sensibility had ossified. 'Homosexuality is becoming as normal as blueberry-pie,'[59] Coward had written in his diaries in 1960, hyperbolically alluding to the veiled discussion of a subject he had never publicly discussed. *A Song at Twilight* may have been inspired by the blueberry-pie tendency, but it is an evasive, pessimistic piece of writing in which Coward discards the coding and ambiguity of a lifetime in his choice of subject matter. The emotions, long-denied and ignored, at least as far as their public presentation was concerned, could no longer be tapped. This late, last play does not regard homosexual desire with Osborne's contempt or Dyer's derision. In *A Song at Twilight* Sir Hugo Latymer sacrifices a homosexual relationship for a sexless marriage and literary success. But he emerges as very similar to that figure of late Victorian drama, The Woman with a Past.

The play's crisis is precipitated when Carlotta looms out of

Latymer's past to remind him of the two-year affair they had conducted long ago, when he was supposed to be tasting the joys of heterosexuality. Carlotta brings news of the long-forgotten letters of the long-dead Perry Sheldon, the man who was 'the only true love of your life' (1.46). But Carlotta is also a purposeless blackmailer, who lacks a clear motive for bringing Latymer out of his closet, and persuading him that he has lived a life-lie.

> He [Perry] loved you, looked after you and waited on you hand and foot. For years he travelled the wide world with you. And yet in your [autobiographical] book you dismiss him in a few lines as 'an adequate secretary'. Having corrupted his character, destroyed his ambition and deprived him of hope, you wrote him off like a bad debt.
>
> (2.63–4)

Coward, made up in the role of Sir Hugo to look like Somerset Maugham, was accusing his *alter ego* of sexual opportunism and sexual ruthlessness, while Carlotta acted as a voice of conscience. Or was Coward accusing the predominantly homosexual Maugham of ruining his lover, Gerald Haxton?[60] At the play's conclusion there has been no indication of how Sir Hugo 'corrupted' his homosexual lover. But Latymer's wife, Hilde, announces that Perry was 'foolish, conceited, dishonest and self-indulgent' (3.84). It is a judgement that Carlotta does not dispute, despite her early impassioned advocacy of the lover. Latymer's treatment of his secretary-lover is never truly explained, and for no dramatically negotiated or argued reason she returns the love-letters to him. Homosexuality is thus in Coward's play the excuse for a dramatic action rather than the justification of it.

What the play does offer is glimpses of a man elegantly concealing his sexual identity. In the very first scene, Latymer alone in his suite with a 'startlingly handsome' young waiter, conducts what is a surreptitious flirtation (1.2). It is replete with compliments and allusions that he would not make in front of his wife – 'You look as though you should be a good swimmer with those shoulders,' he says of the man, who is described in the stage directions in far more detail and appreciation than allowed for Latymer's wife (1.15). Yet when, just after she has arrived, Carlotta comments on the allure of these same shoulders Hugo remarks 'I've never noticed them' (1.37). Here is the old-fashioned homosexual life-lie.

In Latymer's speech, which justifies and explains his wish to preserve the fiction of his heterosexuality, Coward argues the credo of closetry. He envisages a future when homosexuality between consenting males would cease to be an offence against the law (a future, in fact, just one year away). 'Even when the actual law ceases to exist there will be a stigma attached to the "love that dares not speak its name" in the mind of millions of people for generations to come,' Sir Hugo claims. 'It takes more than a few outspoken books and plays and speeches in parliament, to uproot moral prejudice from the Anglo Saxon mind' (2.61–2). But to accept bigotry without attempting to oppose it is merely the soft, easy option. Coward has solved his own problem of identity, the play makes apparent, by creating a camp one. Coward, John Lahr wrote, 'had posed as a romantic comedian and turned his fantasy of heterosexual conquest into a showbiz legend. Instead of being explorations of consciousness the majority of his plays remained exploitations of self-consciousness.'[61] So *A Song at Twilight* assesses the emotional and psychological damage done, damage that Coward seemed not to realize had affected him as well.

Sir Hugo, dressed in 'an emerald green velvet smoking jacket over dark trousers . . . a cream silk shirt and . . . slippers . . . monogrammed in gold' is attired like a vulgar, precious old queen (1.20). But there is no indication that Coward realises what these accoutrements denote. There seems to be a gulf between his perception and ours. Coward himself seemed to be heterosexual but lived as a homosexual. Latymer appeared as heterosexual in public, and tried to live as one. What, then, late in his life, was Coward trying to say and do? Was he merely trying to entertain with a play that reverberated upon, say, Maugham himself or, as has been suggested, Max Beerbohm, who once received a visitor with a mission like Carlotta's? I think not. 'My inner feelings are my own affair,' Hugo tells Carlotta (1.27). It is just what Coward would say, did say, though in different words. Long ago he had revelled in the febrilely concocted rumours of his own decadence. *The Vortex*, with its discreetly coked-out, mother-fixated, anti-hero, who might well be interpreted as gay in the modern sense of the word, inspired frissons of sexual speculation. After the shocked response to the fripperies and feints of *Fallen Angels* (1925), Coward noted jubilantly in an interview, 'The realisation that I am hopelessly depraved, vicious and decadent has for two days ruined my morning break of opium. I find I no longer enjoy my four o'clock cocaine tablets.'[62]

He was happy to assist in the private game of deceiving the public, dreaming up implausible versions of his 'decadence'. By their sheer implausibility the games distracted and diverted from speculation about Coward's sexuality. Later he would pose as the sophisticated heterosexual, never quite finding the ideal woman. He lived off and through façades. In public he was all perfect pose. In an important sense this did not matter. He was success incarnate to the point of resounding fame, fortune and, for a time, fashionability. What connection has Sir Hugo with Sir Noël, if much at all? There are clues. At the close of the play Hilde delivers a pompous, quite unspeakable, epitaph upon her husband. 'The conflict within him, between his natural instincts and the laws of society, has been for most of his life a perpetual problem that he has had to grapple with alone' (3.90). And Sir Hugo is last seen, 'deeply moved', reading one of those love-letters, and he covers his eyes with a hand (3.90). The old pretender rediscovers his true self – a self and identity denied.

Coward shows himself unable to deal with profound personal emotion as expressed through direct utterance on stage. His plays in general – and, it appears, his personality – petrified early on, after an interesting start. Thereafter there was neither true change nor development, merely variants and elaborations. He was not so much forever young as forever frozen-over. Love, that great and often anguishing business, which has rarely occupied the heart or the other vital organs of Sir Hugo, may have concerned Coward mightily in private. But his triumphant success in playing his public role, his life-part, impacted upon his later plays: cool, brittle artificialities characterise the comedies. The plays succeeded, but something crucial was always missing. In *A Song at Twilight* Sir Hugo shows no signs of the problem that beats at the heart of his existence, until the play's close. Latymer could not be, or express, himself. Coward, similarly, shows no sign of a real self in his writing. There he had long lost touch with deep emotional feelings or states of mind. *A Song at Twilight* mourns a loss, without quite knowing what had gone missing or why. It is an important warning. More important, in this context, the play ranks in the terminal stage of that theatrical tradition in which homosexuals were pitiable problem people, and homosexuality a life-curse.

In view of Peter Hall's pioneering London production of *Cat on a Hot Tin Roof* in 1958, and of André Gide's confessional autobiography, *The Immoralist*, Sir Peter's decision to stage Charles Dyer's *Staircase* for the Royal Shakespeare Company in 1966 seems bizarre. The RSC was liberal and modernist. *Staircase* retailed the sexual politics and conventions of Coward's generation. The play represented one of the last stands in the theatre of that English music hall, revue and cabaret tradition in which effete and camp stereotypes of male homosexuality were held up for the amusement of heterosexual audiences and as targets for their ridicule.

By the 1970s, many American lesbians, gay men and feminists had arrived at the view that transvestite performances, of which English pub and club drag was a manifestation, made a caricature of men and women. But English affection for drag – whether among heterosexual or gay audiences – had endured, just as television has continued to satisfy a mass demand for the sight of the effeminate male in situation comedy. For a nation whose fear and hatred of homosexuality surpasses that of all Europe, both drag and effeminacy have provided an acceptable face of homosexuality. Their appeal has to do with the misogyny of the British male, since the principles of drag and the techniques of the effeminate or camp actor, subject femininity to ridicule. Their derogatory aspects impart artifice and affectation to women, often suggesting these conceal a rampant sexuality that cannot be admitted. The performances' popularity lies in the way that they exploit a particularly English conception of female erotic pudeur. At the same time the performer often seeks to signal a kind of desexualising complicity with his audience, by signalling that while he may be behaving like an effeminate, homosexual man, he is a real heterosexual underneath the make-up. Dick Emery, Danny La Rue and Stanley Baxter all do or did this.

Dyer's *Staircase* at least suggests that effeminate men, or men who enjoy dressing up as women, may indeed be homosexual.

Although Dyer's Charlie earns his living as a barber, he still regards himself as an artiste, specialising in drag roles. When he imagines giving evidence in court he describes himself as 'an established member of the theatrical profession in good standing' whose 'whole act is based upon the uproarious antics of my female impersonations'. It may be five years since his 'farewell debut', but he has gone on waiting for the call to perform and escape from the life of a 'small-time, back street hair-dresser' (1.i.17).

The play does offer alluring opportunities for serious actors to show off a kind of versatility as camp comedians and suffering queens. In Britain the fact that such a major classical actor as Paul Scofield took the part of Charles, and Patrick Magee, a Beckett specialist, played Harry, suggested Sir Peter wanted to treat the play as serious; in contrast the 1968 Broadway production at the Bilmore, with Eli Wallach and Milo O'Shea, simply recreated the play as a series of slapstick turns.

Sir Peter now admits that the play was not remarkable.[63] But he was attracted by Dyer's attempt, the first on the British stage, to show a domestic, homosexual relationship. And what a relationship. Here was a pair of middle-aged barbers, lamenting through the course of a Saturday night that fate had damned them homosexual, and had arranged they should live together in bickering, asexual discontent. The play was another symptom of the way in which homosexuals, as far as the theatre was concerned, could be accepted if pitied, their lives held up as awful warnings of an inherent doom waiting to catch them in middle age. Frustration and loneliness, failure and ostracism characterise these homosexual lives. The barbers are a world and a generation away from the new variety of homosexual who would emerge from the Stonewall riots across the great water. Instead, they are victims of early 1960s England, who have introjected prevailing attitudes to homosexuality. Harry and Charlie seem to be predominantly the caricatures of heterosexual imagination, and Scofield's preening, nasal, camping performance was the apotheosis of homosexual cliché, while Magee's more masculine assumption was insistently grotesque.

The play's strategy and its novelty, as Hall says, is to use the stage for the purpose of showing a homosexual relationship as well as the problem of homosexual desire. Harry's chronic depression, which precipitates a melodramatic attempt to gas himself, and Charlie's dread of the court case in which he will be charged with importuning, while dressed in women's clothes – in a homosexual bar – are the play's indices of how grim it was to be gay in the England of the early 1960s, and how hard to be 'deviant'. Charlie, the superannuated actor, believing his time will come again, is, at least, merely pathetic.

Dyer's vision of these two middle-aged wrecks, drifting through the squall of their domestic lives, looks back to the 1950s socio-medical version of the 'ageing homosexual'. D.J.West, the psychotherapist, in cautionary melodrama and parable, saw the homosexual, in middle age, as a character in a 'preordained tragedy' losing 'contact with the normal world', becoming 'more and more taken up with homosexual groups', his 'short-lived affairs' brought to a conclusion by the coming on of age and flesh.[64] At last

> the ageing homosexual finds himself on the shelf, lonely, without home or family, left pathetically and compulsively hanging about lavatories or trailing his old haunts, trying to bribe himself into the company of young men. The normal man, restricted as he may be by the routine of family life, has no cause for envy.

This discourse dehumanises homosexuals and imagines that their lives are bounded by a sexuality that literally causes them to be ostracised and ruined. Dyer queries parts of such a sexual fiction and accepts others. Charlie and Harry have at least lived together for years, apparently defying the idea that all homosexual relationships are fated to be impermanent. But there is scant sense that their relationship has ever been sexual. They are fellow-sufferers, rather than former lovers, who are kept close by loneliness, surviving in dejected symbiosis.

Harry – bald, fat, bewigged – conveys the pathos of a middle-aged Peter Pan who still wants to romp with the boys. 'I'm finished, even though I'm the same inside. I'm wearing tiddly briefs inside, Charlie, and my heart can still dance, but who knows it? Who'd want me on a beach? A yellowing sow's ear.' The homosexual, in this imagining, has no interests beyond sex. Harry also speaks as if his relationship with Charlie did not exist. 'Trouble with our sort, you're never left with anyone. It's an impossibility. It's

an empty room when whatever friends you've got, go first'
(2.43).

This sense of solitariness is not surprising. An explanatory
clue is loudly dropped in the play's closing scene. Harry
(full name, Harry C. Leeds) realises that his name is an
anagram of Charles Dyer, the 'Charlie' who lives with him.
And in an afterword Dyer explains that in the course of the
play he came to believe that there is only one character on
stage, that the second person is an imaginary figment of a
lonely, fantasising mind. Of course, the play could be staged
as an expressionistic homosexual monodrama, but Peter Hall
in the original production did not impose any such gloss
upon it. Dyer lays greater stress upon the sadomasochistic
tendencies that animate the relationship between the two men,
although Hall ignored these aspects also. The procedure is
made vivid in a sequence when Harry finally dons his new
wig and insists upon punishment with the lash of Charlie's
tongue.

> HARRY. I'd rather you said one of your cruel thrusts. Go on,
>   Charlie, get it off your chest.
> CHARLIE. The wig's fine, dear. Fine.
> HARRY. Charlie, Charlie. I don't mind. Tell me the truth. Be
>   yourself.
> CHARLIE. Where are you going to keep it at night – in
>   a cage?
> HARRY. Yes, that's you. That's my old you. Go on, more . . .
> CHARLIE. Well – it looks like you've spat ink on a hot
>   boiled egg.
> [*But this is too much for Harry*]
> HARRY. Oh, you bastard. You're cruel and vicious.
>
> (2.i.45)

There could be no cruder exposé of Harry's need to be degraded.
Not only does their relationship fail to provide them with either
comfort or joy; Dyer belabours the two men's sense of being
outcast from ordinary life and society. Both men have surviving
mothers with whom they cannot communicate. Harry has been
expelled not only from the bosom of his family, but even from
leading a scout-troop, since homosexuality is here reckoned a
close relation of paedophilia. Charlie, who once managed to
marry and sire a daughter, has been ignominiously cut off from

wife and child. So oppressive was Peter Hall's production that you waited in constant anticipation of cancer or a heart attack finishing the duo. No such bad luck attends them. Instead, Dyer keeps them clenched in stereotype's embrace and in tears. Charlie, after news of his court case, is found 'slumped in his chair, shawl around his shoulder', in fits of sobbing (1.ii.18). Harry with a bald head, which is no advertisement for a barber selling hair-restorer and hair-tonic, 'flings himself to the ground sobbing bitterly' at the sheer state of his hairless head (1.ii.25). Dyer saw and believed what his generation had largely been conditioned to believe. And the approving reviews that greeted *Staircase*, both in London and New York, indicate the extent to which critics expected homosexual characters to be disparaged.

John Russell Taylor writing in *Plays and Players* was one of the few reviewers to criticise Dyer for pandering to such stereotypical views. 'It is calculated', he wrote of the play,

> with almost uncanny precision to hit precisely that place in the spectrum of public taste where essentially square and conservative audiences can be pleasantly, superficially outraged, and go out of the theatre with all their original received ideas comfortably reaffirmed.

He was convinced that Dyer had organised his play to leave audiences feeling 'If we're all in a pretty bad way, queers are worse off than most.' When the play reached New York, two years later, Walter Kerr in the *Sunday New York Times*, Richard P. Cooke of the *Wall Street Journal* and Martin Gottfried in *Women's Wear Daily* were concerned about the delicate subject of homosexuality. Kerr, as if heaving a sigh of relief, found the evening and the occasion 'unsqueamish' – the 'most honest treatment' of homosexuality he had seen upon the stage. Cooke warned that the very subject would still be 'offensive' to many theatre-goers, and Gottfried applauded Dyer for daring to deal with the 'homosexual plight' sensitively and adroitly.[65] None of them noted that the two barbers were pathetic and absurd, wretched and anxious. Such things, of course, were reckoned the natural lot of homosexuals.

SIGNS OF COMMUNITY

Mart Crowley's *The Boys in the Band* (Plate 5), as we have seen, belongs both in that world which regards homosexuality as sin and cause of stigma, and in the new one in which homosexual identity is proclaimed in Gay Liberation. That the play opened off-Broadway in 1968, rather than on it, suggests a doubt about its commercial potential or a realization that it was dangerously daring for Broadway's traditional audiences. Clive Barnes, the critic of the *New York Times* in 1968, recognised the sensational significance of what was being enacted. 'This is not a play about a homosexual, but a play that takes the homosexual milieu and the homosexual way of life totally for granted and uses this as a valid basis of human experience,' he wrote. 'Thus it is a homosexual play not a play about homosexuality.'[66] He was recognising what had not been generally recognised before and had not been depicted on stage, except in the sensationalism of Mae West's *The Drag*. But there the drag queens at the party were outsiders. Here there are signs of genuine identity and community, however tempered by signs of stress.

The play also provided just the kind of portrayal of homosexuals that heterosexual theatre critics in New York wished to see. They had complained before that some homosexual playwrights had practised gross deception by creating supposedly heterosexual characters who were endowed with homosexual characteristics. This time there were no regrets. Walter Kerr in his review in the *Sunday New York Times* diagnosed a specifically camp and homosexual diction and form of behaviour, common to a defined gay group. 'They deal with pain by laughing shrilly, ostentatiously, savagely . . . agonies that cannot be acknowledged as agonies but must be everlastingly managed as jests, may be the harshest of all'.[67]

The play depends upon a version of camp that is a savage form of defensiveness and self-protection, upon a mode of living in which emotions that cannot be appeased have to be transformed by wit and humour. It is this New York camp, a creative form of wit, that Crowley retails. It is one of the defining aspects of what will come to be categorised as gay identity. The anti-hero's final collapse, when he gives way to real feeling – 'If we . . . if we could just learn not to hate ourselves so much' –

133

anticipates a tenet of Gay liberation (2.101-2). Defensive camp will be outdated. It will survive as a remnant of the valiant but bad old times.

But the very title of the play suggests the signs of the impending new. The eight or nine young men who assemble in an expensive East Fifties, and thus socially smart, Manhattan apartment are gay; to British eyes and ears they appear to be roughly middle-class. One of them is black. One of them has been married. And only one of them is effeminate. Alan, the married and presumably heterosexual, man who comes into their midst when the chaps are dancing a chorus line together, is only able to discern that one of them, Emory, is gay. The rest of them *look* heterosexual; that is to say, they seem stereotypically masculine. But in their free and spontaneous conversations they do not sound so. And some of them manifest what we may describe as stereotypically gay attitudes, behaviour and beliefs. A question is at once raised. Are we to interpret them as new stereotypes, representatives of a new generation where the signs of homosexuality are apparent in that which is learned, rather than that which is inherent? It is not inappropriate to begin to discard the word 'homosexual' with its medical connotations and replace it with 'gay', that self-chosen word of identity.

The stereotype is a characteristic form, a caricature of the archetype, by which society identifies members of a group. Such a procedure is achieved by emphasizing and designating a series of signs and behaviours as indices of membership of a particular group. These characteristics may be innate or acquired. The stereotype has not merely been used to identify groups, such as homosexuals; it has been applied wherever particular groups, castes or communities can be generally recognised through the generality of signs. For much of this century the homosexual was stereotyped in negative and malign terms, which some homosexuals accepted and others contemptuously rejected.

As homosexual identity and community began to be created in the new atmospheres of the 1960s a reaction to the old stereotype of femininity occurred, as a result of which numbers of homosexuals began consciously to adopt some behaviours that were regarded as indices of masculinity. The 'clone', a form of stereotype itself, was an American homosexual's stereotype of masculinity, expressed through the medium of a working's man costume, moustache, muscularity. It was associated with signs of archetypical masculinity, of laconic, unemotional assertiveness. At the same time the stereotypes of homosexual sexuality began to evolve through a series of behavioural and attitudinal signs, which emerged from an embryonic gay culture. *The Boys in the Band* reflects, though not fully, the nature of these alterations. Crowley lays particular stress upon what his characters wear for the party. He is right to do so. For costume has always been one of those governing signs on which stereotyping depends. Gay people have traditionally depended upon a series of visual, secret codes, whose meanings would only be understood by initiates. Gay costume and gay signs became both private code and public property in the America of the 1960s, even though there were some indicators whose meaning was chiefly discernible to gay people. The sexual signs revealed by the placing of keys and handkerchiefs is an example.

The Boys in the Band pay fastidious attention to their clothes. Donald, dressed in khakis and a Lacoste shirt, and Cowboy, the hustler hired for the night, 'a muscle-bound young man, wearing boots, tight Levis, a calico handkerchief and a cowboy hat', are both, in their completely divergent styles, wearing stereotypically homosexual clothes. But there is nothing of the old feminising stereotype about them: the khakis, with their military connotations, the developed muscles, the cowboy hat, the 'tight' Levis all function to lay stress upon the new stereotype of masculinity. Bernard, in contrast, the only black man at the party, wears 'Ivy league clothes'. He chooses to pass as heterosexual. And Hank, the formerly married man, is similarly attired in conventional heterosexual style (1.4). Emory, the old stereotype of homosexuality, revels in effeminacy, stressing its particular qualities as well as a form of accentuated verbal camp.

But since stereotypes do not depend upon signs alone, it soon becomes apparent that not all Crowley's *Boys in the Band* have renounced the old stereotypical aspects of homosexuality. Michael, the eternal youth, and Harold, for whom the party is held, are obsessed by their appearance. They are both convinced that their desirability will pass in their thirties.

Michael endlessly combs his thinning hair, and changes his sweater over and over again. Harold treats his face as if it were a disaster area, and arrives late, after subjecting it to the blandishments of ointments, salves, creams and masks. Both of them dread the first intimation of older age, with all the dread of a young show-girl whose legs will not be relished, and whose face will no longer serve as her fortune, once she has passed 25.

The play's governing diction, its supposedly 'fag humour', was admired by heterosexual critics as if they were proclaiming their sophistication. 'I love wisecrack humour,' one critic wrote,

And when it is fag style it has the added texture of desperation and irony. These imply the self-contempt and frustration these homosexuals must fight every day of their lives – not sexual frustration, but the frustration of being condemned for doing the only thing that satisfied them.[68]

The comment and the analysis are reflective of the traditional view of the self-hating homosexual man whose only interests are erotic. This New York critic suggests that a peculiar gay humour was born of self-loathing, a grim laughter achieved while scrabbling through the wreckage of one's homosexual life. But he reveals his expectations with his reference to the 'added texture of desperation'. For the supposed 'fag' humour is the exaltation of a useful form of camp. It is a form of defence before attack.

The play is not totally pessimistic, despite the example of homosexual self-loathing that Michael, the play's party-giver, so amply and destructively projects. Michael, and in some sense Donald, Emory, Bernard and Hal, are all representatives of those gay men of the 1960s who admit their homosexual desires, who have active sex-lives and take up what is on offer in the subcultural gay world of bars, clubs and private parties. But they are not easy in this new dispensation. They disparage themselves efficiently. They lack self-esteem. Crowley accordingly allows them to articulate self-abasing critiques. Michael, true to the late 1960s fashion for encounter groups, announces that he is responsible for his own life. Jaded, bored and noisily despairing, he falls back upon

Freud. Donald, long flat upon a psychiatrist's couch, may not complain about his lot, but Crowley hints that some breakdown, precipitated by homosexual desire, has caused this well-educated man to leave the city and resort to menial work. Homosexuality has left both of them resorting to alcohol or psychiatry.

Accordingly, the play's second-act crisis is induced by Michael's novelettish, juvenile truth-game, and powered by malice; his spite and his desire to embarrass or cause pain are rendered as the tactics of the stereotypically embittered homosexual. His game requires each man to telephone the one love of his life and to confess this supposedly shaming fact. For Michael's governing assumption is that truth and homosexual passion are incompatible. To speak the truth is to admit a weakness, particularly when the confession is made in the presence of others. Both Bernard and Emory bolster Michael's theory. They are fixated upon heterosexual love-objects from adolescence, suffering unrequited love through the years – victims of the long-standing, long-running crush. They know only the love that dares not speak its name, let alone confess it on the telephone.

It is thus almost possible to interpret *The Boys in the Band* as a play that equates homosexuality with despair. Most of the Boys are in hot pursuit of romantic love that has never arrived or passed away. And Michael, having failed to show up Alan as a closeted homosexual, sinks into dejection, as if his only happiness was in bringing out misery in others. Michael is the first and thorough example of the modern, metropolitan homosexual male who cannot come to terms with the nature of his desires. Money has brought him nothing but access to pleasure-zones, one-night stands and years-long dissatisfaction. Having given up on pills, alcohol and his psychiatrist, he is on his own, and suffering withdrawal symptoms. Sexual guilt is the nagging anxiety. 'Guilt, unfathomable guilt – either real or imagined – from that split second your eyes pop open and you say, "Oh my God, what did I do last night?"' (1.18).

Harold, in the play's closing scene, analyses the cause of this life-distress in terms that are not as pessimistic as they at first seem. 'You are a sad and pathetic man,' he judges:

You're a homosexual and you don't want to be. But there is nothing you can do to change it. Not all your prayers to your God, not all the analysis you can buy in all the years you've got left to live. You may very well one day be able to know a heterosexual life, if you want it desperately enough – if you pursue it with the fervour with which you annihilate – but you will always be homosexual as well. Always, Michael, always. Until the day you die.

(2.99)

The speech, as chillingly delivered by Leonard Frey, both on Broadway and in the film of the play, sounded like a judgement against which there was no appeal. The references to Michael's analysis and to the chances he has of living as a heterosexual are surely influenced by contemporary psychoanalytic theories about homosexuality. The New York Academy of Medicine's 1964 report, and Laurence Bieber's psychoanalytic study two years earlier, had secured much attention with its suggestion that homosexuality as 'an acquired illness is susceptible to cure'.[69] Harold offers a furious denial of this argument. No wonder. Crowley sees Michael as belonging to the old world.

There are, however, homosexual role models in the play who have revolted against the tyranny of judging oneself according to heterosexual values. Larry voices the views and beliefs of the new generation. He has none of Michael's gluttonous appetite for guilt. He wins the truth-game. He can admit to his lover that he loves him, but he refuses to accept a monogamous relationship based upon heterosexual models of commitment and faithfulness. To be homosexual, he suggests, is to have different options and opportunities, as well as to suffer limitations. 'It's my right to lead my sex life without answering to anybody – Hank included,' he insists, 'And if those terms are not acceptable, then we must not live together . . .' (2.88–9).

What he offers is a permanent commitment to his lover, but within an open relationship that allows other sexual contacts. Hank, having once conformed to society's expectations, has taken the chance offered to him by the new mood of the 1960s. By the end of the play's evening of revelation and plain-speaking, he has come to accept the conditions for living with Larry. This couple serve as positive role models, antidotes to Michael's misery, and affirm the value of Harold's shock therapy addressed to the party-giver. The values and standards of the 1950s are, however, in Crowley's play, more potent than those which are set to usurp them. The Boys may have a gay party, but Alan, Michael's once-best friend, cannot be allowed to see that this is a gay night-in. Deception and subterfuge is necessary. Not until the second act can it be admitted to the heterosexual visitor that Hank and Larry are lovers. Homosexual men, in Crowley's view of fashionable New York, may admit to their gay friends they are gay; but coming out to heterosexuals remains a fearful process. *The Boys in the Band* are, at least and at last (some of them), the first Liberation victors who have revolted successfully against the governing orthodoxies, and have come through happily. Hank and Larry are individualists in a conformist society. They have revolted against those ideologies, familial, social and sexual, in which they have been schooled. They have shaped identities for themselves that within months will come to be described as 'gay'. The other *boys in the band* are living in the past. Hank and Larry are part of the future. For them it works.

5

'SIMPLY THE THING I AM SHALL MAKE ME LIVE': 1969–1981

NEW VIEWS, NEW POWERS

Even the commercial playhouses of New York and the West End are not immune to the forces of political and cultural change. Both in this theatre system and in its radical, studio alternatives the signs of the changing perceptions of homosexuality were clearly on view: in the world beyond the theatre some American states repealed their sodomy laws; in England and Wales, in 1967, homosexual acts in private between two consenting adult males over 21 were exempted from prosecution. In 1973 the American psychiatric association ruled that homosexuality could no longer be classified a mental disorder. Both the American and the British civil services terminated their ban on the employment of gay men and lesbians, though in Britain's case with significant exceptions.

The effect of these changes was to begin to alter the identity of the homosexual as publicly perceived. He was no longer to be regarded as sick, no longer to be automatically classified as criminal or outcast. The Gay Liberationists of the late 1960s revalued Freud and the influential Marxist, Herbert Marcuse, argued that heterosexuality was socially engineered and that homosexuality was a legitimate rebellion against 'procreative genital sexuality'. Heterosexuality, in Marcuse's urging, did not have to take procreation as its justifying aim. Pleasure without reproduction was, he asserted, a valid heterosexual principle.[1] A newly fortified gay subculture, absorbed within the capitalistic system, developed in clubs, bars and bathhouses. It catered for that pleasure principle which became a focal part of the new gay identity. The Gay Liberation movements, in establishing this new sense of identity, assisted in the destruction of one of the theatre's favourite signifiers of homosexuality – the homosexual stereotype. The Liberation movements rejected the system of reducing lesbians and gay men to a series of signs and behaviours that caricatured masculinity and femininity. They argued that there were no archetypical signs of homosexuality, even though some lesbians might be masculine in manner and some gay men effete; but these were not typical of all, since the 'all' comprised within the designation could not be accommodated within such a crude diagnostic system.

The exaltation of the male archetype and the celebration of the qualities of maleness are usually characteristic of patrist societies. Fascist forms of government – with a reverence for the male warrior, while the female is down-graded, valued solely for her procreative, nurturing and domestic capacities – are quintessentially patrist. The matrist-orientated movements of the 1960s in America and Britain emphasised the dangers of exalting archetypically male qualities, arguing that the healthy society was one that integrated and balanced the archetypically masculine and feminine qualities. And the Gay Liberation movements suggested that the gay man might combine and reconcile aspects of the male and female archetype. He was liable to be both sexually active and receptive, an emblem of the versatile and malleable. Lesbians and gay men, when they came into general view, did prove to be people of infinite variety. They could not be categorised within a stereotypical frame any more than heterosexuals could. One of the most powerful assaults upon the old notion of homosexual stereotyping occurs in David Rabe's deep-chill drama, *Streamers*: none of the soldiers in the cadre can accept that one of their number is gay, despite the blatant sexual interest he shows in a black, blue-collar negro soldier. For the gay desirer seems to be what the heterosexual conceives as the model of approved masculinity. Times have changed. It is 1976. A gay man may reveal his sexuality, but his identity is not necessarily accepted, or acceptable.

The idea of gay sensibility – those perceptions inspired and shaped by an individual's sense of being gay – was also popularised in the 1970s as a new mode of gay positivism. Such a sensibility had been detected as early as the 1890s, reflecting the 'attitudes, moods, thoughts, and emotions' of an oppressed section of society.[2] As such that sensibility was (and is) fluid, evolving and socially conditioned. There are, for example, signs of gay sensibility in both Tennessee Williams and Joe Orton, but the forms of its expression are radically different. In both writers there are critiques of the enforcers of social orthodoxy, of the family as a principal agent of that orthodoxy, and a sympathetic identification with the outsider and the outcast. And Orton's use of camp helps to strengthen his mockery of the agents of conformity. The sensibility of both men is apparent in their wildly different treatment of males celebrated as objects of desire.

In the early summer of 1968, when London was hot and heady with the flowering of the Counter Culture, when flower-power and hippies decorated the streets of London, the Lord Chamberlain was asked to license a new American 'love-rock' musical called *Hair*. Although the Chamberlain's control of the theatre was due to terminate within months, he dutifully refused two versions of the musical a licence. His examiner submitted in the margins of his diatribe that the British Medical Association had ruled in the 1950s that homosexuality was catching and the musical posed a variety of sexual threats to decency.[3] *Hair* was cut and cut again until its producer, James Verner, hit upon a neat way out. He decided to open *Hair* on 26 September, the very day that the Lord Chamberlain's power to repress and control the stage was terminated by the passing of the Theatres Act.

The following year Mark Crowley's *The Boys in the Band* arrived in town from Broadway, to be presented at the Wyndham's theatre: its journey from Broadway to the West End would have been impossible just months earlier. And by 1971 Tom Eyen's provocatively entitled *The Dirtiest Show in Town*, preceded by synthetic alarms and fabricated controversy, jauntily tested the stage's new-won freedom. There was commerce and money in the new liberality, since the Theatres Act of 1968, as we have seen, provided the theatre with the substantial protections already afforded to literature by the Obscene Publications Acts of 1959 and 1964.

Charles Marowitz, the American director of London's leading fringe theatre, the Open Space, sent a contemptuous message home, in the form of a review for the *Village Voice* of *The Dirtiest Show in Town*. 'A traditional camp revue', he sneered, 'with generous dollops of nudity, [provided] in the full knowledge that sex would enhance (if not insure) the commercial success of the show.' The production, he complained, was well endowed – with 'a bogus kind of social commentary which is presumably intended to sell these 42nd Street titillations to the intellectuals as well as the plastic mac set'.[4]

But Marowitz's pricking of pretensions, his charge of hypocrisy and commercial exploitation, missed the significance of what was happening to the West End theatre which was in the infancy of freedom. Like some precocious child, it relished its new-found freedom to be naughty; it profited from the sure-fire commercial allure of what had been so recently banned. The hippie generation was there to be wooed. New York's ban on plays dealing with homosexuality had been lifted in 1965. The London theatre was following on.

The entire theatrical structures of both Britain and America were also being subjected to profound change. In Britain, with increased governmental subsidy of the performing arts, the commercial theatre was losing its salience. The fringe – London's equivalent of off-off-Broadway, springing up in pubs and cellars, and sometimes receiving Arts Council financial support – was free to show and discuss the sexual. Marowitz, exulting in the licence for what had previously been unlicensable, presented John Herbert's *Fortune and Men's Eyes* at the Open Space, with its raw, rank homosexing, its sex-power games played out in a Canadian prison. Long-barred holds were now unbarred.

The new alternative theatre of America, was not simply an antidote to Broadway and to its ideology (the star-struck celebration of the status quo); it was fired by the culture of protest of which Gay Liberation was now a flourishing example. This new theatre, whether off-off-Broadway or in other cities, relied upon a new aesthetic and techniques. Its adherence to the radical, and the liberation theories and life-styles of the hippie generation, became an inspirational source for the commercial theatre, still stranded in old times: *The Boys in the Band*, which began off-off-Broadway, and Julian Mitchell's *Another Country* made the transition from the fringe to the mainstream, and reached the cinema screen.

The post-Gay Liberation plays about homosexuality, presented in altered contexts, were fresh in theme and in ideology. The old sexual iconography was discredited. The governing stereotype of the stage homosexual, with his disdained sexuality, began to vanish. Ian McKellen in Martin Sherman's *Bent* or Richie in *Streamers*, key plays about homosexuality in the 1970s, bear no comparison with the sensitive, artistic neurotics of *Tea and Sympathy* or the camp, tear-laden barbers of *Staircase*. The theatre was reflecting and responding to the new sense that homosexuals had of themselves as an oppressed minority, emancipating themselves from shame and misery.

An authentic gay theatre in the 1970s emerged, created by gay companies presenting plays to gay audiences. This theatre discarded the negative myths engulfing homosexuality. The Playhouse of the Ridiculous and The Ridiculous Theatre Company crossed the boundaries of gender and mocked all idea of the great divide, revelling in drag and show-business camp. They were manifestations of a gay counter culture, expressed in theatrical forms to challenge sexual orthodoxy.

The prime plays about homosexuality, in the mainstream theatre and before the AIDS epidemic, examined and reinterpreted a past that had been refracted through the sensibilities of censorious heterosexuals. *Bent*, Julian Mitchell's *Another Country* and Hugh Whitemore's *Breaking the Code* were the key works in this new process. All these plays were written from what we may call a post-Liberation perspective. And the star actors who agreed to play these homosexual roles – Ian McKellen in *Bent*, Rupert Everett and Daniel Day Lewis in *Another Country* and Derek Jacobi in *Breaking the Code* – broke the mould of the homosexual stereotype as the theatre had helped to fashion it.

These plays not only related gay private lives to the worlds that had shaped and limited them. They created and celebrated suitable gay heroes; they rescued from obloquy supposed gay villains. In all these three plays rebellious homosexuals attempt to assert a homosexual identity and to live their sexual lives in societies that outlawed such sexuality. In *Bent*, set during the first phase of Hitler's regime, homosexuality becomes a death-warrant. In *Breaking the Code* a mathematical genius finds that his obstinate determination to lead an openly homosexual life imposes such stresses and penalties that his life becomes insupportable. In *Another Country* a young homosexual realises that his homosexuality will outcast him from the position he craves, and the play leads the audience to forecast that he will achieve a retaliatory vengeance by betraying his country.

The principal characters in each of the plays are, in some way, homosexual heroes: for they battle against the penalising forces of conformity. That late-Shakespearean aspiration in *All's Well That Ends Well* – 'Simply to be the thing I am shall make me live' (IV.iv) – becomes a reigning aspiration. Thus an Ibsen hero like Brand, who lives out Ibsen's process of ranging individual conscience against the institutions and enforcers of orthodoxy, bears relationship with the first, unlikely heroes of this new drama centred upon homosexual desire. The spirit of defiance permeating this new drama is transmuted by homosexuals who struggled for a personal (though not general) liberation, against the ordained arrangements of relationship, at a time when to assume such a Lutheran 'here I stand' individualism was liable to be self-destructive. Their heterodoxy is described as valiant self-assertion rather than defended with any special pleading for the pariah and the pitiful oppressed. And each of these plays ends up upon the commercial stage, brought there by the drawing power of star players prepared to identify themselves with gay heroes.

ABOUT GAY HEROES

Of this trio *Bent* (Plate 6) is the most remarkable, remarkable for the way in which it enabled the theatre to fulfil a rare function. It illuminated what had been carefully obscured. It is also one of the most significant plays produced in the post-Second World War theatre. The difficulty that Martin Sherman experienced in bringing his play to the stage illustrates the reluctance of directors and producers to see commercial value or social significance in plays trading in homosexual history. But its eventual production, and world-wide success upon the commercial stage, is bright evidence of how social, economic and cultural changes were beginning to transform the theatres of London and New York.

If it had not been for the new mood and consciousness engendered by the liberal movement of the late 1960s and 1970s, Sherman would never have had the spur to write *Bent*.

145

And if it had not been for the creation in Britain of a new form of state-subsidised theatre, which treated the theatre as a forum to deal with serious issues and did not put commercial consideration before all else, *Bent* would never have emerged out of the cold. Sherman originally wrote *Bent* for the company that inspired his interest in the subject and had imbued him with a belief in himself as a dramatist – Gay Sweatshop. The company was founded in 1975, in London, to counteract a still-prevailing conception in the mainstream theatre of what homosexuals were like, and to oppose 'the way in which gay people working in the theatre were often put into a position of colluding with those portrayals'.[5] Gay Sweatshop came to life with a season of lunchtime plays at a makeshift studio theatre, the Almost Free in central London. One of the first plays to be produced by Gay Sweatshop, *Passing By*, was written by Sherman. It was notable in its time for the way in which it showed a gay love-affair – 'completely easy and open and never a problem', as the author described it. Such affirmations seemed daring and fresh in those theatrical days, when young American actors were still reluctant to play 'happy' homosexuals and preferred to offer limp or even slit wrists.[6]

For Sherman the production, in which the gay actor Simon Callow played one of the two lovers, was 'a revelation and a turning point'. There he was, an American abroad, rootless and hopeless. 'Writing for the theatre until then', he said in a happy retrospect eight years later,

> filled me with despair; I was penniless, I was usually unproduced, and when I was produced it was improperly so. For the first time my work came truly alive on a stage. The director and actors were strong, tender, humane and technically accomplished, and the producing company had a guiding vision.

Sherman believes that Sweatshop had a 'subtle and subliminal' affect on many while its impact upon him was 'enormous and quite direct'.[7] He was delighted, therefore, when two years later, he was invited to attend rehearsals for Sweatshop's new play, *As Time Goes By*, which Drew Griffiths had written with Noël Greig. The play's idea was to attempt an explanation of contemporary hostility to homosexuals by depicting those influences and attitudes that had created such animosity. The play's three sections looked back to late-Victorian England, Berlin in the early 1930s and New York on the verge of the Stonewall riot of 1969.

Sherman was there to help with the American accents. Just a few casual words in the second section fired his imagination.

> At some point the ultimate fate of Germany's gays in the concentration camps was mentioned, and a cartoonist's drawings of that rehearsal scene would have put a lightening flash above my head, because it was like that, truly like that. I knew immediately that I wanted to write a play on the subject. A couple of sentences about 'pink triangles' triggered things in me I'd been thinking of writing for a long time.[8]

The Berlin section of *As Time Goes By* also 'struck a nerve' about the 'freedom' the new gay communities were enjoying in the 1970s. For Sherman this sense of liberation was illusory. It lacked any statutory basis. 'The whole gay scene was very commercial, very fashion-conscious, but it all seemed to me totally false. There was no real political freedom.' Sodomy was outlawed in many American states and the impact of such legislation was immense. 'When you're an outlaw, you behave like an outlaw.'[9] The gay men of America, manifesting 'a certain hardness, an inability to admit to the purity of loving', were preoccupied, caught up in the pursuit of those sexual pleasures that were now blatantly on show.

The new openness, Sherman believed, had disturbing repercussions. 'People had begun appearing on the streets of the [Greenwich] village in Nazi uniforms, which was then considered sexually titillating.' For the playwright it was a sign of the gay community's lack of historical perspective, of its insularity, of its lack of concern for other minorities. 'The illusion of freedom kept them from thinking they were themselves an abused minority. The Castro Community in San Francisco, for example, was busily evicting the black community.'

Sherman saw a connection with the young homosexuals of Germany at the close of the Weimar Republic and the beginning of Hitler's regime. And his play tacitly, disturbingly makes a series of comparisons between the politically unaware hedonists of Berlin in 1934 and metropolitan gay men in the 1970s.

> I saw a subject that was important to me as a gay man and as a Jew. When orthodox Jews were going around saying homosexuals should be killed, it seemed to me to say, 'if you are not politically free, you're not free at all'. Germany was full of similar illusions that could be wiped away in a second.

Griffiths encouraged him in his idea and committed Sweatshop to producing the play. Months later Sherman sent Griffiths his version of *Bent*, which he had completed while back on a visit to America. Griffiths's response was fine and altruistic. He told Sherman that Sweatshop could only provide a limited audience and urged Sherman to try to place his play in front of the world – in the conventional theatre. This was where the difficulty began. Most plays have to battle themselves into production. Sherman's, with its sexual candour and gay diction, was one thing, but its violent, shocking subject-matter was another.

Peggy Ramsay, who had been Orton's agent and was now Sherman's, was 'furious' that the playwright had even contemplated giving the play to Gay Sweatshop. She sent it to the Hampstead Theatre, then one of the main fringe and subsidised theatres in London devoted to new writing. Its American director Michael Rudman was, Sherman gratefully remembers, 'the first person in a position of power to give me any recognition'.[10] Rudman had already produced a short play of Sherman's at Edinburgh's Traverse Theatre and had originally recommended his *Passing By* to Gay Sweatshop. Rudman turned out to be one of the few heterosexual and Jewish theatre men involved with *Bent* who provided support. He read the play and was eager to do it at Hampstead. 'But he thought the director should be gay.'

Throughout 1978 Rudman sent the play to directors who were gay. 'If I'd known just what he was doing I would have said "stop!"' Sherman says now. For the directors to whom Rudman was sending *Bent* were 'a group of people who were extremely radical in some areas, but stayed not only in the closet but were nervous about gay politics. They were also people who would have been upset by the emotional part of the play.'

Sherman was determined London would see *Bent* first. 'I had had terrible theatre experiences in New York.' But while he was waiting for something to happen he was urged to send the script to the Eugene O'Neill Memorial Centre in America where for four weeks every year a series of staged readings of new plays were presented. 'You have wonderful actors there and the readings are intricately done, so that after two days' rehearsals the readings seem amazingly close to production. All the major American playwrights of the last twenty years started at the O'Neill.'

Bent, however, was turned down. And it was only when a play-script by the American poet Michael McClure, whose *The Beard* at the Royal Court put cunnilingus on stage in 1968, was dropped at short notice, that *Bent* had its chance. 'It caused a sensation,' Sherman recalls. 'They'd resisted and resisted doing it. And here I was getting a lot of offers from regional American theatres and one Broadway producer actually said he wanted to produce it.'

Meanwhile Hampstead had failed to find a gay director and Rudman had departed, to be succeeded by David Aukin. Although Aukin admired the play highly, he suggested Sherman should try somewhere else. Sherman was now faced with a dilemma. Should he commit to the Broadway producer who seemed convinced that he could present the play? Sherman was very doubtful. There was another consideration as well. 'I'd always had an image of Ian McKellen in my mind. But they could not get through to him. People said "He's at the Royal Shakespeare Company. You won't get him." And Peggy [Ramsay] said "Take the American offer."' But the night before Sherman returned to America in 1978 he met the English director Robert Chetwyn at a party. Chetwyn had seen and read a script of Sherman's play, and told Sherman he wanted to direct it. Then he said something strangely fortuitous. 'It's almost as though it's written for Ian McKellen. I'd like to do it with him. I directed his Hamlet.'

A copy was sent to McKellen, then a most closeted gay actor, who was on a RSC tour. For six weeks they waited. The Broadway producer pressed his own case. Sherman asked for a little more time. Still nothing was heard. Then immediately after an ultimatum had been given by the American, Sherman had the message for which he was longing. McKellen had spent the last weeks brooding over whether he should leave the RSC and take on the production. He had decided to take the daring chance.

But who would present the play? Chetywn decided to approach Eddie Kulukundis, a fairly new London producer who had arrived from Greece to work in London with funds from his family shipping firm. Kulukundis went to the Royal Court; he was clearly aware how unwilling the coterie of producers who controlled the West End would be to present such a sexually controversial play. McKellen, although reckoned one of the leading classical actors of his generation, was not the greatest commercial draw at that time.

The Royal Court, with its radical reputation, ought to have welcomed the play with open arms. But according to Sherman it did not.

> I know there was a lot of dissent about doing the play. And I know Max Stafford-Clark (now artistic director) who was then an associate, was very much in favour. There was a lot of tension. But Eddie put up a lot of money. They needed the money so I think they put it on somewhat reluctantly. But at the first preview the audience response was so good that they relaxed.

They were right. It had required the efforts of the subsidised theatre, the discovery of a director who was not afraid of the play's sexuality, and the promptings of a resourceful heterosexual producer, to bring *Bent* in from the cold.

Not until 1972 had any book been published that dealt through historical research in the archives with the Nazi persecution and systematic murder of homosexuals. Rudiger Lautmann's *Homosexuality and Society*, ignored in America and England, was the first book to provide statistics on the fate of homosexuals in the Nazi regime. Five years earlier Heinz Heger's *The Men with the Pink Triangle* had given a personal account of life as a homosexual man within a Nazi death camp. It was Richard Plant's *The Pink Triangle: The Nazi War against Homosexuals* that revealed with a full scholarly approach how the Nazis set out to denounce homosexuals and plan their extermination.

Plant generously acknowledges that as a dramatist Sherman achieved what historians had not:

> *Bent* opened the forbidden closet a crack, and put the world on notice that indeed the Nazis had hounded all contragenics; that gays had been classified with criminals, asocials, the Jews, as deviant subhumans, the cosmic lice that Hitler and Himmler had vowed to exterminate.

Almost all histories of the Third Reich, Plant finds, ignore this aspect of Nazi activity. 'One can only conclude that for most historians, there was and still is a taboo in effect.'[11]

Bent, therefore, is more than theatre-history. It records the progress of young Max from gay life in the Berlin of 1934 to that inferno of the concentration camp to which his homosexuality dooms him. On the journey there he only survives by repudiating his homosexuality and then by successfully asserting a heterosexual identity through an act of heterosexual necrophilia. This ghastly scene recalls the great test to which Brecht's Mother Courage is put when called upon to identify her son's corpse. To claim him as her own would be to betray herself and her other children to the enemy. So she defies kinship, watches as the corpse is taken to be thrown away, and then, as incarnated by Helen Weigel, a legendary, soundless scream shatters the auditorium. Weigel's mouth, agape, signifies the imagined noise of grief. *Bent*'s hero, Max, in a process more harrowing than that suffered by Mother Courage, is forced by a Nazi officer to gaze at the body of his 'semi-conscious ... bloody ... mutilated' lover, Rudi, and to punch the dying man. Six times he is challenged to admit that Rudi is indeed his 'friend' and six times he denies it (1.v.36). To admit his love, and thus to affirm his gay identity, would be akin to signing his own death-warrant. He is, in effect, being asked to repudiate his homosexuality, and to assist in murdering his lover. He does so. He denies his identity to survive. He seems to prove he is not 'queer'.

Not only does he assume a heterosexual identity, he takes on a Jewish one as well, which is less stigmatised by the Nazis than a homosexual one. 'And I said, "I'm not queer." And they laughed. And I said "Give me a yellow star." And they said "Sure, make him a Jew. He's not queer!"' (1.vi.43). For the Nazis, Sherman shows, what you appear to be could be of saving importance, not what you secretly feel or what you secretly are. Thus the essential dilemma of the homosexual is depicted. Your outcast status may be assigned on the basis of external signs and by behaviour. To be homosexual in your fantasies does not necessarily invite an extreme penalty.

In the play's second act two triumphant gay affirmations are made. In the concentration camp Max's homosexual love-affair is achieved and he reasserts his homosexual identity, which is affirmed in death and through death. Max and Horst are not allowed to look at each other or to touch while they work in the stone quarry. But they can speak in the open air where they labour, because they cannot be heard. They can, therefore, fantasise together. In the play's one erotic scene they bring each other to orgasm while the guards watch them. Fantasy, the secret index of gay desire, becomes the means by which they can be homosexual, without manifesting the signs which would condemn them. The gulf between being and doing is bridged.

The second affirmation is more significant. Max, in Ian McKellen's boyish performance, has led a rich, pampered life, seeking after hot sensations; cocaine by evening, sex and S&M by night, hangovers the morning after. He has enjoyed the good, gay things that awaited a rich young homosexual in Berlin before the Night of the Long Knives, that anti-homosexual purge with which the play begins. 'I was always drunk. There was always coke. Nothing seemed to matter much,' he explains to Horst, in words which might have been echoed forty years on in Greenwich Village, New York, 'Queers aren't meant to love. I know. They don't want us to . . . Hate me . . . don't love me' (2.iii.61). But the old familiar sound of homosexual self-hatred is drowned out. The homosexual love-affair becomes symbiotic. It transcends the erotic interchanges by which it was initiated. It is a serious commitment.

At the play's culmination, Max chooses to claim his sexual identity and to die for it. The decision cannot be accounted some romantic, fatal gesture, imposed nearly forty years on by a dramatist seeking to impose his own fantasy of love triumphant upon doomed homosexuals. In the extremities of the death camp suicide and the strangest manifestations of the wish to die were pervasive. 'Moslem' was the generic name given to those who simply gave up the struggle to live in the camps, refusing to eat, drink or speak, and committing a slow suicide. The Moslem suffered fatal reactive depression. Max has been forced to watch his lover killed and his inveterate instinct for survival fizzles out. From the pit where he has been obliged to place the corpse of his lover, he takes Horst's jacket, with its distinguishing emblem, the pink star awarded to homosexuals, and puts it on. In death he will at last proclaim his true identity, having set aside his Jewish disguise. Posthumously he wears that badge which the Nazis regard as the terminal mark of ignominity, with pride. In death he has a kind of victory.

I still remember, eleven years on, the unique sense of raw shock and disgust that *Bent* engendered. It returned the electricity of surprise to the stage and a physical sense of revulsion and horror I have never experienced before or since. Most of the critics who reviewed the play thought otherwise. 'The reviews were not good,' Sherman admits. There was no dividing line between critics who were heterosexual and those who were gay. In fact, the only four reviewers who applauded – Michael Billington of the *Guardian*, Sheridan Morley of *Punch*, Benedict Nightingale of the *New Statesman* and Steve Grant of *Time Out* – were all heterosexual. 'The *Financial Times* and the *Sunday Telegraph* were vituperative,' Sherman rightly recollects. And he was glad that both *The Times* and *Sunday Times* were then not being published. But both Irving Wardle of *The Times* and James Fenton of the *Sunday Times* subsequently made clear their dislike of the play.[12]

Michael Coveney, the theatre critic of the *Financial Times*, voiced an unease that was not untypical. 'It', he wrote of the play, 'prompts discussion as to how to re-enact terrible aberrations of history without celebrating them.' *Bent* was

> less memorable for its writing than for its sensationalism
> ... Wolf's throat being cut, as the storm-troopers burst
> in to purge the city of homosexuals; Max beating the
> dancer to death in order to survive; Max's account of
> how he gained a yellow star instead of a pink triangle
> ... by committing an act of necrophilia ... the grizzly
> electrocution at the end.[13]

The *Daily Telegraph*'s John Barber also accused Sherman of a 'sensationalism' but of a different sort. *'Bent'*, he asserted,

> seeks to glamorise homosexual love by presenting it as coming to valiant birth amidst the most succulent horrors in recent history. I admit that the play packs a thrilling punch, but it seems to argue that being a homo is all right because it [homosexuality? Love?] blossomed even in Hitler's torture chambers. The torture chambers are too hideously alive in the century's experience to be used to promote any sort of thrill.[14]

The charges relate to sensationalism and glamorisation. The simulation of violence upon the modern English stage had only twice in the last quarter of a century inspired a greater outburst of criticism. The stoning to death of a baby in Edward Bond's *Saved* provoked the critic J.W. Lambert, in the *Sunday Times*, to declare that the bounds of seemliness had been rudely breached.[15] In 1975 when Howard Brenton's *The Romans in Britain* was presented at the National Theatre, with a scene of simulated homosexual rape, a private prosecution by Mrs Mary Whitehouse charged the play's director, Michael Bogdanov, with conspiracy to procure an act of gross indecency. Both these reactions suggest that it is likely that there will be condemnatory responses to simulated violence on stage where that violence occurs in modern theatrical writing, but not to classic texts where violence is contained within a formal or poetic diction.

The critics' unease was very strange indeed. Coveney characterised as sensational a reminiscence of being forced to take part in necrophilia; a throat-cutting which was most briefly suggested, and an electrocution scene necessarily mimed. They are all brief enactments, whose horrors were stringently minimised. They are presented in the course of a play otherwise lacking in violent or sensational incident. They occur within a violent context. They are scrupulously related to the circumstances in which they occur, and the incidents are thematically and dramatically integral.

Barber's objections are difficult to follow. How many people would argue that homosexual love achieved in a concentration camp is glamorous? Those who abominate homosexuals – and neither Coveney nor Barber are thought to be anti-gay – might find a grim appropriateness in gay love consigned to such a place and blossoming in such hideous circumstances. Both critics seem to object to a process by which homosexuals are subjected to extreme suffering and achieve a kind of superlative fortitude and transcendence, though such bravery was not, in fact, uncommon.

Further, the so-called 'sensationalism' of Sherman's play palls into insignificance when compared with the actual atrocities inflicted upon homosexual men in the camps. Plant unearths evidence from former inmates that men wearing the pink triangles were to be placed in the lowest of all concentration-camp categories. Eugen Kogon, a political prisoner who was in Buchenwald for six years, came out alive and wrote *The Theory and Practice of Hell*, stressing the particularly horrific experiences of homosexual men.[16]

Sherman was also dispelling a myth that the Nazis were homosexual, almost to a man. Philip Osment, one of Gay Sweatshop's actors at the time, recalls friends saying to him 'Weren't most of the Nazis gay anyway?'.[17] The Night of the Long Knives, when Hitler purged all those known to be homosexual from Ernst Röhm's brownshirts and killed the homosexual Röhm, formed little part of the general English consciousness. But the homosexual SS guard or the Brownshirt had become a familiar film stereotype.

The response to the play was so strong and enthusiastic that a transfer was considered. The Society of West End Theatres, which represents the interests of those who control the commercial playhouses and present plays in them, is a notoriously reclusive and clublike organisation. There is no doubt that several of the senior members of SWET were unwilling to make their theatres available to Kulukundis for *Bent*. Doors were closed. But Thelma Holt, who then ran the Round House, the converted Victorian engine shed in north London, was determined that the play should not die with its Royal Court season. She offered a run at the Round House. Even as the deal was being discussed Eddie Kulukundis arrived in high delight: 'We've got a theatre,' he said. Ian Albery had offered the Criterion, but it was not the ideal place since another show was already booked for December 1979. *Bent* had to give way to Neil Simon's

The Last of the Red Hot Mommas. Nowhere else was available.[18]

With the commercial excitement generated by *Bent* in London, it was not hard to set up a production on Broadway. The play by then was hot property. Everyone said that the Broadway director Bob Ackermann would never persuade Richard Gere to take McKellen's role. 'He read it in a day and said yes,' Sherman recalls. 'But he was straight, so it was easier for him than it was for McKellen.' And Broadway, given what it wanted – a star in his celluloid prime – flocked for months. American critics quite lacked the reservations of their British counterparts. Walter Kerr, whose Catholicism, Sherman believed, would preclude any favourable response to the play, turned out to be Broadway's chief champion of it.

Julian Mitchell's *Another Country*, set in the same decade as *Bent*, but staged within the confines of an English public school, offered an analogous struggle towards homosexual identity. Of course, homosexuals in the England of the 1930s, although liable to prosecution and blackmail, existed in infinitely better circumstances than those who ended up in concentration camps. But Mitchell, like Sherman, suggests that sexual identity is affected by social context. In *Another Country* the figure of the homosexual spy and traitor, demonised in the 1950s, is depicted as the willed creation of a Britain that treated homosexuals as an underclass. The remarkable commercial success of *Another Country* may owe something to its milieu, the 1930s upper-class public school of the sort with which West End audiences were still fondly familiar. Yet the play could not easily find a theatre or a producer. It was thought to be too immersed in the rituals and rites of the public school to appeal to the Royal Court or any of the other principal subsidised theatres. And it only found a place at a most unfashionable playhouse, the Greenwich Theatre, with only one well-known player, Rupert Everett, who took the principal role.

The bonfire-night première in November 1981 was, however, greeted by the national newspaper critics in approving terms that suggested Mitchell was exploiting the old familiar trappings of the public school for fiery accusations against the values that they transmitted and instilled. Jack Tinker, a reliable early-warning system for the kind of play that would draw conventional middle-brow readers of the *Daily Mail* readership, and a critic often subtly at variance with the paper's editorial stance, captured the essence of *Another Country*'s appeal. The fact that Anthony Blunt, Keeper of the Queen's pictures, had recently been exposed as a Soviet agent of the 1930s also imparted a stinging contemporaneity to the play, even if its young heterosexual Marxist seemed close to amiable carica-ture. 'Julian Mitchell', Tinker wrote, 'persuasively examines the seeds of tribal snobberies sown in the pre-war hey-day of the British public school and repeated in a harvest of spy scandals in top places . . . a fiendish picture of the establishment in embryo'.[19]

The clear if implicit inspiration for Mitchell's play was the homosexual diplomat Guy Burgess, here named Bennett, who spied for Russia and defected in 1951. By creating this semi-fictional character, Mitchell was able to achieve an imaginative reconstruction of the kind of motives that might have inspired English men of Burgess's generation into betrayal. Guy Bennett, branded as a life outcast because of his homosexuality, decides in retaliation to take revenge upon his school, his class, his country.

Mitchell does not, however, seek by Bennett's example, to make homosexuality facilely synonymous with treachery and espionage. The play is neither simplistic nor determinist. A specific conjunction of circumstances – Bennett's sexual orien-tation, the cultural and social orthodoxies of upper-middle-class England in the 1930s, and sheer chance – all combine and conspire to persuade Bennett into his choice of espionage as a career. Only when he comes to realise his homosexuality and to appreciate that his desires are not the transient passions of adolescence in a sexually segregated school, does he make his political decision. His plan to become a secret agent is not the result of any sudden access of Marxist sympathy or visionary recognition of Communism's socio-political legitimacy. In dis-covering his sexual identity he does not undergo any authentic political conversion. For Bennett, Marxist-Leninism may have been simply the way of paying back and punishing Britain for what it did to him. The real Guy Burgess, by contrast, insisted that he kept his Marxist-Leninist faith even while he hankered for those English things and experiences of which he had been deprived by his defection to Russia.

Mitchell prefaces his play with Cyril Connolly's famous assertion in *The Enemies of Promise* that public schoolboys' experience of the 'glories and disappointments' of these institutions comes 'to dominate their lives and to arrest their development'. It follows, Connolly argues, 'that the greater part of the ruling class remains adolescent, school-minded, cowardly, sentimental and in the last analysis homosexual'.[20] Mitchell's analysis relates to Connolly's, since he shows the public school observing the codes of sexual hypocrisy of the outer world where appearance is rated far more significant than reality. And it is that hypocrisy which Bennett will not, and Burgess did not, accept.

So the school's values are typical of the English ruling class that these adolescents will soon become. The point is stressed in the play's closing scene where Bennett condemns Martineau, the schoolboy who had hanged himself after being caught by a schoolmaster in a position of gay abandon. 'He was just the sort of pathetic dope who'd've got caught the whole time. Spent his life in prison, being sent down every few months by magistrates called Barclay and Delahay,' he says, alluding by name to the Head of House and a member of Twenty Two, the school's high-peak society (2.vi.95). The prefects and the élite of the Twenty Two are the heirs-in-waiting to privilege, poised to step into the magic circle. Homosexuals like Guy are forever outside it.

Martineau's suicide precipitates a chain reaction, a series of responses, stratagems and realisations which terminate with Bennett's decision to become a spy. First, the prefectorial reaction to Martineau's suicide reveals discrepant attitudes to schoolboy homosexuality. It is either 'immorality' to be beaten out of boys by prefects or a familiar school happening that you must take care to practise out of sight (1.ii.27). The prying eyes of those entrusted with moral surveillance are always on the look out. Delahay, the Games Captain, represents this pragmatic form of morality. School rules are there to be flouted if you can; otherwise, 'watch out' (1.iii.34).

Bennett, however, manifests an exceptional attitude to this sexual behaviour. 'Everyone gives in in the end,' he insists, 'if only out of boredom or loneliness' (1.iii.35). It is mere recreational relief. But his attitude is in combative contrast to the prevailing behaviour. Many of Mitchell's schoolboys have succumbed or do succumb to gay activity, but do not regard the subject as 'something people should talk about' (2.i.52). Bennett, refusing to conform sexually, still wants the school's marks of status as a preliminary to some brilliant diplomatic career. But his disregard for orthodoxy sabotages his grand advance. He may be able to trade in public-school blackmail but in the end sexual desire and performance catch him fatally out. What he says – and both Rupert Everett and Daniel Day Lewis made this speech the angry heart of the play's matter – imparts a late-twentieth-century consciousness to 1930s man. This *cri de cœur* also echoes distantly from Ibsen, and from Williams's conception of a new 'structure of feeling', though not precisely in his terms: Bennett does not assert the primacy of the individual will. In his case, an unexceptional man courageously revolts against the common condition. 'I'm sick of pretending,' he says, 'I'm never going to love women' (2.v.93), 'All this acting up – making a joke of it even to myself – it was only a way or trying to pretend it wasn't true' (2.vi.94).

The form of the Bennett revolt is private, self-related: the public school has already provided Guy with ideal training in the arts of dissimulation. 'You can't beat a good public school for learning to conceal your true feelings,' Bennett notes (2.ii.77). And from this shrewd belief springs his plan by which he will appear as the flamboyantly unconventional diplomat – 'Let them think what they like – let them despise you,' – but be the hoodwinking betrayer (2.vi.99).

In the 1950s, the homosexual was reckoned a security risk because his temperament was stereotyped as 'emotionally unstable'. Bennett/Burgess sets out to destabilise a society that refuses to admit that he could ever be stable. If it is an immature or emotional act, then he has been conditioned into it. He is a product of his times and its sexual orthodoxy. The veteran critic, John Barber, in the *Daily Telegraph*, appreciated the point, seeing 'a play which ... showed how admirably a great public school may prepare a boy for life and in some cases, how disastrously'.[21] *Daily Telegraph* readers would as a result of this judgement have their prejudices confirmed. But Barber's own liberality and his perception of Mitchell's intention sneak through at the end: 'In adopting his friend's communism he can be true to his [Bennett's] nature and fight a bigoted society from within.'

When Hugh Whitemore's *Breaking the Code* was first staged, at the Haymarket theatre in London in 1986, the gay writer and critic Adam Mars-Jones wrote, perhaps with a touch of condescension, that it was not easy to claim the play's hero, Alan Turing, as 'a gay martyr'.[22] Ordinary martyrs refuse to renounce Christian faith and take the ultimate penalty for so refusing. But in the sense that Turing preferred to take his life, or probably did so, rather than accept surveillance of his homosexual behaviour and restrictions upon it, he does seem a kind of martyr. That is not Whitemore's point.

At first, it looks as if the simplest of theatrical messages is being conveyed. The title refers neatly to the way in which Turing both cracked the Germans' Enigma coding of the Second World War and broke the primary code of refusing to live conventionally. Whitemore, in theatrically reconstructing the life of Turing, inspired by a reading of Andrew Hodges' biography – 'one of the most remarkable books and accounts of a life which I've ever read' – created a play involving a highly critical revaluation of the social and legal pressures upon homosexual life in the immediate post-war decades.[23] But he does something more, and not from a gay perspective or from a post-Gay Liberation consciousness. Whitemore interprets Turing as a child of his time, his personality shaped and limited by the fierce codes of British orthodoxy in which he was reared. And he sees the malign impact of that orthodoxy affecting not only homosexuals but heterosexuals as well.

> I think Turing stopped growing emotionally at the age of 14. His tragedy was his inability to make adult sexual relationships. It happened, it happens all the time with heterosexual men as well, but heterosexuals can slip into a social slot and not be put under the microscope. Family life covers things and binds people together.

The sexually orthodox, Whitemore suggests, may conceal what he analyses as a peculiarly British, and essentially male, form of developmental arrest.

It's much easier to be heterosexual. I think – I don't know – I would imagine that there are many unsatisfactory heterosexual marriages where the emotional problem which afflicted Turing – the problem of not being dragged out of adolescence – becomes absorbed by marriage and kids. The social and family structure becomes immense.

Further, Whitemore depicts Turing as a man flawed 'by a Jungian gap between thinking and feeling. Half of his tragedy – and it applies to both heterosexuals and homosexuals – was that he was driven by his sexual energies; but could not relate them to his intellectual life.' Mars-Jones's shrewd review sensed that: 'Turing's sex life was mechanical rather than passionate . . . Sex was part of Turing's disconnection not his antidote to it.' The mechanical, affectionate but detached nature of Turing's sexuality, as the play reveals it with pick-ups was, Whitemore believes, a symptom of his sexually and emotionally inhibited personality: 'I'm 54. When I was a teenager in the late 1940s and 1950s there was a sexual repression of a strong sort – no matter what you were. It was something to be ashamed and frightened of.'

So Whitemore sees himself and Turing as similar casualties of the period, emotionally held in adolescence. But Turing's child-like lack of sophistication had devastating repercussions, of the sort that would not affect a heterosexual in the England of the 1980s. Robbed by one of his pick-ups, he implicates himself sexually and sets in train a series of events that will lead him to court. There is more to this than impetuous lack of sophistication. Turing refuses to accept the codes of conformity. At Bletchley during the Second World War, he transgresses the class boundaries by becoming involved with 'a pretty young [male] engineer' (2.ii.52). Worse, he refuses to conceal the signs of this attachment. The heterosexual majority suffer, he is told, 'Fear . . . anger . . . pain . . . real pain', when they are forcibly made aware of homosexuality. 'Compromises have to be reached,' he is warned. 'I b-b-beg to differ,' Turing retorts (2.ii.54 and 55).

This begging to differ emerges as a foolish form of heroism, an obstinate refusing to bow to the pressures imposed upon him. Even when sentenced to a course of hormone treatment – that useless, dangerous and inhumane treatment imposed in the law courts of 1950s to abate gay desires – Turing suffers manfully and without complaint. 'Nobody seems to know whether or not I'll have to wear a b-b-bra' (2.v.66) It is not so much in breaking the heterosexual code that Turing shows his implacable courage, but in his insistence that he will not pretend to conform in the 1950s style. 'In the long run, all things considered, it's not breaking the code that matters,' he says, 'It's where you go from there' (2.vii.78).

The one important defect of Whitemore's play is its failure to establish a strong sense of those witch-hunting Cold War times. But even so, there is no missing the play's inference that it was the close surveillance under which Turing was placed, with the intelligence services aspiring to limit his sexual freedom, that may have precipitated suicide. Furthermore, Whitemore leaves a lurking doubt that it may have been the intelligence services, fearful that Turing would betray state secrets to a sexual partner, who arranged Turing's death to look like suicide. In either instance, his death, in the powerful consummation of *Breaking the Code*, was precipitated by his refusal to compromise his sexual identity. There is also an underlying intellectual and sexual pathos in the play's subsidiary account of Turing's search for some abstract form of intelligence, existing in detachment from those desires or the senses: the quest is like a metaphor for Turing's need, not his wish, to escape the consequences of erotic desires he would neither disown nor deny. It was a quest engaged with recklessness, endured with bravery. Frank Rich, the *New York Times*'s critic exactly caught the significance of this process: 'When the story of a badgered non-conformist is told as a tale of proud self-assertion rather than maudlin self-pity one finds not a saintly victim, but a stirring hero, at centre stage.'[24]

IDENTITY FOUND

In his study of Joe Orton, Simon Shepherd suggests that homosexuals of the 1950s were schooled to discipline their desires 'to conform to the dominant marriage-based codes of sexual behaviour' or not to have sexual relations at all. And 'the status of blackmail as a homosexual nightmare . . . gave force to the notion that homosexual desire is always in tension with, always threatening to subvert one's moral and social status.'[25] This state of precariousness to which Shepherd alludes shows the extent to which homosexual identity in the 1950s was commensurate with chronic insecurity.

Shepherd, however, exaggerates the sense in which the homosexual of the 1950s was encouraged into 'marriage-based' relationships. For the chief concern then was to cure the world of homosexuality completely, not to channel it into any marriage-imitative forms. 'Almost every homosexual would benefit from some form of psychotherapy', Gordon Westwood advised in a 1952 guide to homosexuality. For homosexuality, being 'a disorder of the mind', required long analytical psychotherapy. But while Westwood could reveal 'there are many cases on record where successful cures have been made,' there were many for whom there was 'little hope'.[26]

Twenty years later, with homosexuality redefined and its forms no longer universally taken as either sickness or abberation, the stage began to produce plays that no longer dealt with the crisis and problems of gay desiring. But how were gay men, freed from primary modes of repression, to relate to each other? It came as no surprise that the most popular play on either side of the Atlantic which dealt with the subject, and to which we will return in this chapter, should be Harvey Fierstein's *Torch Song Trilogy* (Plate 7). Fierstein's hero wants what every mother wants for her boy – a happy marriage and children. Here, however, the hero is a drag queen who wants marriage to a man. He wishes to homosexualise the heterosexual marriage. There were other, less conservative, aspirations but these tended to be suggestions insufficiently popular to reach the commercial stage.

Coming Clean, Kevin Elyot's award-winning play on the fringe, at the Bush Theatre in 1982, mirrors the new conflict sharply. It juxtaposes the domestic and emotional aspirations of two young male lovers, living together, but wanting clean different things from their relationship. Greg and Tony proclaim themselves as models of the new gay freedom. Both men have one-night stands, away from home, while preserving their sexual relationship intact. 'The prospect of a new body's always exciting,' Tony says as if he were an advertising agent for Gay Promiscuity (1.15). When Robert, a young out-of-work actor, arrives to clean their home, it is not long before he ends up in secret sexual combination with Greg, who aspires to maintain relations with both men.

I remember, at the first night, that frisson of excitement streaked with embarrassment, during the scene when Tony arrives home unexpectedly and only just misses finding Robert with his legs in the air. Tony's discovery that Greg has a new sexual commitment rends the stable gay relationship asunder. Home truths come home to roost. 'I want you for myself,' Tony proclaims to a bewildered Greg, who asks 'Why have you suddenly decided you're not in a mood for sharing? We've shared each other around half the gay scene in London' (6.61–2). But while Greg is representative of those gay men who wish for sexual variety, Tony does not. Their happiness has been founded upon Tony's deception. He has played the game of promiscuity. 'The only thing I've ever wanted is to be with you,' he says, 'Every time I knew you were with a trick I felt sick ... I'm tired of all the bars and clubs, tired of looking around, of competing, pretending I need other men, when all I want is you' (6; 63). Since Greg has vetoed such romantic and sexual single-mindedness, Tony has tolerated his lover's one-night stands, on the grounds that they pose no threat to their domestic existence. The dilemma is at once complicated and simplified by the fact that the men's sexual relationship is rigidly defined, with Tony the sexually passive partner and Greg solely active. The relationship will only survive if Tony abandons his conception of their relationship as a variant of a very free heterosexual marriage. But the play manages a quasi-optimistic resolution, when Tony blissfully succumbs to a one-night stand, as if at last he were settling down to enjoy casual sex as a necessary component of his relationship with Greg.

Greg, never described in the stage directions, emerged in Pip Donaghy's performance at the Bush Theatre as the thoroughly modern clone, the epitome of the masculine homosexual. Mustachioed and unemotional, withdrawn and assertive, he represents the subculture's metropolitan gay man who will not model his life upon heterosexual counterparts, but wishes to exploit the freedom his gayness offers. The modes of the 1950s and 1960s, when posing as heterosexual, have been exchanged with new, confident signifiers of homosexuality.

The couple's friend, William, has a sexual problem that runs in counterpoint to theirs. He cruises endlessly through the bars searching for his ideal sex-object, but always lights upon caricatures of masculinity. 'Big, hairy, brutal, verging upon the psychopathic. Just your type,' says Tony of William's latest sex partner (1.11). But these superficial signs, which lead William to imagine that they are emblems of a rough, tough version of masculinity, turn out to be intentionally misleading.

> All those monosyllabic grunts he breathed down my ear in the club soon disappeared when we were sat in the taxi. Crystal-clear enunciation – Oxford English . . . He went on and on about some opera or other . . . I expected him to talk about lorry-driving or hod-carrying or oil-rigs . . . I thought I'd tricked with Steve McQueen, but I ended up with a leather-clad Richard Baker.
>
> (1.11).

The new homosexual iconography may mislead as well as illuminate. But the wit is traditionally sharp.

William appears, bloodied and beaten, in the midst of the play, having succumbed to a man in leather who proves to be rougher and more dangerous than his emblems and demeanour suggest. *Coming Clean*, therefore, argues against those depending for their sense of gay identity and security upon commitment to sexual partners who seem, just seem, to embody erotic or romantic fantasies. William and Tony, in their differing fashions, do just this and are in different ways harmed.

The most sensational depiction of a gay relationship to be staged in the liberation aftermath, and amidst the sabotaging of the myths about homosexuality, was also one of the earliest. This play also attempts to show a struggle to define and achieve gay identity. Charles Marowitz, a heterosexual director keen to take advantage of the freedoms gained through the termination of the Lord Chamberlain's control over the stage, presented John Hopkins's *Find Your Way Home* on the fringe, at the Open Space, in May 1970. It was one of the first plays I reviewed and, naïve and green, I, like the rest of the reviewers, failed to appreciate what was being suggested at the play's climax. Hopkins's diction, freed from the Lord Chamberlain's restraining blue pencil, introduced the language of homosex in a form we had never heard before. It was raw, it was rank, it was real. But neither this fact nor the play's sexual apology was discussed by reviewers – myself included. I can, in retrospect, only plead delayed innocence.

Find Your Way Home suggests, as a signal to the changed times, that a young homosexual masochist may find content in ritualised S&M, rather than in anonymous acts of humiliation. And the young man's history of sexual degradation is eventually identified as a sign of the way he has introjected society's contemptuous view of the likes of him. In view of the stigma attaching to sado-masochism it seems strange now that the play aroused so little condemnation or comment. But that may be because Hopkins concentrated upon the masochistic despair of one partner, only clearly showing, at the conclusion, that the young man's masochistic impulses might be satisfied by a sado-masochistic relationship with his married lover.

Some contemporary analysts argue now that sado-masochistic forms of sexual exchange are 'perfectly valid' methods of achieving individuation, that process by which inaccessible self-potential is realised in relationships. 'A person projects on to the partner and actively seeks in him or her, the unactualised or inadequately incarnated archetypical potential (masculine/feminine or dominance/submission) components of the self.'[27] But in 1970 such a perception was controversial and calculated to shock in a way that it is not today. Even today in the UK a 1990 Old Bailey judgment suggests that consent to homosexual sadomasochistic acts is no defence.

The play's title alludes metaphorically to the process that the two central characters undergo. A 47-year-old married man, Harrison, finally realises and affirms his true sexual identity, or is able to take advantage of new sexual freedoms. And his lover, Weston, achieves an analogous coming home, when the bisexual older man decides to come to live with him. There were instant sexual shock-waves from the very first scene. The form in which Weston addressed last night's one-night stand the morning after was like a lightning flash in the auditorium: 'You think I'm going to let you fuck me? I mean – now? What are you, some sort of raving sex maniac! I wouldn't let you fuck me – as long as you live – you'll never, ever, ever, ever – get into me again . . . Do you want to know about last night . . . Truthfully I've had fellas make you look like a girl' (1.15). Crude, taunting, vehement and cruel, this sex-speak introduced a characteristic gay diction of the metropolitan subculture that had emerged in the 1960s. The furtive discretion of the gentlemanly clubs of the 1950s had given way to the more uninhibited discotheques and pubs of the new decade. Peter Wildeblood had described the homosexual meeting places in 1950s London as 'extraordinarily quiet and well behaved . . . most of the men did not go there primarily to drink, but to relax in an atmosphere where it was not necessary to keep up pretences.'[28] You could almost hear a tie-pin dropped or a cravate removed.

The passing of the 1967 Act 'did nothing to eliminate the hard core of bigotry and hatred', but it at least allowed for a freer socialising of gay men, in places which did not have to maintain themselves in a total, furtive anonymity.[29] Weston, as a beneficiary of these changed times, is free to be screwed liberally and lavishly. But the sexual freedom, it transpires, has turned out to be imprisoning. Weston, both hard-bitten in the sexual war and a lost romantic, is all dead-pan self-mockery. 'My main preoccupation', he explains, 'is waiting for Mr Right to come along – riding his great, white charger, wearing his silver, shining armour – and waving his ten foot lance in my direction' (1; 23). He mocks his own romanticism. The masochistic tendency is a response to it. Masochism, suggests Erich Fromm, cannot be simply understood in terms of physical action. It is, he says, a 'passive form of attachment' in a 'symbiotic union' where the 'masochistic person escapes from the unbearable feeling of isolation and separateness, by making himself part and parcel of another person who directs him'. When sexual desire is involved in the process 'the person . . . makes himself the instrument of somebody or something outside himself . . . he is not yet fully born.'[30]

Weston has gone in for a form of hectic gay abandon that involves just such a masochism – an unrelenting quest for sexual pain and submission. 'I've been fucked . . . in dirty lavatories – by men who would just as soon fuck sheep . . . I've been spread across tables in transport cafes . . . fucked in the dark by frightened little men,' he confesses (1.43–4). The romantic longing is assuaged by the sexual action which is a parody of the action for which he longs and of which he is ashamed.

There is potential for change, a chance of being 'born'. Weston, true to masochistic type, has relished the sweet painfulness of relationship with a married, and thus often absent, man. It is only when Harrison, at last committed to a new life, is read extracts from Weston's secret diary that he becomes aware of his lover's sexual animus. 'I want to hurt you,' Harrison remarks at the end of the play, having taken to heart and mind the messages gleaned from the diaries. 'Please don't hurt me more than you have to,' Weston replies (2.91). This ritual-request signals the new form of their relationship. They may each be discovering hard-won gay identities, literally through pain and suffering.

In the 1950s when doctors, sociologists, judges and clerics were busily defining homosexuality as analogous to 'heroin addiction', 'a proselytising religion' for a 'secret society of addicts' and 'corroding practices', the homosexual was presumed to fester luridly in twilight haunts.[31] Homosexuals, according to an influential sociologist, rejected not only the sexual code but moral and ethical values as well. Accordingly, most levels of homosexual society were 'sordid if not frankly anti-social'. The best-known, most-eagerly anatomised figure in this sordid underworld was the male prostitute. 'They despise the people who pay for the lease of their bodies and do not enjoy sexual relations outside their professional activities any more than a road sweeper would enjoy sweeping the road without payment,' this sociologist of the London streets remarked.[32] Twenty years later in 1974 when the book *Streetboy, Swinging London* was subject to obscenity charges at the Old Bailey, I vividly remember, while reporting the proceedings, that Counsel for the Prosecution turned gravely to the jury and referred in hushed tones to real-life male prostitutes. In the end they became, he said, 'diseased, perverted, rotten, little chaps'.[33]

Michael Wilcox's *Rents* provides a radically different perspective, from a gay vantage point. He rescues rent boys from the grand status they had been accorded for decades and strips them down to size, giving them a new identity; he frees them from guilt, as he does homosexuality from moral obloquy. The amateur rent boy of the Edinburgh 1970s emerges, in terms neither sentimental nor glamorising, as a student speculator no more dangerously on the make than an average city financier or property dealer. He fulfils a not very enviable role with jaunty, comic aplomb. Unlike the financier he cannot be accused of making huge profits, at least not in Edinburgh. Wilcox's portrait is partial, but never misses out on the danger and wretchedness. *Rents* also makes a useful point of comparison with *Find Your Way Home*. It suggests the extent of the social and sexual changes forced in the 1970s. Now the boys are more truly in bands than bondage. The glum, gay rhetoric of self-pity and suffering has been discarded. The shabby, bed-sitting room still plays host to young gay men, but there is no longer pervasive despair. And *Rents*'s progress from the Traverse Theatre in 1979, to the Lyric Studio in 1982, and finally to the Lyric's main house in 1984, indicates its growing popularity.

Wilcox's play also marks a zenith of gay self-confidence, described through the lives of Phil and Robert, two impecunious, gay youths, growing up in the later 1970s. The chaps, who supplement their meagre incomes as drama student and shop assistant, are not traditional male prostitutes, furtively on the game. They look upon their middle-class clients, and at the rent-boy business, with jovial cynicism and mockery. Wilcox has organised a rare sexual comedy of manners as he observes the reactions of these needy, put-upon boys who treat their smitten clients to the kind of frankness that the desirable can afford in face of the unattractive desirer.

'Am I boring you?', Thomas the schoolmaster asks, pausing in the midst of post-coital, autobiographical prattle to Robert. 'Tremendously', replies the youth, who has had his fill of the 'theatrical wankers' he services. 'They're all into themselves. They try and talk all posh and intellectual as though they're where it's at . . . but underneath you get the feeling their Y fronts could do with a good wash' (1.13). Façades are recognised as mere façades. Wilcox does nothing to sentimentalise the boys' part-time occupation. Violence, actual and threatened, comes their way. Both young men keep a medicine cupboard, stocked with those armaments against the sexual ailments to which their rent-boy lives make them heir-apparent and heir-frequent. Venereal infections creep up upon the back and front parts of one of them. For both of them sex is routine transaction and commodity, whose infinite variety and excitement has palled through too much trading and insider-dealing.

Guilt and despair are believably absent. The youths are free-lance fantasists, locked in a mutually dependent and no-longer sexual relationship. In the end, Robert escapes in search of a new beginning which will surely fail to occur. Each of them is seeking after male fantasy figures and gay romance. 'I need a man, a real man ... Oh Scotland where has your virility trickled?' Phil asks in the play's opening scene. 'What I want is a worker hot from the production line ... with a day's sweat on him ... I need a Scot, bright-eyed from an oil rig ... a boilermaker ... The best I've done this week was Malcolm from the Golden Wonder factory' (1.7). Gay romance never quite arrives since it is based upon fantasy. That is the crucial point.

All that Robert can achieve is the dogged devotion of a middle-aged lecturer, who comes from an earlier gay generation in whom guilt has been inculcated. He is unassertive, reticent, polite and soft. The lecturer retreats to his music, the certain source of pleasure and reward. His sexual identity has never been established at all. The boys, relatively secure in their gay sexuality, are victims of hard economic times. The gulf between the gay generations yawns, between the shame of the 1950s and the self-assertion of the 1970s.

That sense of self-assertion was apparent when Harvey Fierstein's *Torch Song Trilogy* arrived on Broadway in the summer of 1982, three years after it had begun its existence in off-off-Broadway life at La Mama. There, across the space of four highly theatrical hours, was a Jewish drag queen, penetrated by chance in a backroom bar, but far keener to settle for marriage to a tall and lean male sex-object. But by the time the *Torch Song Trilogy* reached the London stage in 1985, weighed down by awards, Fierstein's manipulation of the supposedly outrageous subject had come to seem highly manipulative of his audiences.

The London critics tended to a grand disdain: 'Rather like Neil Simon written by Barbara Cartland'; 'The typical romantic comedy imported from Broadway'; 'a plot straight out of any Mills and Boon novel'.[34] Their patronising hauteur was in a sense justified. For the *Trilogy* does trade on sentimental fantasy; and by its insistent proclamation that gay men simply want a gay marriage and children, Fierstein tries to suggest that the variety of homosexual wishes and desires can be subsumed within heterosexual forms. That is a highly conservative theory of gay identity. But two critics did catch the significant aspect of the play. 'Arnold's wish to be an adoptive parent is largely pie in the sky', Jim Hiley wrote in The *Listener*. 'In most parts of America like the rest of the world, gays are kept away from children including their own.' 'It shows what courage it takes', John Barber judged in the *Daily Telegraph* 'to be true to your chromosal [sic] nature in a society sometimes violently alienated against you.'[35]

Hiley's analysis and Barber's reference to courage and truth suggest the surviving, intermittent vitality of Fierstein's wistful gay romance. In constructing or trying to construct his gay identity (and however conservative it may be), Fierstein's drag queen is still a daring and derided outsider, trying and finally managing to achieve his own heterodox, grand design. The happy ending, the triumph of the outsider, up against it, made the *Torch Song Trilogy* the first popular drama about homosexuality. The romantic triumphalism is overwhelming, a gay fairy-tale for the theatre. Not only is Arnold a professional drag queen, he has also so strongly identified with his mother that he wants to be a mummy himself. His instincts are maternal rather than paternal. He has a mother complex *par excellence*. In a style as dream-possessed as the most escapist Hollywood movie, Arnold ends up as a mother-figure to the gay adolescent with whom he has been entrusted by the local welfare department, and who even calls him 'Ma'. That is not all. His long-lost bisexual lover returns from the world of heterosexuality to claim Arnold as lover.

This is a highly American process, dependent upon American support for the individual's battle against the odds, with happiness won through struggle and self-belief. Arnold, fat and sensitive, has only his wit and his courage going for him. He's a game underdog. His stereotypical feminine tendencies, however, run in tandem with some stereotypical masculine ones. He has sufficient fighting spirit to go for what he wants. He is not afraid to make an ample fool of himself. He has the resilience to struggle alone for years, though Fierstein strangely does not depict this crucial sequence. In short, the play marks the homosexualising of the American dream of hard-won success.

But what has it to say about gay identity? Fierstein's aspiration is to emphasise gay affinities with heterosexuals rather than differences. The quest for identity is almost entirely conducted in a fairyland where Arnold is construed both as a plump, neurotic drag queen and as an *homme fatale*. The most attractive men fell for him mightily. At some New York gay bar, he attracts the attentions of Ed Reiss, a bisexual schoolteacher who is described in the introduction as 'very handsome, masculine, with a boyish charm, all in one, and at the age of 34' (1.3).

In the second play the signs of Arnold's sexual success have become even greater. He has graduated from Ed to Alan, a 'shamefully beautiful' male model, equipped with blond hair and blue eyes, and aged just 18. The relationship is passionately erotic, forever perfect, and satisfies Arnold's maternal aspirations. 'Get your fat ass out of bed and get me something to eat' are Alan's first commanding words (2.26). He is 18 going on 8, enabling Arnold to be mummy to him. 'Come on, what frightened you?' asks Arnold, taking the boy in his arms (2.27).

Since this pair of blissful lovers is unbelievably visiting the home of Ed and his girlfriend Laura, the opportunity occurs for Alan to talk with his host about the man they have both had, Arnold Beckoff himself. Alan recollects that the first time he saw his beloved drag queen was from a recumbent vantage point, when he was lying on a table in a lower-east-side bar, with a knife wielded by a black man, held inches away from his neck: 'A beautiful, not like pretty beautiful, but like mountain beautiful', woman cut her way through the crowd to save him. 'She put her hand out to the black guy . . . and he just handed over the knife and disappeared' (2; 39). Magic of course. The point of this anecdote is not to suggest that Arnold can manifest supposedly masculine courage and potency, when dressed as a majestic woman, but that he is considered beautiful and powerful through force of personality. Arnold is, in fact, Fierstein's projection of a gay myth, in which femininity, overwhelming sexual appeal, physical presence and maternal compassion are all fused in one drag queen. The character does not have to search for gay identity. The character is a wet-dream of desirability. Just as in pornography desirable people achieve perfect, endless feats of orgasmic ingenuity, so Arnold moves through life overwhelming men who want him as a sex-object or as mother-figure. He hardly belongs in real life.

In the final part of the *Trilogy*, *Widows and Children First*, the elements of fantasy fuse to achieve the happy ending. Arnold has helped his gay foster-son, David, to achieve 'a positive attitude to his homosexuality', and Ed has arrived stale from four years' marriage (3.73). Although Ed can scarcely accept his homosexual desires, he is quite prepared to accept Arnold's plan for the future, with David becoming their 'son' (3.iv.80). David, of course, a gay problem adolescent, has miraculously adjusted. Thus by the end of the play Arnold has discovered his form of gay identity, although it has taken a fantasy to achieve it. Yet in his major, late speech of defiance, with its references to the death of his former lover, murdered by gaybashers, and its claims to self-sufficiency, Arnold does acquire a certain pathos. Fantasy is overwhelming reality, but there is no missing a truth as well: 'You made fun of my crocheting before. You think it's a cute little effeminate thing to do,' he tells Mrs Beckoff.

> Let me tell you something: I have taught myself to sew, cook, fix plumbing, do taxes, build furniture . . . I can even pat myself on the back when necessary. I don't have to ask for anything. There is nothing I need from anyone except love and respect. And anyone who can't give me those two, has no place in my life.
>
> (3.iii.73)

Gay individualism has won out. The drag queen has recreated and extended himself. He is that cherished American thing – the man who fights to come through. As he speaks in anger to his mother the relationship with her is rent asunder; the spell which she holds over him is broken. She has lost her primacy, while retaining her dignity, and the mother-complex is overwhelmed. For Arnold has found himself. It is a moving, seductive process; I do not entirely believe in its truth.

Fierstein has created fantasy rather than recreated life. He seduces theatre audiences into accepting this gay young man as an admirable and amusing human being. You cannot fail to notice however, that Arnold's intellectual self is shrewd and developed, while his emotional self is adolescent and, therefore, retarded. The process by which he achieves a sort of maturity, and establishes his right to be different, involves suffering. We do not see this process, for, in the last analysis, in *Torch Song*

Trilogy fantasy leaves little room for the hard, complex facts of human interrelating.

In Fierstein's musical, *La Cage aux Folles*, two middle-aged male lovers, one of whom is a professional drag queen, are shown as a surrogate heterosexual couple. 'The musical', according to Robert Brustein, 'might have been a real break through had it been more honest about the range of homosexual lifestyles, instead of suggesting that these are merely differences of costume or manners.'[36] The spouse in *La Cage aux Folles*, 'who applies mascara, wears women's clothes and puts on high heels', is a man, but otherwise a perfect wife. To ensure that no offence is given to heterosexuals in the audience this couple do nothing more than gaze wistfully into each others eyes. They behave with all the decorum of a middle-aged heterosexual couple. Brustein implies that Fierstein's representations are 'pretty evasions' of what is 'the sometimes bleak truth'. He argues, therefore, against the idea that a gay identity can be achieved through adopting or professing the styles and manners of heterosexuals. He is right, though the Brustein view is clearly informed by the belief that gay life is inherently bleak and lonely. In so saying he speaks as an elderly man, whose views of homosexuals and homosexuality were shaped by the period and the place in which he grew up. Fierstein's fantasies are not required to show Brustein wrong. Liberation consciousness has effected changes, which accommodate fantasies, but are not ruled by them. A sense of gay identity has been achieved.

6

THE RETURN OF THE OUTCAST: 1981–1985

THE MESSAGE OF PLAGUES

In the winter of 1597 the plague broke out in Cranbrook, Kent. By the time one hundred and ninety people had succumbed to it, the Vicar of St Dunstan's church felt it his duty to explain the cause of the epidemic. Writing in the parish register, he blithely attributed the outbreak to divine judgement for the sinfulness of the people of Cranbrook, and particularly for 'that vice of drunkenness which did abound here'. Thieving and prostitution had also played their part in prompting retribution. Had not the plague made its first appearance in the home of a well-known thief and ended in the dwelling place of 'one Henry Grymocke, who was a pot companion, and his wife [who was] noted for much incontinency?', he asked. The plague had also advanced through the inns and 'victualling houses' of Cranbrook, which were 'places of great disorder'. God had simply chosen 'to punish that Himself which others did neglect and not regard'.[1]

In attributing the incidence of plague to nemesis the Vicar of St Dunstan's was invoking the ideology of the post-Reformation. It is just such a dogma of retribution that has been revived by some shapers of religious and political orthodoxy to explain the significance of the AIDS pandemic, nearly four hundred years later. AIDS is the first post-second-world-war, world-wide epidemic whose dissemination has been particularly attributed to some forms of biblically anathematised sexual intercourse. It has thus been exploited by those seeking to show a causal connection between biblical conceptions of sinfulness and supposed divine retribution. An editorial in the *Southern Medical*

175

Journal of 1984, deliberating upon the epidemic, shows up this method of imputing blame. 'Might we be witnessing, in fact, in the form of a modern communicable disorder, a fulfilment of St Paul's pronouncement "the due penalty of their error?"', the journal hopefully asked.[2]

Keith Thomas powerfully demonstrates, in *Religion and the Decline of Magic*, how 'all post-Reformation theologians taught that nothing would happen in this world without God's permission. If there was a common theme which ran through their writings it was the denial of the very possibility of chance or accident.'[3] Sickness, whether in individual cases or the outbreak of plague, was not believed to be caused by the vagaries of natural phenomena but by God's judgement. The epidemics of sexually transmitted disease in late-Elizabethan and Stuart England were attributed by surgeons to divine intervention. The late-Elizabethan William Clowes thus ascribed the spread of what was clearly a sexually transmitted disease to the 'notable testimonie of the just wrath of God'.[4]

In the late nineteenth century analogous religious and medical theories abounded. Sexually transmitted disease was interpreted 'as a symbol for a society characterised by a 'corrupt sexuality', and an emblem of 'a decaying social order'. One social historian, working in the mid-1980s, explains the process of blaming and scapegoating homosexuals very clearly: 'Because AIDS is perceived as an illness intrinsic to homosexuals, it can be interpreted as their just reward for flouting the law of God, and by extension, when it afflicts others, this can be explained by homosexual perfidy.'[5]

The reference to homosexual 'perfidy' is crucial. It refers, without elucidation, to the inveterate heterosexual fear of seduction by the homosexual. In the 1970s, while homosexual men could be seen as an isolated or self-detached series of pseudo-communities, they did not arouse that much direct hostility. But AIDS provoked a process of blaming. Bisexual males have formed one of those links between the principal sufferers from the virus and heterosexuals; drug-addicts, prostitutes, homosexuals and prisoners are the other supposed and revealed disseminators. Each of these constituencies is perceived as a component of a stigmatised and anti-social minority group: the dangerous Other. The scapegoating of homosexuals as the begetters of a gay plague has meant that this minority could be discerned as disseminators of a fatal syndrome. One psychologist has accordingly articulated a theory of general reaction to moral panics, which lead to a

taking up of absolutist positions ... the emergence of an imaginary solution – in tougher laws, moral isolation, a symbolic court action, followed by the subsidence of the anxiety, with its victims left to endure the new proscriptions, social climate or legal penalties.[6]

Simon Watney, in his study of the media treatment of AIDS, has extended this in his analysis. He argues that the pandemoniums engendered by the epidemic are the 'latest variation in the spectacle of the defensive ideological rear-guard action which has been mounted on behalf of "the family" for more than a century'. Newspapers habitually constructed 'an ideal audience of national family units, surrounded by the threatening spectacle of the mad, the foreign, the criminal and the perverted'.[7] Such commentary may be a little shrill, but it indicates the extent to which AIDS has been assigned a peculiar identity. The reaction to the epidemic and to gay men seems to be the expression of punitive anxiety, in which dread of both a fatal illness and its disseminators is expressed.

In America of the 1930s there was an analogous though less specific process of creating a dangerous Other: frequently cited figures suggested that one out of every ten Americans suffered from syphilis, but even though the infection could by then be substantially controlled, doctors still had to contend with 'syphilophobia', the equivalent of homophobia. So intense was the fear of syphilis that its infectious potency was grossly exaggerated. And city and state health departments passed legislation and ordinances stipulating that 'domestics and food-handlers' would have to be examined for sexually transmitted disease.[8]

Similarly in the response to AIDS, inveterate beliefs and mythic assumptions have been recalled to life. A moral text was cursorily but efficiently assembled, in which gay men by succumbing to forbidden desire were the authors of their own demise. A new right-wing constituency was created in America, assembled from groups constituted to defend The Family. It was gathered from Evangelicals and capitalists, business and corporation communities. The pro-family movement, opposed to abortion, to homosexuality and to contraception sought to characterise the new matrist-orientated America as cruel, impersonal and pleasure-prone, teetering towards anarchy. In this analysis homosexuality could be represented as a vibrant threat to the security of the family unit. AIDS, therefore, arrived to be absorbed into the matrix where homosexuality was created as an infectious disease.

The Christian right reacted to AIDS by pandering to panic, by constructing a series of new myths by which AIDS and homosexuals could be interpreted as direct and specific threats to heterosexuals. There are by now too many, and depressingly characteristic, examples of the way in which the HIV virus has falsely been credited with contagious potential. In Tulsa city officials 'drained a municipal swimming pool following a rental to a gay group in 1983 . . . a Florida hospital dumped a person with AIDS on an aeroplane with a one-way ticket to San Francisco, some medical personnel refused to work with AIDS patients.'[9] Many similar responses have been reported in Britain. Police raided a gay pub in London in December 1986, some of them wearing rubber gloves. Dan Air, the British-based airline, the *Daily Telegraph* reported on 3 February 1987, was to refuse to recruit men as cabin staff 'because it feared many would be homosexuals who would increase the risk of AIDS to passengers'.

Perhaps most significantly, Section 28 of the Local Government Act of 1988, which forbade local councils intentionally to promote homosexuality, was said to have been enacted to prevent the further activities of councils which attempted to 'glamorise' homosexuality.[10] The AIDS epidemic may have played a contributory role in bringing the Section to the statute book, but the mythic conceptions of homosexuality were what inspired right-wing parliamentarians. These theories are old and discredited: homosexual desire could be promoted, it was argued, since the adolescent and the child were vulnerable to sexual suggestion and eager sexually to experiment. By describing homosexuality in terms that were positive or permissive some might succumb to homosexual desires. Section 28 sought by implication to identify homosexuality as an activity or way of life that removed you from the family unit and general approval. The effect of the Section, as far as the arts are concerned, has been to create what the

Director of Gay Sweatshop, David Benedict, has described as a 'climate of confusion and fear'. Councils, he writes, have run scared of the Section, and drawn back from funding what might be termed homosexual works of art. Photography and exhibitions have been banned and theatre companies have lost bookings.[11]

There have been worse repercussions engendered by the New Fear. Once gay men had been stigmatised in the press, radio and television, by politicians and preachers, as the begetters and disseminators of a lethal virus, violent attacks upon homosexuals were theoretically condoned, and the incidence of violent attacks upon gay men increased in number both in Britain and America. The *Advocate* reported that, in August 1988 in New York, there were seventy-two reported cases of violence against gay men and lesbians, with two fatally injured. This was 'an all-time record' for such attacks. 'Last year we were more likely to see people struck or punched. This year we're getting more and more cases of physical assault with a real weapon, like a gun, a knife, a bat,' said David Wertheimer, director of the New York City Gay and Lesbian Anti-Violence Project.[12] In London in 1987 the Lesbian and Gay Rights Campaign reported that violent assaults on gay men in the capital had 'increased substantially in the past twelve months'.

Yet these ominous indicators do not mean that all the myths and fictions about homosexuals are being reconstructed. It would be a hard, long and complex business to suppress the signs of gay and lesbian community. The subcultural networks and political groups in America are contending with those forces of orthodoxy that intend to suppress the signs of gay identity. In this emergency plays about AIDS have acquired a more urgent definition, significance and aspiration. They have tried to fulfil that liberating and heterodox role to which Raymond Williams referred in his critique of Ibsen.[13] There are plays in which minority voices battle to fight an orthodoxy that regards AIDS as a mere local difficulty, principally affecting a reviled minority. It is a crucial business. It is a battle for life, and to persuade the orthodox majority to recognise that The Family inevitably includes homosexuals. The theatre, with its traditional elite audiences of persuaders and influences, has a potentially vital role.

TO BE RANKED AMONG THE NORMAL

Larry Kramer's *The Normal Heart* (Plate 8) emerges in this light as one of the most crucial recent plays written about homosexuality. It is an enraged alarm call both to the controlling heterosexual majority and to the gay community, whose political and sexual behaviour he condemns with a rare fury. But it is depressingly significant that the play's commercial success, in New York and in London, has depended principally upon the play's messenger rather than its message.

In New York in 1985 the play was presented with a succession of film stars – Brad Davis, Michael York and Joel Grey – in the principal role. And it was performed at Jo Papp's Public Theatre, which has values and functions remote from Broadway. In London, at the Royal Court in 1986, although the theatre's artistic director, Max Stafford-Clark, decided to do the play because of its social significance, the production was boosted by the decision of another American filmstar, Martin Sheen, to accept the leading role.

The advance for the play was twice as big as for any other play in the Court's history, Stafford-Clark says. 'That's what a star does.'[14] All of the performances were sold out, except for the mid-week matinées. But this burst of interest occurred after the announcement of Sheen's starring role. And when the play moved to the West End, to the Albery theatre, with a less well-known film star, Tom Hulce, the production did not last long.

Originally when Stafford-Clark saw the play in New York he was unimpressed. 'The melodramatic elements of the performance gave it a shallowness I did not like.' And when he returned to see the production four months later he liked it even less. 'The system in New York is rather like Edwardian theatre, the stage-manager is all powerful and he rehearses the replacement actors. The play had deteriorated even more.' But when he read the script, 'I saw the possibility of an alternative production, and what was important was what was moving.' The melodrama of the production, and the American system of bringing in new stars and treating them as mere objects of attraction had had adverse repercussions. He decided to go ahead. There was some opposition from those who thought that the play's melodramatic elements overwhelmed its significance, but the decision to stage it was taken, Stafford-Clark stresses, before they knew about Sheen. 'I was very pleased about that.'

The Normal Heart communicates a strong sense of the American government's lethargy in the face of the epidemic's progress. In David Hayman's hustling London production at the Royal Court, and later at the Albery theatre, the sense of an oppressed, reviled community fighting against the extreme pressures suffered by those involved in the epidemic was overwhelming. The first night was high and hot with rare audience response. A sense of emergency was communicated in a fashion that few other plays I have seen have managed to achieve.

Kramer's critique in *The Normal Heart* of the specifically gay identity so jubilantly claimed and enjoyed by Americans and Europeans is fired by his analysis of gay life ten years earlier. It is an important element in his argument. The 1970s bore witness, in major cities in Europe and America, to a rapid commercialisation of gay life and, in the exuberant liberation ardour, to much gay sexuality, representing 'an ecstatic break with . . . the furtive past we have left behind'.[15] But sexual adventure so joyfully undertaken had little to do with community, except in the sense that such contacts could be achieved in those American bath-houses and back-rooms that commercialised and encouraged gay desires.

In the decades before Gay Liberation, and before some homosexual acts were legalised, impersonal gay sex in public lavatories and open spaces was a popular way of dealing with one's outlawed desire. The speed and the anonymity of such transactions implicitly acknowledged the illegality and danger of what was being done. A gay sexual relationship, as opposed to a brief sexual act with a stranger, was fraught with problems. To be in a gay relationship was to acknowledge your sexuality and accept it as an enduring, daily aspect of your life. Anonymous sex appeased desire and reduced the problem of one's sexuality. It even allowed the possibility of denying gayness to oneself.

The post-Gay Liberation exaltation of multi-sexual activity was a response to the inveterate school of repression and sublimation. Andrew Holleran's *Dancer from the Dance* celebrated the release from repression. It recorded the flourishing of the new gay culture, its manners, its rituals, its styles. John Rechy's *The Sexual Outlaw*, in the same decade, offered an impassioned correlative to Holleran's joyful hedonism. It was a romantic idea of promiscuity as an assertion of freedom and identity. In sex itself the outlaw experienced 'the physical and psychical discharge of the fully awakened, living, defiant body'.[16] Such a romantic-political decoding of the mystery of orgasm imparts an attractive gravity, grandeur and rebelliousness to specific kinds of gay sexual activity, though Rechy never forgets the potential for despair in the endless sex-quest. And he suggests powerfully the sheer excitement of the sexual hunt in dangerous contexts. But no single explanation of the new pattern of sexual behaviour is sufficient or convincing. Male desire, whether heterosexual or homosexual in its object-choice is often strong, constant and demanding. In heterosexual relations such desires are liable to be tempered by a countervailing female search for commitment and monogamy. In gay relations there is often no such search.

Larry Kramer's novel *Faggots*, published in the midst of the new gay surge of hedonism, was an attack upon this new sexual life-style, an attack that would be repeated with greater ferocity and anguish in *The Normal Heart*. For his play and novel alike assert that a gay identity founded upon a celebration of free-ranging sexual expression is dangerous and life-defying. In the 1970s his argument was based upon a series of moral propositions. In *The Normal Heart* his distaste for gay hedonism depends upon a medical argument. (There is no discussion of the role that safer sexual acts may have on gay lives in the midst of the epidemic.) Thus Kramer's hero, Ned Weeks, accuses 'All we've created is generations of guys who can't deal with each other as anything but erections' (1.18). Someone else laments a gay world in which 'guys can only think with their cocks' (1.18). The response to an appeal for a new dispensation in which monogamous gay relationships will replace the practice of random sexuality is simple and direct. 'The entire gay platform is fucking,' retorts the man opposing Weeks's campaign to stir the slumbering consciences of politicians (1.18). The extremism of each of these contentions is typical of a play written as a polemic, a call to action and alarm. Kramer asserts that Gay Liberation has merely created gay promiscuity, and that gay men's only political concern is to fight for the freedom to be promiscuous. To talk in these terms is to dabble in ideological caricature.

But Ned Weeks does so talk. He does not want to be considered different from the heterosexual majority. He searches for some desirable Other with whom he will be able to share his life, in a form which mimics a heterosexual marriage. His dream of discovery is achieved, albeit to a man who contracts AIDS. And Kramer provides at the play's melodramatic, quasi-Victorian death-bed finale an imitation of a marriage ceremony for Ned and his dying lover. Weeks seems unable to appreciate that if you condemn, stigmatise, penalise and even ostracise an entire sexual subgroup, then once it achieves some liberation from its stigmatists, many in that subgroup will reject the forms and behaviours of those who have oppressed them. The play does not consider such an argument.

Gay identity, in the minds and behaviours of post-Stonewall gay men, has often involved different kinds of sexual, social and emotional relationships from the conventional heterosexual models. Kramer stresses affinities with heterosexuals rather than differences. His sense of what is entailed in the idea of gay identity can not simply be described as conservative, although it is clearly revisionist. 'The gay leaders who created this sexual-liberation philosophy in the first place have been the death of us ... Why didn't you guys fight for the right to get married instead of the right to legitimise promiscuity?' rages Weeks (2.30). It is Kramer's commitment to gay monogamy that attracted the heterosexual Sheen to the role. This form of rhetoric ignores the fact that Gay Liberation did not cause AIDS. The dissemination of the HIV virus was assisted by the failure to take seriously the first prognoses of the epidemic's gravity, and by delayed programmes of political education and medical information. And the conception of gay marriages would no more terminate promiscuity than heterosexual marriages necessarily discourage adultery and fornication.

Kramer's credo, dependent on the supposed similarities between heterosexuals and homosexuals, also involves gay candour. Admitting one's sexuality, coming out into the open is, he argues, a crucial personal and political act, which will limit guilt and increase self-esteem. The challenge posed by such openness is recognised by Ned Weeks, and the idea frightens his friends. Benedict Nightingale, in his review of the play's London production, emphasised the dilemma.

How can a minority achieve anything if it's been half-conditioned to apologise for its very existence and is terrified of offending its oppressors with the slightest show of self-assertion? How can a successful lobby be mounted by people as nervous for their jobs, their incomes and place in a straight society as several characters shown here?[17]

Such questions, which sensibly recognise the social and political difficulties of coming out, are never debated in the sweep and rush of Kramer's polemic.

As a result, the author seems guilty of arch simplification. This does not detract from the aptness of his attack upon the Reagan administration, the New York mayor, Ed Koch, and the American Medical Association. They are variously accused of regarding gay lives as valueless, and gay people as citizens who do not merit the respect or concern shown to heterosexuals. In an indictment as provocative as it is emotive, Kramer compares these symptoms of indifference to the half-hearted diplomatic gestures made by American Jews to save their European brethren from Hitler's gas chambers. These same Jews, he points out, were still engaged in futile diplomacy to save endangered Jews when the war was virtually over and the six million slaughtered. But the analogy does not work because the nature of the threat posed by the Nazis is quite different in kind and degree from that which AIDS entails.

Weeks's argument that Gay Liberation went awry from its onset by making a gay identity dependent upon gay sexuality is similarly suspect. 'I belong to a culture,' he announces 'that includes Proust, Henry James, Tchaikovsky, Cole Porter, Plato, Socrates, Aristotle, Alexander the Great, Michelangelo, Leonardo da Vinci, Christopher Marlowe, Lorca, Auden, James Baldwin . . . These were not invisible men' (2.41). What gay men must do, he urges, is to

demand recognition of a culture that isn't just sexual. It's all there – all through history we've been there. But we have to claim it, and identify who was in it, and articulate what's in our minds and hearts and all our creative contributions on this earth. Being defined by our cocks is literally killing us.

(2.42)

184

But Weeks's cocksure argument fails to pass muster. There is no single gay culture, no single unchanging sensibility that unites Cole Porter and Michelangelo or Plato and James Baldwin. The sensibilities of the great gay may be tempered by their homosexuality, but it is implausible to argue that these artists share an identity. It is no more than a conjuring trick to imagine that gay culture sweeps into existence through the naming of great homosexuals in history, when the homosexuals whom he names have a necessarily different sense of their identity, and may not even have a homosexual identity in the sense we understand it. Social contexts shape identity, after all. Homosexual sensibility, and the cultures which that sensibility generates, has changed and developed according to time and circumstance.

William Hoffman's *As Is*, by contrast, has no truck with the kind of gay spiritual identity that Kramer proposes. He celebrates the gay promiscuity that Kramer so deplores and condemns, and views it through nostalgia's distorting filter. The play's sufferer from AIDS, a well-heeled *homme fatale* suitably called Rich, has returned to be nursed by his former lover, whom he had discarded for a new love. The play anatomises gay urban life among the upwardly mobile and forwardly promiscuous. Its people are modish, glib and flippant. In Hoffman's play gay identity is principally a matter of sex and more sex. His characters do not see, or did not, much further than the demanding ends of their sexual organs. But the fact of AIDS has put caution and restraint where once had been gay abandon. 'God, how I love sleaze,' Rich tells the audience. 'Five o'clock in the Mineshaft, with the bathtubs full of men dying to get pissed on and whipped; a subway john full of horny high-school students; Morocco, getting raped on a tombstone in Marrakesh. God how I miss it.'[18]

This is the attitude, this is the kind of sexual identity against which Kramer set his heart, mind and polemical gifts. Here are Hoffman's metropolitan gay males hankering for humiliation, submission and free-range violence in the cause of sexual satisfaction. Some may regard such activities as unaesthetic, degrading and damaging. Hoffman describes experiences where men are seemingly demasculinised – submissive and acted upon, penetrated rather than penetrative –

a repudiation of all that a man is traditionally supposed to be and do.

But where harm is not caused, consensual sexual acts should not require formal seals of approval, at least according to liberal theory. Better, surely, that violence should be ritualised and formalised between consenting partners, than that it should be expressed in wild, criminal activity or outrages inflicted upon the innocent uninvolved. *As Is*, a retrospect upon the age before AIDS, is an inept, unmemorable play. But it is at least unafraid to cast light upon some of the controversial results of gay emancipation. Hoffman does not have the will or the enthusiasm to justify such acts to man or woman, but by alluding to such activity he points out one of the routes to which limited homosexual freedom may lead.

A DIFFERENT JOURNEY TO THE SAME END

One of the early theatrical snapshots to which I referred, taken from Ackerley's *The Prisoners of War* in 1925 showed a post-First World War British army captain, furtively touching the curly head of a younger soldier. The last, a mere word-picture, is loud with the sound of a young American remembering the good old sexual days when he was whipped and raped by other men. It is a curious transformation this, from a furtive, homosexual romantic gesture to the sexy reminiscences of a thoroughly modern gay young American. Some may diagnose a tumultuous moral decline in society in the years between these two snapshots, arguing that gay emancipation has merely assisted in a process by which gay men have rampantly pursued their sexual desires to the point of gross promiscuity, treating their partners as so many pieces of flesh. I have tried to show why such an analysis is incomplete and superficial.

The process of change, which this survey has attempted to reflect, is implicit in its title. The taboo engulfing discussion and depiction of gay desire has been eroded in gradual, irregular sequences of change. But there still survives an unwillingness to recognise that gay relationships may have enduring validity and value, or provide sources of satisfaction and enrichment over a period of time. And there may always be difficulties of adjustment and acceptance for some gay people in a heterosexual world. Gay desire is a recognised fact of existence; gay love is not. When Benjamin Britten died in 1986 the *Guardian* was the only national British newspaper to allude to the fact that Peter Pears had been the composer's lover rather than 'his life-long companion' or 'friend'. The euphemistic designations are sure signs of embarrassment and a refusal to accept that a gay or lesbian lover be given the accolade of public recognition. For there is still no pervasive acceptance of the Freudian contention that human sexuality is various, changing and inconstant. Barriers of apprehension and prejudice separate the heterosexual from the homosexual, when neither truly belongs rigidly in his or her designated accommodation. Since heterosexuals are the prime bringers of homosexuals into existence, heterosexuals continue to wish that their children follow their own sexual traditions. And those who fail to repeat the heterosexual pattern are still subject to condemnation. When Oscar Wilde was despatched to prison, news of his sentence was greeted with cries of delight by jubilant prostitutes. A little less than a hundred years on, Section 28 of the Local Government Act suggests that homosexuality must actively be discouraged. Homosexuality is 'against public policy'. The Section implies that homosexual relations are the active, negative aspect of heterosexuality. Sexual uniformity and sexual orthodoxy in which heterosexual marriage is the prevailing, universal mode of transaction has once more become the single desired consummation.

Even the writer Bernard Levin, a right-wing heterosexual polemicist, is disturbed by the signs of the times, signs of which Section 28 is but one: 'On all sides the baying of the hounds can be heard, with eager voices urging them on,' he has written.

> Homosexuals are being portrayed – portrayed literally as well as metaphorically – as creatures scarcely human; they are being abused not just in the old mocking way but in the foulest terms, meant with deadly seriousness; they are experiencing an increasing discrimination over a wide range of situations; already voices have been raised to demand the 'cleansing' of schools as they have been for purging of the church.[19]

AIDS has become the goad by which the process of reaction has been given a spurious legitimacy. The gay man has been reinterpreted, and the myths by which he was identified in the nineteenth century have been reaffirmed. Yet the theatre has not greatly or even occasionally treated or responded to the issues and the implications of such a reversion. This should not be the cause of surprise. For in the sixty years with which this book has been concerned, the theatre's treatment of homosexuality has followed conservative and mythic lines of belief. Even in the last two decades plays about homosexuality in mainstream theatre have reflected the theatre's prevailing middle-class concerns and appeal. Love and passion, or the pursuit of these elemental things, has generally characterised the action of these plays. Not many dramatists have delved further, deeper or wider. Sherman, Mitchell, Kramer and Whitemore have been exceptions. There have been few attempts to deal with the legal, social or cultural problems against which generations of gay men and lesbian women have contended, or many plays that have depicted the way in which homosexuality has been interpreted as an impediment to career or happiness. There have been too few efforts to rebut or contend with the assumptions and prejudices on which heterosexuals have continued to depend and in which they still believe; too few attempts to relate the political to the personal-sexual. Sexual bigotry has had its way in the theatre, while reform and modest change have been achieved by those who fought from the 1960s to change those laws and myths that made gay lives hard, unhappy and limited.

Yet homosexuality is a matter for heterosexuals. Homosexuality exists in almost every family. To persecute and to try to instil guilt and self-loathing into homosexuals, to make the context of gay lives threatening and oppressive, is not a mature or civilised behaviour. The stigmatising of homosexuality has had to do with a devaluing and dread of the feminine. It has been inspired by an overvaluation of the male archetype. Yet re-emergent patrist systems of government, with their exaltation of archetypal male qualities of aggression, power and even brute force, have helped bring us, at the closing of the twentieth century, to a condition that leaves the world's future in doubt. A grossly overpopulated, polluted and hungry planet, its resources insufficient to cater for need, is a reproach to the patrist supremacy, a supremacy insufficiently tempered by the redemptive female archetype and its nurturing, pacific and empathising aspects.

Our stages and our cinemas are not immune to the influence of this patrism, of this reverencing of the qualities of the young rather than the mature male. A nadir of false judging is reached, has been reached, when Sylvester Stallone's Rambo, flaunting his abnormal muscular development and his stunted intellect, has become one of the cinema's most seductive role models for young men. The prescriptive, censored theatres between 1925 and 1970, in portraying the homosexual as a puny, affected caricature of femininity, all masculinity gone, were influenced by a similar false accounting of manliness. So pervasive has this reverence for aspects of the male become that the tomboyish androgynous female heroine – a Dietrich, a Garbo or a Hepburn – is admired for incorporating aspects of the opposite sex.

The taboo relating to homosexuality is, in part, controlled by this reverencing of aspects of the male archetype. For the stigmatising of homosexuals has not simply to do with biblical anathematisation of buggery. Even if there were no such practice, homosexual attachments and desire would still induce outrage. For while the signs of heterosexual desire or attachment, as publicly displayed in the form of a kiss or the holding of hands are completely acceptable, if these same acts are perpetrated in either Britain or America in a public place by two men or two women, they are liable to be interpreted as a prosecutable offence. We are conditioned and schooled to regard the signs of gay desire, as depicted upon stage or screen, with a far greater sense of outrage and disgust than the graphic enactment of violence. John Schlesinger's film of 1971, *Sunday, Bloody Sunday*, engendered revulsion in hundreds of cinemas when the actors Peter Finch and Murray Head were shown in the grip of an extended, erotic kiss. Twenty years later the actor Michael Cashman reminded us how powerful the taboo against such mimetic and actual displays of gay feeling remains. In his BBC TV documentary, *A Kiss Is Not a Kiss* (1991) he noted that the minor gay kiss he was required to bestow in the TV soap opera *EastEnders* caused almost as much uproar as the meeting of the lips of Finch and Head had inspired twenty years earlier.

The signs of gay affection, let alone of desire, are clearly understood to subvert and threaten received ideas of manliness. But the potency of a taboo only survives in full efficiency as long as that taboo is observed and honoured. The theatre and the cinema, from the 1920s, has, even where creating false and malevolent images of male and female homosexuality, helped to erode the taboo engulfing such sexuality. The unspeakable gradually became discussable. In the 1980s, a trio of British Actors – Ian McKellen, Antony Sher and Simon Callow – revealed that they were gay. And their careers in the theatre appear not to have suffered as a result of such revelations, although if they had been international film stars such candour might have proved damaging. More than a generation earlier Michael Redgrave, celebrated as an icon of the British upper-middle class male on screen and as a classical actor, seems to have been very much a man of his theatrical times. He was an anguished bisexual, whose homosexual desires and relations were characterised by secrecy, guilt and sadness. Homophobia is not what it was.

Yet there remains a sense in which homosexuality remains the something that must not be shown in front of an audience. The signs of homosexual affection and desire, as they are perfunctorily rendered on stage and screen, still retain their capacity to shock and offend. Homosexuals and lesbians are still liable to be outcasts from their own families. The theatre, which since Ibsen has dealt with the crises of family relations, and of the heterodox in opposition to the orthodox, still has significant sexual business to conduct. This business is not a matter of ideology; it has to do with the task of demystifying homosexual love and enabling gay men and lesbians to be part of both the families into which they are born and the complementary sexual worlds into which they go.

Noël Coward and Terence Rattigan, whose homosexual sensibilities were diverted but not thwarted by stage censorship, could not deal openly with such things. Rodney Ackland, their contemporary, wanted to be candid in his 1952 play *The Pink Room*. Homosexuality was part of his picture. That element had to be excised and was only restored when the play was revived, retitled *Absolute Hell*, at a little fringe theatre, the Orange Tree, in 1988. It is therefore a theatre of sexual candour, and a theatre demystifying homosexuality, which we still require.

NOTES

1 FROM THE PLAYHOUSE TO THE OLD BAILEY

In the text and notes, the reference 1.26 refers to Act 1, page 26; 1.ii.54 refers to Act 1, scene ii, page 54.

1 Mae West, *The Drag* (unpublished manuscript in Library of Congress, Washington, DC, dated February 1927), Act 1, p.6. The play is discussed in Kaier Curtin, *We Can Always Call Them Bulgarians*, Boston, Alyson Publications, 1987, pp.68–88. His book is subtitled *The Emergence of Lesbians and Gay Men on the American Stage*, and contains much information on the period 1926–39, relating to Broadway productions.
2 Mordaunt Shairp, *The Green Bay Tree*, 1.i.56. The play is published in *Gay Plays*, selected and introduced by Michael Wilcox, London and New York, Methuen, 1984.
3 Robert Anderson, *Tea and Sympathy*, London, Heinemann, 1957.
4 John Osborne, *A Patriot for Me*, London and Boston, Faber & Faber, 1983, 3.v.98.
5 Harvey Fierstein, *Torch Song Trilogy*, London, Methuen, 1984, *Prologue to Fugue in a Nursery*, the second play in the trilogy, p.23.
6 Larry Kramer, *The Normal Heart*, London, Methuen, 1986, 2.xiv.42.
7 Susan Sontag, *A Susan Sontag Reader*, Harmondsworth, Penguin, 1982, p.105. Susan Sontag's essay *Notes on Camp*, from which this quotation is taken, is the best short explanation on the subject.
8 The process is revealed in detail in the newspaper extracts assembled in Jonathan Katz (ed.) *Gay American History*, New York, Avon Books, 1978, pp.139–81.
9 Alan Bray, *Homosexuality in Renaissance England*, London, Gay Men's Press, 1982, p.31. Bray's interpretation of the significance of sexual relations between males in the sixteenth century and thereafter is unsurpassed.
10 Bray, op. cit., pp.31–2.
11 Keith Thomas, *Religion and the Decline of Magic*, Harmondsworth, Penguin, 1973, p.97.
12 See A.N. Gilbert, 'Conceptions of Homosexuality and Sodomy in

191

Western History' in Salvatore J. Licata and Robert P. Peterson (eds) *The Gay Past*, New York and London, Harrington Park Press, 1985, pp.57–67.

13 Anthony Stevens, *Archetype*, London, Routledge, 1982, p.235.
14 Bray, op. cit., pp.13 and 34.
15 Stephen Gosson, *The Schoole of Abuse*, London, 1579, p.10.
16 Edward Guilpin, *Skialetheia*, London, The Shakespeare Association, Facsimile no.2, 1931, p.BIV.
17 Philip Stubbes, *Anatomie of Abuses*, ed. W.B.D.O. Turnbull, London and Edinburgh, 1836, p.166.
18 *Great Thoughts*, 1 January 1898, pp.228–30.
19 *Daily Mirror*, 10 April 1990.
20 Edward Ward, *The History of London Clubs*, London, 1709, p.284.
21 *Select Trials for Murder, Robberies, Rapes, Sodomy, Coining, Frauds, and Other Offences at the Session-House in the Old Bailey*, 3 vols, London, 1742, vol.2, pp.257–8.
22 Bray, op. cit., p.86.
23 Jeffrey Weeks, *Sex, Politics and Society*, London and New York, Longman, 1986, pp.38–56.
24 Op. cit. p.45.
25 William Archer, *English Dramatists of Today*, London, 1882, p.17.
26 Howard Taubman, *The Making of the American Theatre*, London, Longmans, 1967, p.83.
27 ibid., p.126.
28 ibid.
29 *Report of Joint Committee on Censorship of the Theatre*, London, HMSO, 1967, p.185. Curtin, op. cit., p.101.
30 Raymond Williams, *Drama from Ibsen to Brecht*, Harmondsworth, Penguin, 1973, p.34.

2 THE DEVIANT, THE DAMNED AND THE DANDIFIED:
1925–1939

1 Jeffrey Meyers, *Homosexuality and Literature 1890–1930*, London, Athlone Press, 1977, p.1.
2 J. Katz (ed.) *Gay American History*, New York, Avon Books, 1978, p.90.
3 Meyers, op. cit., p.26.
4 Richard Ellman, *Oscar Wilde*, London, Hamish Hamilton, 1987, p.297.
5 Michael Bell (ed.) *The Context of English Literature*, London, Methuen, 1980, p.215.
6 *Letters of Sigmund Freud 1873–1939*, ed. Ernst Freud, London, Hogarth Press, 1961, p.227.
7 Laurence Olivier, *On Acting*, London, Weidenfeld & Nicolson, 1986, pp.48–9.
8 Tyrone Guthrie, *A Life in the Theatre*, London, Columbus Books, 1987, p.173. Olivier, in his book *On Acting* does not mention the fact that he and Guthrie agreed that Iago should be homosexually

in love with the Moor. But he writes that he emphasised Iago's honesty. 'Then when I got to the soliloquy, I'd have my syringe ready and let the audience have it straight up the arse' (op. cit., p.101).

9 Gordon Westwood, *Society and the Homosexual*, London, Gollancz, 1952, pp.44–50.

10 John Johnston, *The Lord Chamberlain's Blue Pencil*, London, Hodder & Stoughton, 1990, p.86. The Lord Chamberlain's files relating to his function as the licenser and censor of plays in the period 1901–68, were placed in the British Library just as this book was going to press. It was too late for me to take advantage of much information in these files relating to plays about homosexuality. The Lord Chamberlain and his staff were convinced in the 1950s that homosexuality was catching. There is evidence to this effect in relation to the production of *A Patriot for Me* by John Osborne (see further Chapter 4).

11 G. Robertson, *Obscenity*, London, Weidenfeld & Nicolson, 1979, p.36.

12 ibid., p.34.

13 Vito Russo, *The Celluloid Closet*, New York, Harper & Row, 1981, pp.26 and 32; Jeffrey Richards, *The Age of the Dream Palace*, London, Routledge & Kegan Paul, 1984, p.107.

14 Gyles Brandreth, *John Gielgud*, London, Pavilion Books, 1984, p.14.

15 Notes written by Sir John, to accompany the publication of Johnston, op. cit., and circulated to the media.

16 Martin Green, *Children of the Sun*, London, Constable, 1977.

17 ibid., pp.32–3.

18 Peter Parker, *Ackerley*, London, Constable, 1989, p.90.

19 ibid., p.90.

20 Julian Symons, *The Thirties, A Dream Revolved*, London, Faber & Faber, 1975, p.40.

21 In an interview with the author, April 1990; all references to Harris are taken from this interview.

22 J.R. Ackerley, *My Father and Myself*, London, The Bodley Head, 1968, pp.216–17.

23 ibid., pp.18, 127 and 134. Ackerley's misogyny to which he admits in *My Father and Myself* was partial. He had a guilty and very intense relationship with his sister Nancy who was probably in love with him. And his liking for his aunt, who lived with him and Nancy during the later stages of his life, was pronounced.

24 *The Ackerley Letters*, ed. Neville Braybrooke, New York, Harcourt Brace Jovanovich, 1975, p.13.

25 James Agate, *The Contemporary Theatre*, London, Chapman and Hall, 1926, pp.110–11.

26 Frederick Lonsdale, *Spring Cleaning*, London, Chapman and Hall, 1925.

27 Kaier Curtin, *We Can Always Call Them Bulgarians*, Boston, Alyson Publications, 1987, p.215.

28 *Gay Plays, The First Collection*, ed. William M. Hoffman, New York, Avon Books, 1979, p.36.

29 Mae West, *The Drag* (unpublished manuscript on file in Library of Congress, Washington, DC, dated February 1927), Act 3, p.7.

30 Edouard Bourdet, *The Captive*, New York, Bretano's, 1926, p.145.

31 Curtin, op. cit., p.93.

32 *The Drag*, Act 1, p.6.

33 John Gielgud, *Early Stages*, London, Falcon Press, 1948: Gielgud describes Vosper and the actress Laura Cowie, who played Claudius and Gertrude to his 1934 Hamlet at the Old Vic as like 'a pair of cruel, monstrous cats' (p.192).

34 *Gay Plays*, ed. M. Wilcox, London and New York, Methuen, 1984, p.53; *New York Times*, 21 October 1933.

35 *Gay Plays*, ed. Wilcox, p.6.

36 In an interview with the author, July 1990.

37 Johnston, op. cit., p.175.

38 *Daily Telegraph*, 30 September 1936; *The Times*, 30 September 1936; Curtin, op. cit., pp.240–6.

39 *New York Times*, 16 October 1938.

40 Chester Erskine, *The Good* (manuscript in Lincoln Center Library, New York).

41 *Variety*, 30 March 1938.

3 THE ENEMY WITHIN: 1949–1958

1 Jack Lait and Lee Mortimer, *Washington Confidential*, New York, Crown, 1951, pp.90 and 94.

2 *New York Times*, 19 April 1950. Jonathan Katz in *Gay American History*, New York, Avon Books, 1978, gives a comprehensive account, culled from contemporary newspapers and books, of the Cold War witch-hunt against homosexuals.

3 Haynes Johnson and Benard M. Gwertzman, *Fulbright the Dissenter*, London, Hutchinson, 1969, p.129.

4 Gordon Westwood, *Society and the Homosexual*, London, Gollancz, 1952, pp. 105–6; Jeffrey Weeks, *Sex, Politics and Society*, London and New York, Longman, 1986, p.238 and *passim*.

5 Katz, op. cit., pp.151–5; *New York Times*, 16 December 1950.

6 Andrew Boyle, *The Climate of Treason*, London, Hutchinson, 1979, p.184.

7 John D'Emilio, *Sexual Politics, Sexual Communities*, Chicago and London, University of Chicago Press, p.37.

8 ibid.

9 Peter Wildeblood, *Against the Law*, Harmondsworth, Penguin, 1955, p.50.

10 ibid.

11 Kenneth Tynan, *Tynan on Theatre*, Harmondsworth, Penguin, 1964, p.16.

12 ibid., p.42.

13 ibid., p.58.

14 Irving Wardle, *The Theatres of George Devine*, London, Jonathan Cape, 1978, p.169.

15 Henry Ritchie, *Success Stories*, London, Faber & Faber, 1988, pp.26–7.

16 J. Tudor Rees and Marley V. Usill (eds) *They Stand Apart*, London, Heinemann, 1955, p.vii. This collection of essays, including one by Lord Hailsham, gives a vivid impression of the British establishment attitude to homosexuals and homosexuality in the 1950s, an attitude characterised by ignorance, hysteria, misinformation and simple fear.

17 ibid., p.24.

18 *The Times*, 26 April 1957.

19 *New York Times*, 1 October 1953.

20 In an interview with the author, January 1991.

21 B.A. Young, *The Rattigan Version*, London, Hamish Hamilton, 1986, p.102.

22 Michael Darlow and Gillian Hodson, *Terence Rattigan, the Man and His Work*, London, Quartet, 1979, p.202.

23 *Sunday Times*, 11 April 1958; *Observer* 11 April 1958.

24 *Observer*, 8 September 1963; *Sunday Times*, 8 September 1963.

25 Darlow and Hodson, op. cit., p.281.

26 ibid., pp.227–8. Rattigan's quotation is taken from an interview with the virulently anti-homosexual critic, John Simon, in *Theatre Arts*, April 1962, p.

27 Darlow and Hodson, op. cit., p.227.

28 ibid., p.228.

29 Hilary Spurling, *Daily Telegraph*, 22 March 1988.

30 Rodney Ackland, *Absolute Hell*, London, Oberon Books, 1990: Introduction by Nicholas Dromgoole, p.9.

31 *New York Post*, 9 February 1954.

32 C.A. Tripp, *The Homosexual Matrix*, London, Quartet, 1977, pp.172 and 171.

33 Vito Russo, *The Celluloid Closet*, New York, Harper & Row, 1981, p.113.

34 D.J. West, *Homosexuality*, Harmondsworth, Penguin, 1960, p.132.

35 *Gay Plays*, ed M. Wilcox, volume 2, London and New York, Methuen, 1985, pp. 11 and 9.

36 Westwood, op. cit., p.42.

37 Harold Hobson, *Theatre in Britain*, Oxford, Phaidon Press, 1984, p.151.

38 An anthology of the first-night reviews of the London production are published in Bernard Braden, *Kindness of Strangers*, London, Hodder & Stoughton, 1990, pp. 88–9. Braden played the part of Mitch in the original London production; Donald Spoto, *The Kindness of Strangers*, New York, Ballantine Books, 1985, p. 151.

39 Alexander Walker, *Vivien Leigh*, London, Weidenfeld & Nicolson, 1987, p.196.

40 Tennessee Williams, *Memoirs*, London, W.H. Allen, 1976, p.230.

41 C.W.E. Bigsby, *A Critical Introduction to Twentieth Century American*

Drama, volume 2, Cambridge and New York, Cambridge University Press, 1987, p.3.

42 Williams, op. cit., p.100.

43 Tennessee Williams, *Sweet Bird of Youth,* Harmondsworth, Penguin, 1976, Foreword, pp.9–10; Spoto, op. cit., p.153.

44 Molly Haskell, *From Reverence to Rape: The Treatment of Women in the Movies,* New York, Penguin, 1974, p.251; Richard Dyer (ed.) *Gays and Film,* New York, Zoetrope, 1984, p.53.

45 Spoto, op. cit., p.270.

46 Roger Boxill, *Tennessee Williams,* London, Macmillan, 1987, pp.35–6. Boxill's interesting account falters when he succumbs entirely to Freudian exegesis and argues that the plays are re-enactments of Oedipal fixation and confirmation that homosexuality is a form of narcissism.

47 Spoto, op. cit., pp.243–8.

48 ibid., pp.355 and 356.

49 Bigsby, op. cit., p.86.

50 West, op. cit., p.150.

51 *New York Times,* 25 March 1955.

52 *New York Journal American,* and *New York Herald Tribune,* 25 March 1955.

53 *The Times,* 30 January 1958.

54 *New York Daily Mirror,* 25 March 1955.

55 In an interview with the author, January 1991.

56 Spoto, op. cit., p.240.

57 The *Observer,* 7 April 1957.

58 West, op. cit., p.181.

59 In a letter to the author, 3 November 1987.

4 OUT OF BONDAGE TOWARDS BEING: 1958–1969

1 John D'Emilio, *Sexual Politics, Sexual Communities,* Chicago and London, University of Chicago Press, 1983, p.237.

2 ibid., p.153; see also the rest of the chapter.

3 Geoffrey Robertson, *Obscenity,* London, Weidenfeld & Nicolson, 1979, p.248.

4 The Lord Chamberlain's Files relating to Theatre Censorship were placed in the British Library in February 1991; the file on John Osborne's *A Patriot for Me* (Royal Court, 1965) contains illuminating references to the Lord Chamberlain's perception of the threat to the public posed by homosexuality.

5 Kenneth Tynan, *Tynan on Theatre,* Harmondsworth, Penguin, 1964, pp.84 and 82.

6 ibid., p.88.

7 Lord Chamberlain's file on *A Taste of Honey.*

8 *Daily Telegraph,* 5 May 1964.

9 *The Orton Diaries,* ed. John Lahr, London, Methuen, 1986, p.251.

10 Tennessee Williams, *Memoirs,* London, W.H. Allen, 1976, p.53.

11 *The Orton Diaries,* ed. Lahr, p.125.

12 John Lahr, *Prick Up Your Ears*, London, Allen Lane, 1978, pp.32–3.
13 Simon Shepherd, *Because We're Queers*, London, Gay Men's Press, 1989, p.50.
14 ibid., pp.56 and 29.
15 *Christian Science Monitor*, 19 March 1969.
16 *Observer*, 2 October 1966.
17 Shepherd, op. cit., p.65. Shepherd's chapter 'Boy's Freud and Fathers' very persuasively shows the way in which Orton's sexy hooligan is a child of his time.
18 *The Orton Diaries*, ed. Lahr, p.84.
19 ibid., p.145.
20 ibid., p.107; Lahr, *Prick Up Your Ears*, p.248.
21 *The Orton Diaries*, ed. Lahr, p.125.
22 John Rechy, *The Sexual Outlaw*, London, W.H. Allen, 1978, pp.28 and 31.
23 Lahr, *Prick Up Your Ears*, p.187.
24 John Johnston, *The Lord Chamberlain's Blue Pencil*, London, Hodder & Stoughton, 1990, p.218.
25 Lord Chamberlain's File on *Entertaining Mr Sloane*; Lahr, *Prick Up Your Ears*, pp.207 and 202.
26 Lahr, *Prick Up Your Ears*, p.217.
27 *World Telegraph and Sun*, 13 October 1965; *New York Times*, 13 October 1965.
28 Lahr, *Prick Up Your Ears*, p.53.
29 ibid., p.219.
30 Shepherd, op. cit., p.131.
31 Lahr, *Prick Up Your Ears*, p.324.
32 The actress Sheila Ballantine in a note to Lahr who quotes her in his edited version of *The Orton Diaries* on p.265.
33 The Lord Chamberlain's file on *A Patriot for Me* is revelatory of the attitudes to homosexuality which prevailed in the court and military circles of the 1960s.
34 The complex legal matters are also detailed in the Lord Chamberlain's files.
35 The Director of Public Prosecutions in a letter to the Lord Chamberlain, 27 July 1965.
36 Of all the staff dealing with censorship in the Lord Chamberlain's office Mr Hill was the most strenuously homophobic.
37 Johnston, op. cit., p.207.
38 See the Lord Chamberlain's files on a series of Osborne's plays, but chiefly *A Patriot for Me*.
39 Richard Findlater, *Banned*, London, Panther, 1968, pp.213–14.
40 ibid., p.214.
41 *The Times*, 1 July 1965.
42 *Daily Express*, 9 April 1959.
43 *Daily Express*, 16 April 1959.
44 Anthony Page in an interview with the author, November 1990. All remarks from Page are taken from this interview.
45 Sir John Johnston in a letter to the Royal Court, from the Lord

Chamberlain's office, September 1964. The letter is in the Lord Chamberlain's file for *A Patriot for Me*.

46 Helen Montagu in an interview with the author, October 1990; Irving Wardle, *The Theatres of George Devine*, London, Jonathan Cape, 1978, p.273. The word 'bum-boys' is used by Osborne in *A Patriot for Me* to describe the male prostitutes at the drag ball (2.i.50).

47 *Guardian*, 12 May 1965.

48 Wardle, op. cit., p.275.

49 *The Times*, 1 July 1965.

50 *Sunday Times*, 4 July 1965.

51 *New Statesman*, 9 July 1965.

52 *Observer*, 4 July 1965.

53 *New Statesman*, 9 July 1965.

54 Johnston, op. cit., p.205.

55 Findlater, op. cit., p.203. The Lord Chamberlain's file on *US* is fascinating. It shows exactly how Lord Cobbold tried to persuade the government to intervene over this production.

56 Johnston, op. cit., p.206.

57 ibid., p.207. The Lord Chamberlain's file on *A Patriot for Me* gives a full account of the Department's action over Osborne's play.

58 The play was never published. It can be read in the July and August 1960 editions of *Plays and Players*.

59 *The Noël Coward Diaries*, ed. Graham Payn and Sheridan Morley, London, Weidenfeld & Nicolson, 1982.

60 It may be that the play was inspired by Somerset Maugham's life. See John Lahr, *Coward The Playwright*, London, Methuen, 1982, p.154. But Richard Huggett, *Binkie Beaumont*, London, Hodder & Stoughton, 1989, p.491, suggests Beerbohm was the source of the play's inspiration.

61 Lahr, *Coward*, p.158.

62 *Sunday Chronicle*, 26 April 1925.

63 In an interview with the author, January 1991.

64 D.J. West, *Homosexuality*, Harmondsworth, Penguin, 1960, p.55.

65 *Plays and Players*, January 1967; *Sunday New York Times*, 21 January 1968; *Wall Street Journal*, 12 January 1968; *Women's Wear Daily*, 11 January 1968.

66 *New York Times*, 15 April 1968.

67 *Sunday New York Times*, 18 April 1968.

68 *Women's Wear Daily*, 15 April 1968.

69 John D'Emilio, op. cit., p.162.

5 'SIMPLY THE THING I AM SHALL MAKE ME LIVE': 1969–1981

1 Jeffrey Weeks, *Sexuality and its Discontents*, London, Routledge & Kegan Paul, 1985, pp.165–6.

2 Michael Bronski, *Culture Clash*, Boston, Southend Press, 1984, p.11.

3 Lord Chamberlain's file on *Hair*.

4 Charles Marowitz, *Confessions of a Counterfeit Critic*, London, Eyre Methuen, 1973, p.18

5 *Gay Sweatshop, Four Plays and a Company*, ed. Philip Osment London, Methuen, 1985, p.ix.

6 Sherman, writing in the introduction to his play, *Passing By*, in *Gay Plays*, ed. M. Wilcox, London and New York, Methuen, 1984, p.101.

7 ibid.

8 Article by Carole Woods in the programme for a benefit performance of *Bent*, June 1989. Subsequent quotations from Sherman are also from this article.

9 *Gay Sweatshop*, ed. Osment, p.xxxviii.

10 Sherman, in an interview with the author, November 1990. Subsequent quotations from Sherman are also from this interview.

11 Richard Plant, *The Pink Triangle*, Edinburgh, Mainstream Publishing, 1987, pp.14–15; p.19.

12 Sherman, in an interview with the author.

13 *Financial Times*, 23 July 1979.

14 *Daily Telegraph*, 23 July 1979.

15 Richard Findlater, *Banned*, London, Panther, 1968, p.198.

16 Plant, op. cit., p.167.

17 *Gay Sweatshop*, ed. Osment, p.xxxiv.

18 Sherman, in an interview with the author.

19 *Daily Mail*, 6 November 1981.

20 Cyril Connolly, *Enemies of Promise*, Harmondsworth, Penguin, 1961, p.271.

21 *Daily Telegraph*, 6 November 1981.

22 *The Independent*, 23 October 1986.

23 Hugh Whitemore, in an interview with the author, January 1991; all other quotations from Whitemore are taken from this interview.

24 *New York Times*, 16 November 1987.

25 Simon Shepherd, *Because We're Queers*, London, Gay Men's Press, 1989, pp.37 and 39.

26 Gordon Westwood, *Society and the Homosexual*, London, Gollancz, 1952, pp.71, 69, 64.

27 Anthony Stevens, *Archetype*, London, Routledge & Kegan Paul, 1982, p.198.

28 Peter Wildeblood, *Against the Law*, Harmondsworth, Penguin, 1955, p.16.

29 Richard Davenport-Hines, *Sex, Death and Punishment*, London, Collins, 1990, p.328.

30 Erich Fromm, *The Art of Loving*, London, Unwin Books, 1971, pp.20–1.

31 The phrases are taken from J. Tudor Rees and Harley V. Usill (ed.) *They Stand Apart*, London, Heinemann, 1955, pp.24, 22, xii.

32 Westwood, op. cit., p.183.

33 I reported the 'Street Boy' obscenity case at the Old Bailey in February 1974 for the *Guardian*.

34 *Guardian*, 3 October 1985; *Evening Standard*, 3 October 1985.

35 *Listener,* 10 October 1985; *Daily Telegraph,* 3 October 1985.
36 Robert Brustein, *Who Needs Theatre?,* London, Faber & Faber, 1987, p.5.

6 THE RETURN OF THE OUTCAST: 1981–1986

1 Keith Thomas, *Religion and the Decline of Magic,* Harmondsworth, Penguin, 1973, p.100.
2 James Fletcher, 'Homosexuality: Kick and Kickback', *Southern Medical Journal,* February 1984.
3 Thomas, op. cit., pp.90–1.
4 William Clowes, *A Brief and Necessary Treatise,* London, 1596, p.147.
5 Allen M. Brandt, *No Magic Bullet,* New York and Oxford, Oxford University Press, 1985, p.5; Dennis Altman, *Aids and the New Puritanism,* London and Sydney, Pluto Press, 1986, p.182.
6 Jeffrey Weeks, *Sexuality and its Discontents,* London, Routledge & Kegan Paul, 1985, p.45.
7 Simon Watney, *Policing Desire,* London, Methuen, 1987, pp.43 and 84.
8 Brandt, op. cit., pp.154–8.
9 Barry D. Adam, *The Rise of a Gay and Lesbian Movement,* Boston, Twayne, 1987, p.158.
10 *The Parliamentary Debates* (Hansard), London, HMSO, 1988, House of Lords, 1 February 1988, cols 642–3 (Earl of Caithness, government spokesman on Section 28).
11 David Benedict, writing in the *National Campaign for the Arts Newsletter,* December 1990.
12 *Advocate,* 30 August 1988, p.27.
13 See Chapter 1, note 30.
14 Max Stafford-Clark in an interview with the author, January 1991.
15 Richard Goldstein, 'Heartsick Fear and Loving in the Gay Community', in *Village Voice,* vol.xxvii, no.26, 28 June 1983.
16 John Rechy, *The Sexual Outlaw,* London, W.H.Allen, 1978, p.300.
17 *New Statesman,* 4 April 1986.
18 William Hoffman, *As Is,* unpublished text.
19 *The Times,* 28 December 1987.

BIBLIOGRAPHY

Ackerley, J.R. *The Prisoners of War*, in *Gay Plays*, ed. M. Wilcox, volume 3, London, Methuen, 1988.
Ackerley, J.R. *My Father and Myself*, London, The Bodley Head, 1968.
——*The Ackerley Letters*, ed. N. Braybrooke, New York, Harcourt Brace Jovanovich, 1975.
Ackland, R. *Absolute Hell*, London, Oberon Books, 1990.
Adam, B.D. *The Rise of a Gay and Lesbian Movement*, Boston, Twayne, 1987.
Agate, J. *The Contemporary Theatre*, London, Chapman and Hall, 1926.
Altman, D. *Aids and the New Puritanism*, London and Sydney, Pluto Press, 1986.
Anderson, R. *Tea and Sympathy*, London, Heinemann, 1957.
Archer, W. *English Dramatists of Today*, London, 1882.
Bell, M. (ed.) *The Context of English Literature*, London, Methuen, 1980.
Bigsby, C.W.E. *A Critical Introduction to Twentieth Century American Drama*, volume 2, Cambridge and New York, Cambridge University Press, 1987.
Bourdet, E. *The Captive*, New York, Bretano's 1926.
Boxill, R. *Tennessee Williams*, London, Macmillan, 1987.
Boyle, A. *The Climate of Treason*, London, Hutchinson, 1979.
Braden, B. *Kindness of Strangers*, London, Hodder & Stoughton, 1990.
Brandreth, G. *John Gielgud*, London, Pavilion Books, 1984.
Brandt, A.M. *No Magic Bullet*, New York and Oxford, Oxford University Press, 1987.
Bray, A. *Homosexuality in Renaissance England*, London, Gay Men's Press, 1982.
Bronski, M. *Culture Clash*, Boston, Southend Press, 1984.
Brustein, R. *Who Needs Theatre?*, London, Faber & Faber, 1987.
Clowes, W. *A Brief and Necessary Treatise*, London, 1596.
Connolly, C. *Enemies of Promise*, Harmondsworth, Penguin, 1961.
Coward, N. *Design for Living*, London, Heinemann, 1933.
Coward, N. *A Song at Twilight*, London, Heinemann, 1966.
——*The Noël Coward Diaries*, ed. G. Payne and S. Morley, London, Weidenfeld & Nicolson, 1982.

Crowley, M. *The Boys in the Band*, London and New York, Samuel French, 1968.

Curtin, K. *We Can Always Call Them Bulgarians*, Boston, Alyson Publications, 1987.

Dalton, M. and Hodson, G. *Terence Rattigan, the Man and His Work*, London, Quartet, 1979.

Davenport-Hines, R. *Sex, Death and Punishment*, London, Collins, 1990.

Delaney, S. *A Taste of Honey*, London, Methuen, 1982.

de la Roche, M. *Whiteoaks*, London, Macmillan, 1936.

D'Emilio, J. *Sexual Politics, Sexual Communities*, Chicago and London, University of Chicago Press, 1983.

Dyer, C. *Staircase*, London, Samuel French, 1966.

Dyer, R. (ed.) *Gays and Film*, New York, Zoetrope, 1984.

Ellman, R. *Oscar Wilde*, London, Hamish Hamilton, 1987.

Elyot, K. *Coming Clean*, London, Faber & Faber, 1984.

Erskine, C. *The Good*, manuscript in Lincoln Center Library, New York.

Fierstein, H. *Torch Song Trilogy*, London, Methuen, 1984.

Findlater, R. *Banned*, London, Panther, 1968.

Freud, S. *Letters of Sigmund Freud, 1873–1939*, ed. E. Freud, London, Hogarth Press, 1961.

Fromm, E. *The Art of Loving*, London, Unwin Books, 1971.

Gay Plays, The First Collection, ed. W. Hoffman, New York, Avon Books, 1979.

Gay Plays, ed. M. Wilcox, London and New York, Methuen, 1984.

Gay Plays, Volume 2, ed. M. Wilcox, London and New York, Methuen, 1985.

Gay Plays, Volume 3, ed. M. Wilcox, London and New York, Methuen, 1988.

Gay Sweatshop, Four Plays and a Company, ed. P. Osment, London, Methuen 1985.

Gielgud, J. *Early Stages*, London, Falcon Press, 1948.

Gosson, S. *The Schoole of Abuse*, London, 1579.

Green, M. *Children of the Sun*, London, Constable, 1977.

Guilpin, E. *Skialetheia*, London, The Shakespeare Association, 1931.

Guthrie, T. *A Life in the Theatre*, London, Columbus Books, 1987.

Haskell, M. *From Reverence to Rape: The Treatment of Women in the Movies*, New York, Penguin, 1974.

Henry, J. *Look on Tempests, Plays and Players*, July and August, 1960.

Hobson, H. *Theatre in Britain*, Oxford, Phaidon Press, 1984.

Huggett, R. *Binkie Beaumont*, London, Hodder & Stoughton, 1989.

Ibsen, H. *Ghosts*, Harmondsworth, Penguin, 1964.

Johnson, H. and Gwertzman, B.M. *Fulbright the Dissenter*, London, Hutchinson, 1969.

Johnston, J. *The Lord Chamberlain's Blue Pencil*, London, Hodder & Stoughton, 1990.

Katz, J. (ed.) *Gay American History*, New York, Avon Books, 1978.

Kaufman, G.S. and MacGrath, L., *The Small Hours*, London, Dramatists Play Service Inc., 1951.

King, P. *Serious Charge*, London and New York, Samuel French, 1956.

Kramer, L. *The Normal Heart*, London, Methuen, 1986.

Lahr, J. *Prick Up Your Ears*, London, Allen Lane, 1978.

——*Coward The Playwright*, London, Methuen, 1982.

Lait, J. and Mortimer, L. *Washington Confidential*, New York, Crown, 1951.

Licata, S.J. and Petersen, R.P. (eds) *The Gay Past*, New York and London, Harrington Park Press, 1985.

Lonsdale, F. *Spring Cleaning*, London, Chapman and Hall, 1925.

Marowitz, C. *Confessions of a Counterfeit Critic*, London, Eyre Methuen, 1973.

Meyers, J. *Homosexuality and Literature, 1890–1930*, London, Athlone Press, 1977.

Mitchell, J. *Another Country*, London, Amber Lane Press, 1985.

Olivier, L. *On Acting*, London, Weidenfeld & Nicolson, 1986.

Orton, J. *The Orton Diaries*, ed. J. Lahr, London, Methuen, 1986.

——*The Complete Plays*, London, Methuen, 1990.

Osborne, J. *A Patriot For Me*, London and Boston, Faber & Faber, 1983.

Parker, P. *Ackerley*, London, Constable, 1989.

Plant, R. *The Pink Triangle*, Edinburgh, Mainstream Publishing, 1987.

Rechy, J. *The Sexual Outlaw*, London, W.H. Allen, 1978.

Report of Joint Committee on Censorship of the Theatre, London, HMSO, 1967.

Rees, J.T. and Usill, H.V. (eds) *They Stand Apart*, London, Heinemann, 1955.

Richards, J. *The Age of the Dream Palace*, London, Routledge & Kegan Paul, 1984.

Ritchie, H. *Success Stories*, London, Faber & Faber, 1988.

Robertson, G. *Obscenity*, London, Weidenfeld & Nicolson, 1979.

Russo, V. *The Celluloid Closet*, New York, Harper & Row, 1981.

Shairp, M. *The Green Bay Tree*, in *Gay Plays*, ed. M. Wilcox, London and New York, Methuen, 1984.

Shepherd, S. *Because We're Queers*, London, Gay Men's Press, 1989.

Sherman, M. *Bent*, London, Amber Lane Press, 1979.

Sontag, S. *A Susan Sontag Reader*, Harmondsworth, Penguin, 1982.

Spoto, D. *The Kindness of Strangers*, New York, Ballantine Books, 1985.

Stevens, A. *Archetype*, London, Routledge & Kegan Paul, 1982.

Stokes, L. and S. *Oscar Wilde*, London, Secker & Warburg, 1937.

Stubbes, P. *Anatomie of Abuses*, ed. W.B.D.O. Turnbull, London and Edinburgh, 1836.

Symons, J. *The Thirties, A Dream Revolved*, London, Faber & Faber, 1975.

Taubman, H. *The Making of the American Theatre*, London, Longmans, 1967.

Thomas, K. *Religion and the Decline of Magic*, Harmondsworth, Penguin, 1973.

Tripp, C.A. *The Homosexual Matrix*, London, Quartet, 1977.

Tynan, K. *Tynan on Theatre*, Harmondsworth, Penguin, 1964.

Walker, A. *Vivien Leigh*, London, Weidenfeld & Nicolson, 1987.

Ward, E. *The History of London Clubs*, London, 1709.

Wardle, I. *The Theatres of George Devine*, London, Jonathan Cape, 1978.

Watney, S. *Policing Desire*, London, Methuen, 1987.

Winter, K. *Rats of Norway*, London, Heinemann, 1933.

Weeks, J. *Sexuality and its Discontents*, London, Routledge & Kegan Paul, 1985.

Weeks, Jeffrey, *Sex, Politics and Society*, London and New York, Longman, 1986.

West, M. *The Drag*, unpublished MS in Library of Congress, Washington DC, dated 1927.

West, D.J. *Homosexuality*, Harmondsworth, Penguin, 1960.

Westwood, G. *Society and the Homosexual*, London, Gollancz, 1952.

Whitemore, H. *Breaking the Code*, London, Amber Lane Press, 1987.

Wilcox, M. *Rents*, London and New York, Methuen, 1983.

Wildeblood, P. *Against the Law*, Harmondsworth, Penguin, 1955.

Williams, R. *Drama from Ibsen to Brecht*, Harmondsworth, Penguin, 1973.

Williams, T. *Memoirs*, London, W.H. Allen, 1976.

Williams, T. *Sweet Bird of Youth*, Harmondsworth, Penguin, 1976.

Williams, T. *Suddenly Last Summer*, Edinburgh, Thomas Nelson & Sons.

Williams, T. *Small Craft Warnings*, Harmondsworth, Penguin, 1982.

Williams, T. *Cat on a Hot Tin Roof*, Harmondsworth, Penguin, 1986.

Young, B.A. *The Rattigan Version*, London, Hamish Hamilton, 1986.

INDEX

205